Verse by Verse Commentary on the Book of

1 SAMUEL

Enduring Word Commentary Series

By David Guzik

The grass withers, the flower fades,

but the word of our God stands forever.

Isaiah 40:8

Commentary on First Samuel

Printed in the United States of America

ISBN 1-56599-040-4

Enduring Word Media

USA
Attention: Sheri Guzik
514 Jurupa Avenue
Redlands, CA 92374
USA

(909) 307 0688

Europe
Calvary Chapel Bibelschule
Waldsrasse 6
57290 Neunkirchen
GERMANY

+49 (0)2735-658793

Electronic Mail: ewm@enduringword.com
Internet Home Page: www.enduringword.com

Table of Contents

For Our Son
Jonathan

1 Samuel 1 - The Birth of Samuel

1 and 2 Samuel form one book in the ancient Hebrew manuscripts. They were not divided into two books until the Old Testament was translated into Greek. We don't know who wrote the books; certainly, Samuel was a major contributor, but much of the book takes place after his death in 1 Samuel 25. They are called the books of 1 and 2 Samuel, not because Samuel wrote all of them, but because they describe his great ministry in Israel and the legacy of it.

A. Hannah's barrenness and her vow.

1. (1-2) The family of Elkanah.

Now there was a certain man of Ramathaim Zophim, of the mountains of Ephraim, and his name *was* Elkanah the son of Jeroham, the son of Elihu, the son of Tohu, the son of Zuph, an Ephraimite. And he had two wives: the name of one *was* Hannah, and the name of the other Peninnah. Peninnah had children, but Hannah had no children.

a. **A certain man**: At this strategic time and place, God began His plan as He almost always does - with a person He will use. God can do His work by Himself, or by angels, or by any number of other means; but His normal method is to find **a certain man** and work through him.

b. **Elkanah**: He was a descendant of Zuph, and his family line shows he was a Levite (1 Chronicles 6:16-30). He is called an **Ephraimite** here because his family lived in a Levitical city in the boundaries of Ephraim, not because he was of the *tribe* of Ephraim.

c. **Elkanah . . . had two wives**: Polygamy was a fact of life in the ancient world. However, the Bible never puts polygamy in a favorable light. Strife and conflict always characterize polygamous families in the Bible.

i. There was an intense, competitive relationship between the two wives, **Peninnah** (who had children) and **Hannah** (who had no children).

ii. "Polygamy was ever [always] a sin, though in the patriarchs and ancient saints, a sin of ignorance. 'It was not so from the beginning.' (Matt. xix. 8; Mal. ii. 15)." (Trapp)

2. (3-7) Elkanah and his family journey to the tabernacle.

This man went up from his city yearly to worship and sacrifice to the LORD of hosts in Shiloh. Also the two sons of Eli, Hophni and Phinehas, the priests of the LORD, *were* there. And whenever the time came for Elkanah to make an offering, he would give portions to Peninnah his wife and to all her sons and daughters. But to Hannah he would give a double portion, for he loved Hannah, although the LORD had closed her womb. And her rival also provoked her severely, to make her miserable, because the LORD had closed her womb. So it was, year by year, when she went up to the house of the LORD, that she provoked her; therefore she wept and did not eat.

a. **This man went up from his city**: According to the Law of Moses, Israelites could not worship God through sacrifice at any time and in any way they pleased. They were to bring sacrifices to the tabernacle and the priests, which at this time were at **Shiloh**.

b. **Also the two sons of Eli, Hophni and Phinehas, the priests of the LORD, were there**: These priests are mentioned by name because they were known as notoriously wicked priests (1 Samuel 2:17, 24). Their mention here shows how godly Elkanah was. Even though the priests were wicked, he still offered sacrifices to the LORD, knowing that the wickedness of the priest did not make his own service to the LORD invalid.

c. **He would give portions**: As Elkanah brought his family each year to the tabernacle for sacrifice he ate a ceremonial meal at the tabernacle with his family, giving portions to his wives and their children. He showed his favor and love to Hannah by giving her a **double portion**.

d. **She wept and did not eat**: Because of the conflict between the two wives, Hannah could not enjoy this display of love and favor from Elkanah.

i. It is possible for problems at home to make your time at the house of God miserable. Hannah is at the house of the LORD with a blessed double portion in front of her and she can't enjoy it.

e. **The LORD had closed her womb**: Beyond Hannah's painful trial there was a purpose of God. God used the trial of a closed womb to accomplish something great in her life and to further the whole plan of salvation. Even though things were hard God was still in charge.

i. It seems strange that Peninnah (who seems of a bad character) was blessed with children and Hannah (who seems of a good character) was cursed with barrenness. Often, we don't understand God's ways until He completes His plan.

3. (8-11) Hannah's godly vow.

Then Elkanah her husband said to her, "Hannah, why do you weep? Why do you not eat? And why is your heart grieved? *Am* I not better to you than ten

sons?" So Hannah arose after they had finished eating and drinking in Shiloh. Now Eli the priest was sitting on the seat by the doorpost of the tabernacle of the LORD. And she *was* in bitterness of soul, and prayed to the LORD and wept in anguish. Then she made a vow and said, "O LORD of hosts, if You will indeed look on the affliction of Your maidservant and remember me, and not forget Your maidservant, but will give Your maidservant a male child, then I will give him to the LORD all the days of his life, and no razor shall come upon his head."

a. **Hannah, why do you weep? . . . Am I not better to you than ten sons?** In Elkanah's response to Hannah's sorrow, we see that he really did love her, yet like many men he was insensitive. He did not recognize that she had needs he could not fulfill (such as the desire to be a mother).

b. **Prayed to the LORD**: Hannah **was in bitterness of soul** and great **anguish** yet she did the right thing. Hannah took those bitter and anguished feelings to God honestly in prayer.

c. **O LORD of hosts**: Hannah began her prayer by calling on the **LORD of hosts**. This title is used some 260 times in the Old Testament, and has the idea "LORD of the Mighty Armies." Hannah felt attacked by her rival, so she called on the *LORD of Mighty Armies* to be her protector.

d. **She made a vow**: Hannah promised her son to the work of the LORD, vowing he would be a Nazirite from birth (**I will give him to the LORD all the days of his life, and no razor shall come upon his head**). According to Numbers 6, the vow of a Nazirite included the following:

- Abstinence from any product from a grape vine, signifying distance from all fleshly pleasures
- Taking no part in any mourning for the dead, nor to come near a dead body, because the dead show the corruption and the fruit of sin. Also, this showed that the Nazirite had greater concerns than the ordinary joys and sorrows of life
- Never cutting the hair because it was a public, visible sign to others of the vow
- Typically, the vow of a Nazirite was taken for a set and rather short period of time. Samuel and Samson (Judges 13:5) were unique because they were Nazirites from birth

e. **I will give him to the LORD all the days of his life**: The child was already dedicated as a Levite because God regarded the tribe of Levi as His own special possession. But the time of a Levite's special dedication to the LORD only lasted from the age of 30 to 50 (Numbers 4:2-3). Hannah took something that already belonged to the LORD and gave it again to Him in a greater way - for the whole life, and in the dedication of a Nazirite, which was a greater consecration than a Levite.

i. Even so, we may be dedicated unto the LORD - but it is possible to give God a greater dedication. It would be easy for Hannah to say, "I don't need to dedicate my child to the LORD, because he is already dedicated." But there was a deeper dedication for the LORD to draw out of Hannah.

4. (12-14) Eli, the high priest, watches Hannah's silent prayer.

And it happened, as she continued praying before the LORD, that Eli watched her mouth. Now Hannah spoke in her heart; only her lips moved, but her voice was not heard. Therefore Eli thought she was drunk. So Eli said to her, "How long will you be drunk? Put your wine away from you!"

a. **As she continued praying**: This is literally, "as she multiplied to pray." We only have recorded a bare summary of Hannah's prayer.

b. **Now Hannah spoke in her heart; only her lips moved, but her voice was not heard**: It is often good to pray aloud, because it can help us to better focus our thoughts. Yet this passage shows that prevailing prayer doesn't need to be vocal. Effective prayer can be silent and in the heart.

c. **How long will you be drunk?** Eli misunderstood Hannah, but the fact that he suspected that she was drunk shows that it may not have been unusual for people to become drunk at the "fellowship meals" with the LORD at the tabernacle. The fact that Eli suspected Hannah of drunkenness doesn't speak well for what went on around the tabernacle.

i. "The fact that Eli supposed her to be *drunken*, and the other of the conduct of Eli's sons already mentioned, prove that religion was at this time at a very low ebb in Shiloh; for it seems *drunken women* did come to the place, and *lewd women* were to be found there." (Clarke)

5. (15-18) Hannah responds to Eli's accusation; Eli answers with a blessing.

And Hannah answered and said, "No, my lord, I *am* a woman of sorrowful spirit. I have drunk neither wine nor intoxicating drink, but have poured out my soul before the LORD. "Do not consider your maidservant a wicked woman, for out of the abundance of my complaint and grief I have spoken until now." Then Eli answered and said, "Go in peace, and the God of Israel grant your petition which you have asked of Him." And she said, "Let your maidservant find favor in your sight." So the woman went her way and ate, and her face was no longer *sad*.

a. **No, my lord**: Hannah did not accept Eli's accusation but she did not respond in a haughty or arrogant tone. She would explain herself but she did it remembering that he was her high priest.

b. **I have poured out my soul before the LORD**: This is exactly what Hannah needed to do. Instead of keeping the *bitterness of soul* and the *anguish* in her heart, she **poured** it **out** of her **soul before the LORD**.

c. **The God of Israel grant your petition**: Eli may have spoken this only as a kind wish; but it was in fact a word from the LORD.

d. **Her face was no longer sad**: The change in Hannah's countenance shows that she received the promise with faith, something necessary if we will inherit the promises of God (Hebrews 6:12).

i. Hannah shows how we can regain the joy of fellowship in the house of the LORD again: by pouring out our heart before the LORD and by receiving His word with *faith.*

B. The birth and dedication of Samuel.

1. (19-20) Samuel's miraculous conception and his birth.

Then they rose early in the morning and worshiped before the LORD, and returned and came to their house at Ramah. And Elkanah knew Hannah his wife, and the LORD remembered her. So it came to pass in the process of time that Hannah conceived and bore a son, and called his name Samuel, *saying*, "Because I have asked for him from the LORD."

a. **Then they arose early in the morning and worshipped**: Hannah could genuinely *worship* the LORD in faith while the promise was still not yet fulfilled. This is a glorious pattern of faith.

b. **And the LORD remembered her**: To use the term **remembered** is an *anthropomorphism*, a way of explaining God's actions in human terms that *we* can understand, even if it doesn't perfectly describe God's action. It isn't as if God ever *forgot* Hannah, but it is proper to say He **remembered** her.

c. **It came to pass in the process of time**: It didn't happen right away. Hannah had reason enough to be discouraged, but when the promise of God was spoken she did not lose faith in the promise, even when it took some time. She is a great example of *those who through faith and patience inherit the promises* (Hebrews 6:12).

2. (21-23) Hannah keeps the child until he is weaned.

Now the man Elkanah and all his house went up to offer to the LORD the yearly sacrifice and his vow. But Hannah did not go up, for she said to her husband, "*Not* until the child is weaned; then I will take him, that he may appear before the LORD and remain there forever." And Elkanah her husband said to her, "Do what seems best to you; wait until you have weaned him. Only let the LORD establish His word." So the woman stayed and nursed her son until she had weaned him.

a. **Until the child is weaned**: In that culture, a child was usually not weaned until two years of age, or sometimes three years. It is reasonable to assume that Hannah was in no hurry to wean Samuel.

b. **Only let the Lord establish His word**: This was wonderful counsel from Elkanah. He said, "do everything in obedience to God so we may see His word established among us."

3. (24-28) Hannah dedicates Samuel to God's service.

Now when she had weaned him, she took him up with her, with three bulls, one ephah of flour, and a skin of wine, and brought him to the house of the Lord in Shiloh. And the child *was* young. Then they slaughtered a bull, and brought the child to Eli. And she said, "O my lord! As your soul lives, my lord, I *am* the woman who stood by you here, praying to the Lord. For this child I prayed, and the Lord has granted me my petition which I asked of Him. Therefore I also have lent him to the Lord; as long as he lives he shall be lent to the Lord." So they worshiped the Lord there.

a. **She took him up with her**: This was hard for Hannah and Elkanah. Their willingness to fulfill the vow even at great personal cost is evidence of godliness in Elkanah and Hannah.

b. **With three bulls**: The fact that 1 Samuel 1:24 mentions three bulls brought to Shiloh but 1 Samuel 1:25 mentions only one being sacrificed (with some of the meat available for a fellowship meal) emphasizes that one of the bulls was specifically made as a burnt offering for the cleansing and consecration of little Samuel.

c. **I also have lent him to the Lord**: This could be translated, "And I also made myself to present for the Lord." The idea is not that Hannah "owned" the child and "lent" him to the Lord. Instead, the idea is that the child is her "prayer," or the fulfillment of her prayer to the Lord.

i. The name *Samuel* means "Name of God" but Hannah - as was common among the Hebrews - made a pun on the name by saying that she had "asked the Lord for him." *Asked* in Hebrew sounds like *Samuel*.

d. **So they worshipped the Lord there**: *Worship* is a repeated characteristic of this family (see also 1 Samuel 1:3, 19, 28). Even in difficult situations, they could worship the Lord. Praising God on the day you give your little son away may not be easy but it is praise God is pleased with, even as we are told to bring a *sacrifice of praise* to God (Hebrews 13:15).

1 Samuel 2 - Hannah's Prayer, Eli's Evil Sons

A. Hannah's prayer.

1. (1-2) Thanksgiving and praise.

And Hannah prayed and said:

"My heart rejoices in the LORD; my horn is exalted in the LORD. I smile at my enemies, because I rejoice in Your salvation. No one is holy like the LORD, for *there is* none besides You, nor *is there* any rock like our God."

a. **Hannah prayed and said**: 1 Samuel 1:28 ended, *So they worshipped the LORD there.* This song records the worship Hannah offered on the very day she left her little boy - her only child - at the tabernacle, never for him to live in her home again.

b. **My heart rejoices in the LORD**: Hannah showed a depth of commitment and love for God that may humble us. On the day she made the biggest sacrifice of her life she **rejoices in the LORD**.

i. Notice though, that she **rejoices in the LORD**. She can't rejoice in leaving her son but she can rejoice **in the LORD**. In the most desperate situations, when we have nothing else to rejoice in, we can rejoice **in the LORD**.

c. **My horn is exalted in the LORD**: The **horn** is used often as a picture of strength in the Bible (Psalms 75:4-5 and 92:10). This is because the strength of an ox or a steer could be expressed in its **horn**. Hannah spoke of strength and power being **exalted in the LORD**.

i. "We have often seen that *horn* signifies power, might, and dominion. It is thus constantly used in the Bible, and was so used among the heathens." (Clarke)

d. **I smile at my enemies**: Hannah had a strong sense of vindication over her rival, Elkanah's other wife named Peninnah. Peninnah cruelly brought Hannah low (1 Samuel 1:6-7), but now Hannah rejoiced because the LORD lifted her up.

e. **There is none holy like the LORD**: This shows a classic form of Hebrew poetry - repetitive parallelism. To say the LORD is **holy** is to say He is completely set apart; that He is unique, and not like any other. When she continued in the same verse and said, "**For there is none besides You**," she said the same thing as "**There is none holy like the LORD**," only saying it in different words. When she said, "**Nor is there any rock like our God**," she again says the same thing in different words.

i. In this, Hebrew poetry does not rhyme words by sound as much as it rhymes *ideas*. The ideas of the three lines of 1 Samuel 2:2 all rhyme together, having different words yet "sounding" the same.

2. (3) A warning to the arrogant and proud.

"Talk no more so very proudly; let no arrogance come from your mouth, for the LORD *is* the God of knowledge; and by Him actions are weighed."

a. **Talk no more so very proudly**: Hannah certainly had her rival in mind but she also saw Peninnah as a representative of all the proud and arrogant people in the world. Hannah wisely told the proud to **talk no more** and to **let no arrogance come from your mouth**. Pride can be expressed in many ways, but it usually is expressed by our words. It would be better if proud people just did not talk so much.

b. **For the LORD is the God of knowledge**: This, of course, is the best reason to forsake our pride. Next to God, we know nothing. He knows us, and **by Him actions are weighed**.

3. (4-8a) Hannah's glory to God who humbles the strong and exalts the weak.

"The bows of the mighty men *are* broken, and those who stumbled are girded with strength. *Those who were* full have hired themselves out for bread, and the hungry have ceased *to hunger*. Even the barren has borne seven, and she who has many children has become feeble. The LORD kills and makes alive; He brings down to the grave and brings up. The LORD makes poor and makes rich; He brings low and lifts up.

"He raises the poor from the dust *and* lifts the beggar from the ash heap, to set *them* among princes and make them inherit the throne of glory."

a. **The bows of the mighty men are broken**: We should be humble before God because He knows how to humble the strong. **Those who were full** are now begging and she **who has many children has become feeble**. If we are strong or exalted now, we should keep humble because the LORD can change our place quickly.

b. **Those who stumbled are girded with strength . . . those who were hungry have ceased to hunger . . . even the barren has borne seven**: We should be humble before God because He knows how to exalt the weak. If we are weak or in a low place now we should wait humbly before God and let Him lift us up (Luke 14:7-11).

c. **The Lord makes poor and makes rich; He brings low and lifts up**: Hannah knew she was barren *because the Lord had closed her womb* (1 Samuel 1:6). She knew God first set her low, and then brought her high. She could see the hand of the Lord in it all.

4. (8b-10) Hannah's confidence in the future is confidence in the Lord.

"For the pillars of the earth *are* the Lord's, and He has set the world upon them. He will guard the feet of His saints, but the wicked shall be silent in darkness. For by strength no man shall prevail. The adversaries of the Lord shall be broken in pieces; from heaven He will thunder against them. The Lord will judge the ends of the earth.

"He will give strength to His king, and exalt the horn of His anointed."

a. **For the pillars of the earth are the Lord's**: Hannah was confident in God's ability to humble the strong and exalt the weak because God is *in control*. If God were not in control, then perhaps the strong could do what they wanted and God couldn't stop them. Hannah knew that the foundation of the earth itself (**the pillars of the earth**) belonged to the Lord.

b. **For by strength no man shall prevail. The adversaries of the Lord shall be broken in pieces**: God uses His power to set things right. It isn't enough for us to believe God has this power. We must know He will *use* it for His glory and righteousness.

c. **He will give strength to His king, and exalt the horn of His anointed**: At this time Israel did not have a king and didn't seem to want one. So when Hannah spoke of **His king** she looked ahead to the Messiah, who will finally set all wrongs right. He is **His anointed**.

i. This is the first place in the Bible where Jesus is referred to as the *Messiah*. "She first applied to him the remarkable epithet Messiah in Hebrew, Christ in Greek, and Anointed in English, which was adopted by *David, Nathan, Ethan, Isaiah, Daniel*, and the succeeding prophets of the Old Testament; and by the apostles and inspired writers of the New." (Hales, cited in Clarke)

ii. Zecharias, the father of John the Baptist, quoted Hannah in Luke 1:69 when he prophetically called Jesus *a horn of salvation*, quoting from 1 Samuel 2:10. Mary the mother of Jesus quoted Hannah's song often (Luke 1:46-55).

5. (11) Samuel ministers unto the Lord.

Then Elkanah went to his house at Ramah. But the child ministered to the Lord before Eli the priest.

a. **Then Elkanah went**: They *did* it. It was hard to do, to leave this little son behind, but they did it because they promised God they would do it.

b. **But the child ministered to Lord before Eli the priest**: Young as he was, Samuel had a ministry to the Lord. Our young people can praise and please God and it is often a breakthrough in their walk with the Lord when they experience God in worship.

i. The Living Bible translates it well: *And the child became the Lord's helper.* There are ways that even children can serve God and minister to Him.

B. The wicked sons of Eli, the high priest.

1. (12) The evil character of Eli's sons.

Now the sons of Eli *were* corrupt; they did not know the Lord.

a. **The sons of Eli were corrupt**: Literally, the ancient Hebrew calls them *sons of Belial. Belial* was a pagan god and the phrase *sons of Belial* refers to worthless and wicked men. This was a significant problem, because the **sons of Eli** were in line to succeed him as high priest and they already functioned in the priesthood.

b. **They did not know the Lord**: Even though their father Eli knew the Lord that knowledge was not passed on genetically to his sons. They had to personally know the Lord for themselves.

2. (13-17) Their first offense: stealing what was offered to God.

And the priests' custom with the people *was that* when any man offered a sacrifice, the priest's servant would come with a three-pronged fleshhook in his hand while the meat was boiling. Then he would thrust *it* into the pan, or kettle, or caldron, or pot; and the priest would take for himself all that the fleshhook brought up. So they did in Shiloh to all the Israelites who came there. Also, before they burned the fat, the priest's servant would come and say to the man who sacrificed, "Give meat for roasting to the priest, for he will not take boiled meat from you, but raw." And *if* the man said to him, "They should really burn the fat first; *then* you may take *as much* as your heart desires," he would then answer him, "*No*, but you must give *it* now; and if not, I will take *it* by force." Therefore the sin of the young men was very great before the Lord, for men abhorred the offering of the Lord.

a. **The priests' custom with the people**: With many of the sacrifices brought to the tabernacle, a portion was given to God, a portion was given to the priest, and a portion was kept by the one who brought the offering. According to other passages in the Old Testament, the priest received a portion of the breast and the shoulder. But now, some 400 years after the Law of Moses came, the priestly custom changed - they did not take the prescribed portion of the breast and shoulder, but took whatever the fork (**fleshhook**) brought up out of the pot.

b. **Before they burned the fat**: God's portion was always given first, so it was wrong to take the priest's portion **before they burned the fat**.

i. The **fat** was thought to be the most luxurious, best part of the animal, so they gave it to God. The idea was that God should always get the best, and God should get His portion first. But in their pride the sons of Eli took their portion **before they burned the fat**.

c. **He will not take boiled meat from you, but raw**: Why did the sons of Eli want raw meat? Perhaps it was so they could prepare it anyway they pleased, or more likely, it was because raw meat was easier to sell and they sold the meat and pocketed the money.

d. **No, but you must give it to me now; and if not, I will take it by force**: The greed of Eli's sons was so bad that they did not hesitate to use violence and the threat of violence to get what they wanted.

e. **For men abhorred the offering of the Lord**: The greatness of the sin of Eli's sons was clear because through their greed, violence, and intimidation they made others not want to come and bring offerings to the Lord. It was bad enough what they themselves did; but the greater sin of Eli's sons was in how they hurt other people.

3. (18-21) The purity and service of Samuel is a contrast to the evil character of Eli's sons.

But Samuel ministered before the Lord, *even as* a child, wearing a linen ephod. Moreover his mother used to make him a little robe, and bring *it* to him year by year when she came up with her husband to offer the yearly sacrifice. And Eli would bless Elkanah and his wife, and say, "The Lord give you descendants from this woman for the loan that was given to the Lord." Then they would go to their own home. And the Lord visited Hannah, so that she conceived and bore three sons and two daughters. Meanwhile the child Samuel grew before the Lord.

a. **But Samuel**: As bad as Eli's sons were, Samuel was different. We can say that this is why God raised up Samuel, because of the corruption of Eli's sons. God knew how bad Eli's sons were, so He guided the whole series of events that resulted in Samuel's service at the tabernacle. If Eli's sons were not worthy successors then God would raise up someone else.

i. Ultimately, corrupt ministers do not stop - or even hinder - the work of God. It may look like it; but every time there are men like Eli's sons, God raises up someone like Samuel. God's work does not stop when God's ministers become corrupt.

b. **Wearing a linen ephod**: Even as a child Samuel distinguished himself in his service to the Lord. His service was exceptional enough that he received **a linen ephod**, a priestly garment (Exodus 39:27-29).

i. What did Samuel do? "He did small charges, as setting up lights, laying up vestments, learning music, or the like." (Trapp)

c. **Even as a child**: Though a child, Samuel served the LORD better and in a greater way than the sons of Eli did. What man looks at in the service of God is often not what the LORD looks at.

d. **His mother used to make him a little robe**: Only someone who was really there would describe such a small detail. Though Hannah gave her little boy to the LORD, she never stopped loving him.

e. **The LORD visited Hannah**: He certainly did - three more sons, and two daughters. God will never be a debtor to anyone. Hannah could never say to the LORD, "I gave you my son, but what did you give me?" because God gave her much more in return.

4. (22) The second offense of Eli's sons: sexual immorality.

Now Eli was very old; and he heard everything his sons did to all Israel, and how they lay with the women who assembled at the door of the tabernacle of meeting.

a. **Now Eli was very old**: This passage is not focused on Eli's sons as much as it is on Eli himself. He was old and in no condition to lead Israel as high priest. **He heard everything his sons did** but Eli *only* rebuked them about it.

b. **They lay with the women who assembled at the door of the tabernacle of meeting**: This means the sons of Eli we committing sexual immorality with the women who came to *worship* at the tabernacle. This was an ancient version of the modern "preacher sex scandal."

i. It is possible that the **women who assembled at the door of the tabernacle** were in some way workers at the house of the LORD. Exodus 38:8 refers to *the serving women who assembled at the door of the tabernacle of meeting.*

5. (23-26) The vain, ineffective rebuke of Eli to his sons.

So he said to them, "Why do you do such things? For I hear of your evil dealings from all the people. "No, my sons! For *it is* not a good report that I hear. You make the Lord's people transgress. "If one man sins against another, God will judge him. But if a man sins against the LORD, who will intercede for him?" Nevertheless they did not heed the voice of their father, because the LORD desired to kill them. And the child Samuel grew in stature, and in favor both with the LORD and men.

a. **Why do you do such things?** It is an understandable question, but a needless one. It doesn't matter **why** because there could be no good reason. They can't excuse their sin; they had to be responsible for it instead.

i. Eli did about the worst thing a parent can do in trying to correct their children: *just* talk. All he did was whine about what they did wrong, but he never took the necessary actions to correct the problem. Parents would be better off to yell less, lecture less, and to take sensible action more often, letting the children see the consequences for their disobedience.

ii. Writing from the 17th century, John Trapp advises Eli on what he *should* have said: "Draw near hither, ye sons of the sorceress, the seed of the adulterer and the whore . . . ye degenerate brood and sons of Belial, and not of Eli; ye brats of fathomless perdition . . . It is stark stinking naught that I hear, and woe is me that I yet live to hear it; it had been better that I had died long since, or that you had been buried alive, than this to live and stink above the ground."

b. **You make the LORD's people to transgress**: Again, this was the great sin of Eli's sons. It was bad enough that they stole and indulged their own lusts; but they also, by their corrupt behavior, made people hate to worship God with their offerings at the tabernacle (1 Samuel 2:17), and they led women worshippers into sexual immorality.

c. **If one man sins against another, God will judge him. But if a man sins against the LORD, who will intercede for him?** Fortunately, 1 John 2:1 answers Eli's question: *And if anyone sins, we have an Advocate with the Father, Jesus Christ the righteous.* We thank God that there is someone to **intercede** for us when we sin **against the LORD**.

d. **Nevertheless they did not heed the voice of their father, because the LORD desired to kill them**: This striking statement may seem unfair to some. They picture Eli's sons wanting to repent and listen to their father, but God prevented them. This is not the case at all. God judged Eli's sons this way: He gave them *exactly* what they wanted. They did not want to repent, and God did not work repentance in their hearts.

i. God saw they were corrupt men and wanted to judge them. When **the LORD desired to kill them**, it simply meant that God desired justice towards Eli's sons.

e. **And the child Samuel grew in stature, and in favor both with the LORD and men**: What a contrast to the wickedness of Eli's sons! This shows that although Eli was far from a perfect father, he was not a chronically bad father, because he essentially fathered Samuel and he grew up to be a godly man.

C. The announcement of God's judgment against Eli's house.

1. (27-33) An unknown **man of God** pronounces judgment to Eli: his family will be cut off from the office of high priest.

Then a man of God came to Eli and said to him, "Thus says the LORD: 'Did I not clearly reveal Myself to the house of your father when they were in Egypt in Pharaoh's house? Did I not choose him out of all the tribes of Israel *to be* My priest, to offer upon My altar, to burn incense, and to wear an ephod before Me? And did I not give to the house of your father all the offerings of the children of Israel made by fire? Why do you kick at My sacrifice and My offering which I have commanded *in My* dwelling place, and honor your sons more than Me, to make yourselves fat with the best of all the offerings of Israel My people?' Therefore the LORD God of Israel says: 'I said indeed *that* your house and the house of your father would walk before Me forever.' But now the LORD says: 'Far be it from Me; for those who honor Me I will honor, and those who despise Me shall be lightly esteemed. Behold, the days are coming that I will cut off your arm and the arm of your father's house, so that there will not be an old man in your house. And you will see an enemy *in My* dwelling place, *despite* all the good which God does for Israel. And there shall not be an old man in your house forever. But any of your men *whom* I do not cut off from My altar shall consume your eyes and grieve your heart. And all the descendants of your house shall die in the flower of their age.' "

a. **Then a man of God**: We don't know who this was; this **man of God** is one of the wonderful anonymous characters of the Bible. But it doesn't matter who he was. He was a **man of God**, and God raised him up to speak to Eli and Eli's whole family at this important time.

b. **Did I not clearly reveal Myself to the house of your father**: The **father** referred to is *Aaron*, who was the first High Priest. Since the High Priesthood was a hereditary office, Eli was a descendant of Aaron, whom God had revealed Himself to.

c. 1 Samuel 2:28 is a wonderful summary of some of the duties of the priesthood in Israel.

- **To be My priest**: First and foremost, the job of the High Priest was to minister unto the LORD. Before he served the people, he was a servant of God. He was not *first* the people's priest, he was *first* the priest of God
- **To offer upon My altar**: The priest brought sacrifices for atonement and worship
- **To burn incense**: Burning incense was a picture of prayer, because the smoke and the scent of the incense ascends up to the heavens. The priest was to lead the nation in prayer, and to pray for the nation
- **To wear an ephod before Me**: The priest was clothed in specific garments, *for glory and for beauty* (Exodus 28:2). He was to represent the majesty, dignity, glory, and beauty of God to the people

- **All the offerings**: The priest was also charged with the responsibility to receive the offerings of God's people and to make good use of them

d. **Why do you kick at My sacrifice**: It would have been easy for Eli to say, "I'm not doing it! My sons are!" But Eli had a double accountability for his sons, both as a father (though this was diminished because the sons were adults), and as the High Priest. His sons "worked" for him as priests, and Eli was a bad "boss."

e. **And honor your sons more than Me**: Since Eli did not correct his sons the way he should, he essentially preferred them to the LORD. If Eli were more afraid of offending God and less afraid of offending his sons he would have corrected them as he should have.

i. Eric Liddell was one of Britain's great athletes, and later he gave his life for Jesus on the mission field. In 1924 he was to run for Britain in the Olympics when it was discovered that the preliminary heats of his best event - the 100 meters - would be run on a Sunday. Quietly but firmly, Liddell refused to run. The day of 400 meters race came, and as Liddell went to the starting blocks, an unknown man slipped a piece of paper in his hand with a quotation from 1 Samuel 2:30: **Those who honor Me I will honor**. That day Eric Liddel set a world's record in the 400 meters.

f. **I will cut off your arm**: Not literally, but since the **arm** was a picture of strength and might in Hebrew thinking (Psalms 10:15, 77:15, and 89:10), this said the house of Eli would be left powerless and without strength.

g. **'I said indeed that your house and the house of your father would walk before Me forever'; but now the LORD says**: God promised that the priestly line would not stay with Eli and his descendants, but would pass to another line of descendants from Aaron. This was fulfilled many years later, in Solomon's day. Abiathar (from Eli's family) was deposed as high priest and replaced with Zadok (who was from another family).

i. 1 Kings 2:27 reads, *So Solomon removed Abiathar from being priest to the LORD, that he might fulfill the word of the LORD which He spoke concerning the house of Eli at Shiloh.*

ii. **"I said indeed that your house and the house of your father would walk before Me forever," but now the LORD says**? This is a promise to *Aaron* in passages like Exodus 29:9. God did not remove the priesthood from the line of Aaron, but He did remove it from the line of Eli.

h. **There shall not be an old man in your house forever . . . And all the descendants of your house shall die in the flower of their age**: This idea is repeated twice in these few verses. God wanted to emphasize that He would not bless the descendants of Eli with a long life.

i. **Shall consume your eyes and grieve your heart**: The descendants of Eli who did live a little longer would not live *blessed* lives. Their end would be painful to see.

2. (34-36) The sign and the promise: both sons will die on the same day.

"Now this *shall be* a sign to you that will come upon your two sons, on Hophni and Phinehas: in one day they shall die, both of them. Then I will raise up for Myself a faithful priest *who* shall do according to what *is* in My heart and in My mind. I will build him a sure house, and he shall walk before My anointed forever. And it shall come to pass that everyone who is left in your house will come *and* bow down to him for a piece of silver and a morsel of bread, and say, 'Please, put me in one of the priestly positions, that I may eat a piece of bread.' "

a. **Now this shall be a sign to you**: Since the fulfillment of the judgment would be many years away (in the days of Solomon), God gave Eli an immediate sign to demonstrate His truthfulness. Eli's sons will die **in one day**; Eli will see this and know the judgment of God has come against his house.

b. **Then I will raise up for Myself a faithful priest**: Who is the **faithful priest** predicted here? He was a great priest, because he did **according to what is in** [God's] **heart and in** [God's] **mind**. He was a blessed priest, because God said of him, **I will build him a sure house, and he will walk before My anointed forever**.

- This promise was partially fulfilled in *Samuel*, because he functioned as a godly priest, effectively replacing the ungodly sons of Eli

- The promise was partially fulfilled in *Zadok*, in the days of Solomon, because he replaced Eli's family line in the priesthood

- The promise was ultimately fulfilled in *Jesus Christ*, because He is a priest forever in the order of Melchezedek (Hebrews 7:12-17)

c. **Everyone who is left in your house will come and bow down to him for a piece of silver**: This is a fitting judgment, since much of the sin of Eli's sons was greed and stealing from God's people. Instead of receiving the priestly portions that were rightfully theirs, Eli's family would one day be reduced to begging.

1 Samuel 3 - God Speaks to Samuel

A. Samuel is unable to recognize God's voice.

1. (1) The scarcity of revelation in Israel.

Then the boy Samuel ministered to the Lord before Eli. And the word of the Lord was rare in those days; *there was* no widespread revelation.

a. **The boy Samuel ministered to the Lord**: For the third time it is emphasized that Samuel **ministered to the Lord** (also in 1 Samuel 2:11 and 2:18), just as Aaron and his sons did at their consecration as priests (Exodus 29:1) and just like Paul and Barnabas did before they were sent out as missionaries (Acts 13:1-2).

b. **The word of the Lord was rare in those days**: The only **word of the Lord** we read of in the first two chapters of 1 Samuel is the word of judgment brought by the man of God against Eli. God didn't speak often, and when He did, it was a word of judgment.

i. **The word of the Lord rare in those days** because of the hardness of heart among the people of Israel and the corruption of the priesthood. God will speak, and guide, when His people seek Him, and when His ministers seek to serve Him diligently.

2. (2-4) God's first words to Samuel.

And it came to pass at that time, while Eli *was* lying down in his place, and when his eyes had begun to grow so dim that he could not see, and before the lamp of God went out in the tabernacle of the Lord where the ark of God *was*, and while Samuel was lying down, that the Lord called Samuel. And he answered, "Here I am!"

a. **His eyes had begun to grow so dim that he could not see**: This was true both spiritually and physically of Eli. His age made him an ineffective leader for Israel.

b. **Before the lamp of God went out in the tabernacle of the Lord**: As a figure of speech, this simply means "before dawn." But it is also suggestive of the dark spiritual times of Israel - it is dark, and will probably get darker.

i. Exodus 27:21 refers to the responsibility of the priests to tend the lamps until sunrise, or just before dawn.

c. **While Samuel was laying down to sleep, that the LORD called Samuel**: We don't know for certain how old Samuel was. The ancient Jewish historian Josephus said Samuel was 12 years old. However old he was, God spoke to Samuel.

d. **And he answered, "Here I am!"** This leads us to believe God spoke to Samuel in an audible voice, instead of in an "inner voice," though this is not certain. But Samuel was so impressed by what he heard, he responded by saying, **"Here I am!"**

i. This is a beautiful way to respond to God's Word. It isn't that God does not know where we are, but it tells God and it reminds us we are simply before Him as servants, asking what He wants us to do. Samuel is among several others who also said, "**Here I am**" when the LORD spoke to them: Abraham (Genesis 22:1), Jacob (Genesis 46:2), Moses (Exodus 3:4), Isaiah (Isaiah 6:8), and Ananias (Acts 9:10).

3. (5-9) Samuel doesn't recognize God's voice.

So he ran to Eli and said, "Here I am, for you called me." And he said, "I did not call; lie down again." And he went and lay down. Then the LORD called yet again, "Samuel!" So Samuel arose and went to Eli, and said, "Here I am, for you called me." He answered, "I did not call, my son; lie down again." (Now Samuel did not yet know the LORD, nor was the word of the LORD yet revealed to him.) And the LORD called Samuel again the third time. Then he arose and went to Eli, and said, "Here I am, for you did call me." Then Eli perceived that the LORD had called the boy. Therefore Eli said to Samuel, "Go, lie down; and it shall be, if He calls you, that you must say, 'Speak, LORD, for Your servant hears.' " So Samuel went and lay down in his place.

a. **He ran to Eli**: Samuel was an obedient boy. He was wrong in thinking Eli spoke to him, but he was right in what he did. Samuel came to Eli quickly because he knew Eli was blind and might need help.

b. **And the LORD called yet again**: When speaking to us, God almost always confirms His word again and again. It is generally wrong to do something dramatic in response to a single "inner voice" from the LORD. If God speaks He will confirm, and often in a variety of ways.

c. **Samuel did not yet know the LORD**: Samuel was a godly and obedient boy, serving God wonderfully. Yet, he had not yet given his heart to the LORD. Even children raised in a godly home must be converted by the Spirit of God.

d. **Speak, LORD, for Your servant hears**: Eli gave Samuel wise counsel. Eli told Samuel to:

- Make himself available for God to speak (**Go, lie down**)
- Not be presumptuous about God speaking (**if He calls you**)
- Respond to the word of God (**Speak, LORD**)
- Humble himself before God and His word (**Your servant hears**)

e. **Speak, LORD**: We must hear from God. The preacher may speak, our parents may speak, our friends may speak, our teachers may speak, those on the radio or television may speak. That is all fine, but their voices mean nothing for eternity unless God speaks through them.

B. God's message to Samuel.

1. (10) Samuel responds just as Eli told him.

Now the LORD came and stood and called as at other times, "Samuel! Samuel!" And Samuel answered, "Speak, for Your servant hears."

a. **Then the LORD came and stood and called**: This seems to have been audible and because it says the LORD **stood**, it may be that this was a unique *appearing* of the LORD, perhaps in the person of Jesus before Bethlehem. This was not a dream or a state of altered consciousness.

2. (11-14) God's message to Samuel: the coming judgment on Eli and his house.

Then the LORD said to Samuel: "Behold, I will do something in Israel at which both ears of everyone who hears it will tingle. "In that day I will perform against Eli all that I have spoken concerning his house, from beginning to end. For I have told him that I will judge his house forever for the iniquity which he knows, because his sons made themselves vile, and he did not restrain them. And therefore I have sworn to the house of Eli that the iniquity of Eli's house shall not be atoned for by sacrifice or offering forever."

a. **Both ears of everyone who hears it will tingle**: God will give young Samuel spectacular news. In other places in the Old Testament, *tingling ears* are signs of an especially severe judgment (2 Kings 21:12, Jeremiah 19:3).

b. **For I have told him that I will judge his house**: Through the word of the *man of God* in 1 Samuel 2:27-36, Eli already heard of the judgment to come. This word to young Samuel was a word to *confirm* the previous message from God.

i. "The Lord sends him a word of threatening by a child; for God has many messengers." (Spurgeon)

c. **For the iniquity which he knows, because his sons made themselves vile**: Eli knew of this iniquity from his own observation and from the reports of the people, but especially because God made it known by the message of the *man of God.*

d. **And he did not restrain them**: Eli's responsibility to restrain his sons was not only or even mainly because he was their father. These were adult sons, no longer under Eli's authority as they were when they were younger. Eli's main responsibility to restrain his sons was as their "boss" because he was the high priest and his sons were priests under his supervision. However, Eli's indulgence towards his sons as a *boss* was no doubt connected to his prior indulgence of them as a *parent*.

e. **The iniquity of Eli's house shall not be atoned for by sacrifice or offering forever**: What a terrible judgment! This means, "It's too late. Now the opportunity for repentance is past. The judgment is sealed."

i. Probably, the judgment declared by the *man of God* in 1 Samuel 2:27-36 was a warning, inviting repentance. Because there was no repentance God confirmed the word of judgment through Samuel. Or, perhaps Eli pleaded that God might withhold His judgment, and this is God's answer to that pleading.

ii. Do we ever come to a place where our sin cannot be **atoned for by sacrifice or offering forever**? Only if we reject the sacrifice of Jesus for our sin. As Hebrews 10:26 says, if we reject the work of Jesus for us, *there no longer remains a sacrifice for sins*.

3. (15-18) Samuel tells Eli the message from God.

So Samuel lay down until morning, and opened the doors of the house of the LORD. And Samuel was afraid to tell Eli the vision. Then Eli called Samuel and said, "Samuel, my son!" And he answered, "Here I am." And he said, "What *is* the word that *the Lord* spoke to you? Please do not hide *it* from me. God do so to you, and more also, if you hide anything from me of all the things that He said to you." Then Samuel told him everything, and hid nothing from him. And he said, "It *is* the LORD. Let Him do what seems good to Him."

a. **Samuel lay down until morning**: Of course, he didn't *sleep* at all. We see young Samuel laying on his bed, ears tingling at the message from God, wondering how he could ever tell Eli such a powerful word of judgment (**Samuel was afraid to tell Eli**).

b. **Opened the doors of the house of the LORD**: Presumably, this was one of Samuel's duties as a servant at the tabernacle.

c. **Samuel, my son!** Eli was not a good boss or a good parent to Hophni and Phinehas. But Samuel came to him as a "second chance," and Eli did a better job of raising Samuel than he did with his sons by birth.

d. **What is the thing that the LORD has said to you?** Eli had an idea of what the message of God to Samuel was. Kindly, he took the initiative and asked Samuel, knowing it was difficult for the young man to tell him.

i. Eli made it clear to Samuel he had the responsibility to bring the message even if it was bad news. With a threat like **God do so to you, and more also**, Samuel was suitably motivated to tell Eli everything.

ii. Eli was admirable, because he was willing to be taught from an unexpected source, he wanted to hear the bad news of his condition, and he wanted to hear *all* God's message.

e. **Then Samuel told him everything**: How hard it is to bring a message of judgment! There may be a few with hard hearts (like Jonah) who are happy to announce God's judgment, but most people find it difficult. Yet it is always the responsibility of God's messenger to bring **everything** God says, not just the "easy" words.

f. **It is the LORD. Let Him do what seems good to Him**: It is hard to know if Eli's response was godly or fatalistic. We should always submit to God's rod of correction. Yet this submission is not totally passive. It is also active in repentance, and in doing what one can to cultivate a godly sorrow.

C. Samuel matures and is established as a prophet.

1. (19-20) Samuel grows, maturing physically and spiritually.

So Samuel grew, and the LORD was with him and let none of his words fall to the ground. And all Israel from Dan to Beersheba knew that Samuel *had been* established as a prophet of the LORD.

a. **The LORD was with him**: Nothing compares to this, to have and to know you have the LORD with you. The Christian can know God is with them: *If God is for us, who can be against us?* (Romans 8:31)

b. **Let none of his words fall to the ground**: This means all of Samuel's prophecies came to pass, and were known to be true words from God. Therefore, **all Israel . . . knew that Samuel had been established as a prophet of the LORD**.

i. Since the days of Moses (some 400 years before the time of Samuel) there were not many prophets in Israel, and certainly no great prophets. At this important time in Israel's history, God raised up Samuel as a prophet.

ii. Coming in this place in Israel's history, Samuel is rightly seen as Israel's last *judge* and first *prophet*. Samuel bridges the gap between the time of the judges, and the time of the monarchy when prophets (such as Nathan, Elijah, and Isaiah) influenced the nation.

c. **From Dan to Beersheba**: This is a way of saying "from northernmost Israel to southernmost Israel." It is a similar idea as saying in the United States, "from New York to California."

2. (21) The word of the LORD comes to Samuel.

Then the LORD appeared again in Shiloh. For the LORD revealed Himself to Samuel in Shiloh by the word of the LORD.

a. **The LORD appeared again in Shiloh**: When did the LORD first appear in Shiloh? We know He appeared to Samuel in 1 Samuel 3:10. Now, in some undescribed way, the LORD appeared again.

b. **The LORD revealed Himself . . . by the word of the LORD.** God reveals Himself by His word. Whenever God is moving, He will reveal Himself **by the word of the LORD.**

1 Samuel 4 - Capture of the Ark of the Covenant

A. The Ark is captured.

1. (1-2) Israel is defeated before the Philistines.

And the word of Samuel came to all Israel. Now Israel went out to battle against the Philistines, and encamped beside Ebenezer; and the Philistines encamped in Aphek. Then the Philistines put themselves in battle array against Israel. And when they joined battle, Israel was defeated by the Philistines, who killed about four thousand men of the army in the field.

a. **Israel went out to battle against the Philistines**: During this time there was no great world power (such as Egypt or Assyria) seeking to dominate the region. So, Israel's battles were waged against her near neighbors, such as the Moabites, the Ammonites, or as here, the **Philistines**.

i. Israel competed on more equal terms with Moab and Ammon but the Philistines had Greek military equipment (such as helmets, shields, chain mail armor, swords and spears) making the Philistines more formidable opponents. The Philistines were the first people in Canaan to process iron and they made the most of it.

ii. The Philistines were an immigrant people from the military aristocracy of the island of Crete (Amos 9:7). Small numbers of Philistines were in the land at the time of Abraham, but they came in larger numbers soon after Israel came to Canaan from Egypt. They were organized into five city-states.

iii. This was a difficult period for Israel. "Never did time seem more hopeless than when Samuel arose. The Philistines, strengthened not merely by a constant influx of immigrants, but by the importation of arms from Greece, were fast reducing Israel to the condition of a subject race." (Smith, *Pulpit Commentary*)

b. **The word of the Samuel came to all Israel . . . now Israel went out to battle**: This doesn't mean the battle was initiated by Samuel. Some manuscript traditions (evident in the Septuagint) make it clear the Philistines started this conflict. Nevertheless, the battle ended in disaster: **Israel was defeated by the Philistines, who killed about four thousand men.**

2. (3-4) The elders of Israel respond with a superstitious trust in the ark.

And when the people had come into the camp, the elders of Israel said, "Why has the LORD defeated us today before the Philistines? Let us bring the Ark of the Covenant of the LORD from Shiloh to us, that when it comes among us it may save us from the hand of our enemies." So the people sent to Shiloh, that they might bring from there the Ark of the Covenant of the LORD of hosts, who dwells *between* the cherubim. And the two sons of Eli, Hophni and Phinehas, *were* there with the Ark of the Covenant of God.

a. **Let us bring the Ark of the Covenant . . . it may save us from the hand of our enemies**: The elders of Israel, after the battle with the Philistines, decided the next battle could be won if they took the **Ark of the Covenant** with their soldiers.

i. The **Ark of the Covenant** was the representation of the throne of God in Israel. Kept in the most holy place of the tabernacle, the people never saw it. Only the high priest entered and saw the ark, and only once a year. The elders wanted to take this representation of the throne of God out of the holy of holies (it could be moved when the tabernacle was to be moved), cover it, and bring it into battle with them. They hoped it would give confidence that God was really with them.

ii. The ark went into battle before. The ark went in front of the marchers around the city of Jericho (Joshua 6:6-8). Moses told the priests to lead the ark into battle against the Midianites (Numbers 31:6). Later, Saul brought the ark into battle (1 Samuel 14:18), as did David (2 Samuel 11:11).

b. **It may save us**: The elders rightly sensed they needed God's help to win the battle. But they were wrong in the way they sought help. Instead of humbly repenting and seeking God, they turned to methods that God never approved. They only cared if it *worked.*

i. They believed the presence of the ark would make God work for them. "Their idea was that God should be *forced* to fight for them. If He was not willing to do it for their sake, He would have to do it for His honour's sake." (Ellison)

ii. No doubt, it seemed like a brilliant suggestion. They were probably pleased to arrive at such a great solution.

c. **That it may save us from the hand of our enemies**: They regarded the ark as the ultimate "good luck charm" and believed they could not lose with it there. They looked to the ark to save them, not to the LORD.

i. "Instead of attempting to get right with God, these Israelites set about devising superstitious means of securing the victory over their foes. In this respect most of us have imitated them. We think of a thousand inventions; but we neglect the one thing needful . . . They forget the main matter, which is to enthrone God in the life, and to seek to do His will by faith in Christ Jesus." (Spurgeon)

ii. "There are plenty of Christians, like these elders, who, when they find themselves beaten by the world and the devil, puzzle their brains to invent all sorts of reasons for God's smiting, except the true one, - their own departure from Him." (Maclaren)

d. **The two sons of Eli, Hophni and Phinehas, were with the Ark of the Covenant of God**: Instead of trusting in the ark, they should be more concerned that the ark was served and carried by priests who had forsaken the LORD.

3. (5) Israel's confidence in the Ark of the Covenant.

And when the Ark of the Covenant of the LORD came into the camp, all Israel shouted so loudly that the earth shook.

a. **All Israel shouted so loudly that the earth shook**: Someone passing by Israel's camp would think something tremendous was happening. Certainly, this would be considered a great church service, and many would think Israel really trusted God. But for all the appearances, it was really *nothing.* All the noise and excitement meant nothing because it wasn't grounded in God's truth.

i. The Israelites probably felt they were better than the Philistines because the Philistines were pagans, worshipping false gods. Yet the Israelites thought and acted just like pagans, thinking they could manipulate God and force Him into doing what they wanted Him to do.

ii. "Had they *humbled* themselves, and *prayed* devoutly and fervently for success, they would have been heard and saved. Their shouting proved both their vanity and irreligion." (Clarke)

b. **The earth shook**: "Now, beloved, when you are worshipping God, shout if you are filled with holy gladness. If the shout comes from your heart, I would not ask you to restrain it. God forbid that we should judge any man's worship! But do not be so foolish as to suppose that because there is loud noise there must also be faith. Faith is a still water, it flows deep. True faith in God may express itself with leaping and with shouting; and it is a happy thing when it does: but it can also sit still before the Lord, and that perhaps is a happier thing still." (Spurgeon)

4. (6-9) The Philistines' fear of the Ark of the Covenant.

Now when the Philistines heard the noise of the shout, they said, "What *does* the sound of this great shout in the camp of the Hebrews *mean*?" Then they understood that the ark of the LORD had come into the camp. So the Philistines were afraid, for they said, "God has come into the camp!" And they said, "Woe to us! For such a thing has never happened before. "Woe to us! Who will deliver us from the hand of these mighty gods? These *are* the gods who struck the Egyptians with all the plagues in the wilderness. Be strong and conduct yourselves like men, you Philistines, that you do not become servants of the Hebrews, as they have been to you. Conduct yourselves like men, and fight!"

a. **God has come into the camp!** We should compliment the Philistines for understanding that the Ark of the Covenant represented the presence of God, and on their knowledge of Israel's history.

i. They knew it was unusual - even unheard of - for the Israelites to bring the ark into battle (**For such a thing has never happened before**), and they knew the God of Israel defeated the Egyptians (**who struck the Egyptians with all the plagues**).

b. **These mighty gods**: Even though they did not understand much about God, the Philistines recognized the superiority of the God of Israel. Yet, they did not submit to God, but simply determined to fight against Him all the more. If they really believed their gods were greater than the God of Israel, they should not have been worried. If they believed the God of Israel was greater than their gods, they should have submitted to Him.

i. We, like them, often know God is greater and deserves our submission. Yet we often resist God as well, instead of submitting to Him. Knowledge wasn't their problem. Submission to God was.

c. **Be strong and conduct yourselves like men, you Philistines**: The presence of the ark did not make the Philistines feel like giving up. Instead, it made them feel they had to fight all the harder to overcome the odds. They had the courage of desperate men.

i. Godless Philistines can teach us something. Christians need to show more of this courage. Instead of giving up when things look bad we should trust the LORD and fight all the harder and decide we will *not* give up. Courage and persistence win many battles, even sometimes for the wrong side.

5. (10-11) The ark goes into battle and Israel is defeated worse than before.

So the Philistines fought, and Israel was defeated, and every man fled to his tent. There was a very great slaughter, and there fell of Israel thirty thousand foot soldiers. Also the ark of God was captured; and the two sons of Eli, Hophni and Phinehas, died.

a. **Israel was defeated**: There were three reasons for this great defeat. First, the Philistines fought with the courage of desperate men. Second, the Israelites felt the battle would be easy with the ark of the Covenant there, and did not try as hard. Finally, God did not bless Israel's superstitious belief in the power of the ark instead of the power of God.

i. We often make the same mistake, believing that if God is with us, we don't need to try so hard. We think if God is on our side, the work will be easy. That may not be true at all.

ii. As it turned out, God did *not* feel obligated to bless the Israelites just because they took the ark into battle. He wouldn't allow His arm to be twisted by the superstitions of the Israelites. God is a Person, not a genie to be summoned at the will of man.

b. **There fell of Israel thirty thousand foot soldiers**: Not only did Israel lose, they lost far worse than they did *before* taking the ark into battle. The loss which prompted them to take the ark resulted in the death of *about four thousand men* of Israel (1 Samuel 4:2). With the ark more than seven times as many men of Israel were killed.

i. In the late 1970's, a five-line inscription was found on a grain silo in the ruins of Izbet Sarteh. When deciphered, it was found to contain a Philistine account of this battle, the capture of the ark, even specifically mentioning the priest Hophni. This is the earliest known extra-biblical reference to an Old Testament event.

c. **The ark of God was captured**: This was worse than just losing a battle. The very "thing" they thought would win the battle was captured. Israel made an idol of the ark and God often deals with our idolatry by taking the idol away.

i. We can make good things idols. There was nothing wrong with the ark itself. God commanded them to make it. It was important to Israel. He told them to put the tablets of the law, a jar of manna, and Aaron's rod that budded, in the ark. Yet, even a good thing like the ark can be made an idol, and God won't tolerate our idols.

ii. The **ark of God was captured**, but the God of the ark was still on the throne in heaven, and guiding these circumstances for His glory. Israel thought they could ignore the God of the ark and find deliverance in the ark of God. God showed He was greater than the ark.

d. **The two sons of Eli, Hophni and Phinehas, died**: The priests who were supposed to supervise the ark were killed in the battle. God promised the two sons of Eli would die on the same day as proof of His ultimate judgment on the house of Eli (1 Samuel 2:34). Now the proof of judgment came.

B. Israel's great anguish at the loss of the ark.

1. (12-18) Eli hears of the loss of the Ark of the Covenant of God and dies.

Then a man of Benjamin ran from the battle line the same day, and came to Shiloh with his clothes torn and dirt on his head. Now when he came, there was Eli, sitting on a seat by the wayside watching, for his heart trembled for the ark of God. And when the man came into the city and told *it*, all the city cried out. When Eli heard the noise of the outcry, he said, "What *does* the sound of this tumult *mean*?" And the man came quickly and told Eli. Eli was ninety-eight years old, and his eyes were so dim that he could not see. Then the man said to Eli, "I *am* he who came from the battle. And I fled today from the battle line." And he said, "What happened, my son?" So the messenger answered and said, "Israel has fled before the Philistines, and there has been a great slaughter among the people. Also your two sons, Hophni and Phinehas, are dead; and the ark of God has been captured." Then it happened, when he made mention of the ark of God, that Eli fell off the seat backward by the side of the gate; and his neck was broken and he died, for the man was old and heavy. And he had judged Israel forty years.

a. **A man of Benjamin ran from the battle line the same day, and came to Shiloh**: The battle was fought near *Aphek* (1 Samuel 4:1), and it was at least 20 miles from Aphek to Shiloh. The messenger had a long way to go, the route was mostly uphill, and he carried very bad news.

i. Because the news was so bad he came **with his clothes torn and dirt on his head**. These were some of the traditional signs of mourning. The messenger brought bad news, and he let his appearance reflect how bad the news was.

ii. According to an unfounded Jewish tradition, this unnamed messenger from the tribe of **Benjamin** was a young man named Saul.

b. **Eli, sitting on a seat by the wayside watching, for his heart trembled for the ark of God**: Eli anxiously waited back at the tabernacle for news of the battle. Eli was rightly more concerned about the fate of the ark than the fate of his sons.

i. Why was he so nervous? Eli knew he let the ark go on an unwise, superstitious errand, and his conscience made him fear it would end in disaster.

c. **Eli fell off the seat backward by the side of the gate; and his neck was broken and he died**: Eli fell over and died at the news of the ark (**when he made mention of the ark of God**). It wasn't the news of Israel's loss in battle, or the slaughter of the army, or even the news of the death of his own sons that killed him. It was hearing the Ark of the Covenant of God was captured.

i. "No sword of a Philistine could have slain him any more powerfully; neither can you say whether his neck or his heart were broken first." (Trapp)

ii. God promised that Eli's two sons would die on the same day as a sign of judgment on the house of Eli (1 Samuel 2:34). God did *not* announce that Eli would also die the same day. God tells us much in prophecy, but not everything. Some is only seen in its fullness after it is fulfilled.

iii. According to other passages, after the Philistines defeated the Israeli army they went on to destroy the city of Shiloh itself (Psalm 78:60-64, Jeremiah 7:12 and 26:9).

2. (19-22) More tragedy among the family of Eli.

Now his daughter-in-law, Phinehas' wife, was with child, *due* to be delivered; and when she heard the news that the ark of God was captured, and that her father-in-law and her husband were dead, she bowed herself and gave birth, for her labor pains came upon her. And about the time of her death the women who stood by her said to her, "Do not fear, for you have borne a son." But she did not answer, nor did she regard *it*. Then she named the child Ichabod, saying, "The glory has departed from Israel!" because the ark of God had been captured and because of her father-in-law and her husband. And she said, "The glory has departed from Israel, for the ark of God has been captured."

a. **When she heard the news**: Poor wife of Phinehas! Pregnant, she heard of the death of her husband, her brother-in-law, her father-in-law, a slaughter among the soldiers of Israel, a lost battle, and the capture of the Ark of the Covenant all on one day. The anguish was too great, and **labor pains came upon her**.

b. **Then she named the child Ichabod**: For a Jewish woman, the birth of a son was wonderful news - but not for the wife of Phinehas on this day. To reflect her anguish and the national tragedy upon Israel she named the child **Ichabod**, meaning, **"The glory has departed from Israel."**

i. **But she did not answer, nor did she regard it**: Her grief was so great, it overcame her maternal joy at the birth of her son. To her, the loss was total and she even lost the desire to live.

c. **The glory has departed**: The glory of God, displayed by the Ark of the Covenant, had departed from Israel. The Philistines now held it.

i. The glory of God *had* departed in one sense. But the glory left when Israel stopped repenting and trusting God and started superstitiously trusting in the ark itself. "The glory of God had indeed departed, but not because the ark of God had been captured; the ark had been captured because the glory had already departed." (Ellison)

ii. How could God allow something so terrible to happen? First, He allowed it as a righteous judgment upon Israel as a nation and the family of Eli. They simply received what they deserved. Secondly, God allowed it as a correction to the nation, so they would not trust in the ark of God, instead of trusting in the God of the ark. Finally, though it seemed so terrible to man, was it all that terrible to God? At that moment, did God wring His hands in heaven, worried about how things would turn out? Worried about His reputation? Worried about the Philistines and their gods? Looking at it this way, the glory had not departed at all. Instead, God was just *beginning* to show His glory.

iii. Many circumstances that we regard as a calamity, God uses in a marvelous way to glorify Himself. Israel was right to be sad at the loss of life and the ark on that day. But they should have been confident, knowing God was well able to take care of Himself.

iv. "Thus as God was no loser by this event, so the Philistines were no gainers by it; and Israel, all things considered, received more good than hurt by it, as we shall see." (Poole)

1 Samuel 5 - The Ark of the Covenant Among the Philistines

A. The ark in the Philistine city of Ashdod.

1. (1-5) God humiliates the idol Dagon.

Then the Philistines took the ark of God and brought it from Ebenezer to Ashdod. When the Philistines took the ark of God, they brought it into the temple of Dagon and set it by Dagon. And when the people of Ashdod arose early in the morning, there was Dagon, fallen on its face to the earth before the ark of the LORD. So they took Dagon and set it in its place again. And when they arose early the next morning, there was Dagon, fallen on its face to the ground before the ark of the LORD. The head of Dagon and both the palms of its hands *were* broken off on the threshold; only Dagon's torso was left of it. Therefore neither the priests of Dagon nor any who come into Dagon's house tread on the threshold of Dagon in Ashdod to this day.

a. **They brought it into the house of Dagon and set it by Dagon**: No doubt, the Philistines were jubilant, and confident in the superiority of their god over the God of Israel. They faced the God of Israel in battle, and believed their god Dagon delivered them and defeated Israel. Now, the Ark of the Covenant of Israel's God stood as a trophy in the temple of their god Dagon. The victory seemed complete.

i. **Dagon** was represented with a half man, half fish figure, and was said to be the father of Baal. "This deity was a personification of the generative and vivifying [life-giving] principle of nature, for which the fish with its innumerable multiplication was especially adapted, to set forth the idea of the giver of all earthly good." (Keil and Delitszch)

b. **There was Dagon, fallen on its face to the ground before the ark of the LORD**: Had the glory of God departed? Not at all. God was more than able to glorify Himself among the Philistines and their pagan gods. God made this statue bow down in worship before Him.

i. God *will* glorify Himself. Sometimes when men disgrace the glory of God, we fear God will go without glory. We think the glory has departed. But when men and women will not glorify God, God will glorify Himself.

c. **The head of Dagon and both the palms of its hands were broken off on the threshold; only the torso of Dagon was left of it**: Imagine the horror of the Philistine priests when they entered the temple of Dagon the *next* morning. They not only saw their god bowing down before the LORD, they also saw the image broken. It was hard to account for such an accident two days in a row and for the broken head and hands of Dagon.

i. After seeing the superiority of the God of Israel, these Philistine priests had a choice. They could turn from their weak, inferior god Dagon and begin serving the mighty, superior LORD of Israel. Or they could make a religious tradition instead. They chose the religious tradition: **Therefore neither the priests of Dagon nor any who come into Dagon's house tread on the threshold of Dagon in Ashdod to this day**.

ii. These Philistine priests, like men confronted with the truth today, rejected God *despite* the evidence, not *because* of the evidence. They wanted to believe it was an accident.

iii. How could they believe something so ridiculous? Because worshipping the LORD instead of Dagon meant a huge change in thinking and living. The Philistine priests were unwilling to make those changes. It was easier when they **took Dagon and set it in its place again**. Setting Dagon up and gluing him together is easier than changing your life and your thinking.

2. (6-8) The LORD afflicts the city of Ashdod with tumors.

But the hand of the LORD was heavy on the people of Ashdod, and He ravaged them and struck them with tumors, *both* Ashdod and its territory. And when the men of Ashdod saw how *it was*, they said, "The ark of the God of Israel must not remain with us, for His hand is harsh toward us and Dagon our god." Therefore they sent and gathered to themselves all the lords of the Philistines, and said, "What shall we do with the ark of the God of Israel?" And they answered, "Let the ark of the God of Israel be carried away to Gath." So they carried the ark of the God of Israel away.

a. **The hand of the LORD was heavy on the people of Ashdod**: They would not listen when God struck down their statue of Dagon; they just set it up again. When we close our ears to God, He often finds another way to speak to us, and we may not like the second way.

b. **He ravaged them and struck them with tumors**: What were these **tumors**? Older commentators often describe them as hemorrhoids, and newer commentators often describe them as signs of the bubonic plague.

i. "According to the Rabbins, swellings on the anus." (Keil and Delitszch) "Beating Dagon upon his own dunghill, and smiting his worshippers on their hinder parts, paying their posteriors, as men used to deal with puny boys." (Trapp) "The word *apholim*, from *aphal*, to be *elevated*, probably means the disease called the *bleeding piles*, which appears to have been accompanied with dysentery, bloody flux, and ulcerated anus." (Clarke)

ii. "Of the numerous suggested identifications of the specific malady that struck the Philistines, bubonic plague remains the most likely: 'It is a disease characterized by an epidemic occurrence, by the appearance of tumours, by the production of panic amongst the affected population, by a high mortality rate, and by an association with mice or rats.'" (Wilkinson cited in Youngblood)

iii. The Septuagint adds this to verse six: "And the cities and the fields of all that region burst up, and mice were produced, and there was the confusion of a great death in the city." Some think this was originally in the Hebrew text, and explains why golden images of rats were included in the return of the ark (1 Samuel 6:5).

iv. In *Legends of the Jews*, Ginzberg is much more graphic: "This new plague consisted in mice crawling forth out of the earth, and jerking the entrails out of the bodies of the Philistines while they eased nature. If the Philistines sought to protect themselves by using brass vessels, the vessels burst at the touch of the mice, and, as before, the Philistines were at their mercy."

c. **Let the ark of the God of Israel be carried away to Gath**: Instead of submitting to the God of Israel, they decided to get rid of Him. Yet we can't get rid of God. We can do things to push Him away but even the best of those attempts are temporary. We must all face God and stand before Him one day.

B. The ark of God in Gath and Ekron.

1. (9) The Ark of the Covenant in the Philistine city of Gath.

So it was, after they had carried it away, that the hand of the LORD was against the city with a very great destruction; and He struck the men of the city, both small and great, and tumors broke out on them.

a. **The hand of the LORD was against the city with a very great destruction**: The city of Gath didn't do any better than the city of Ashdod. More of the destructive and painful **tumors broke out on them**.

2. (10-12) The Ark of the Covenant in the Philistine city of Ekron.

Therefore they sent the ark of God to Ekron. So it was, as the ark of God came to Ekron, that the Ekronites cried out, saying, "They have brought the ark of the God of Israel to us, to kill us and our people!" So they sent and gathered together all the lords of the Philistines, and said, "Send away the ark of the God of Israel, and let it go back to its own place, so that it does not kill us and our people." For there was a deadly destruction throughout all the city; the hand of God was very heavy there. And the men who did not die were stricken with the tumors, and the cry of the city went up to heaven.

a. **Therefore they sent the ark of God to Ekron**: The Ark of the Covenant was now among the Philistines like a "hot potato," in the children's game, burning every city where it stayed. The **Ekronites** were not happy to see the ark but they still wouldn't submit to the LORD God of Israel.

b. **Send away the ark of the God of Israel, and let it go back to its own place**: The Philistines, if they had repented and turned towards the LORD, could have *benefited* from the ark. Instead it became a curse and a judgment to them. The same is true of the presence of God among men today, which can be as a fragrance of life to some and the aroma of death to others (2 Corinthians 2:15-16).

1 Samuel 6 - The Ark of the Covenant Is Returned to Israel

A. How will the Philistines get rid of the Ark of the Covenant?

1. (1-6) The priests of the Philistines suggest a way to relieve themselves of the burden of the ark.

Now the ark of the LORD was in the country of the Philistines seven months. And the Philistines called for the priests and the diviners, saying, "What shall we do with the ark of the LORD? Tell us how we should send it to its place." So they said, "If you send away the ark of the God of Israel, do not send it empty; but by all means return *it* to Him *with* a trespass offering. Then you will be healed, and it will be known to you why His hand is not removed from you." Then they said, "What *is* the trespass offering which we shall return to Him?" They answered, "Five golden tumors and five golden rats, *according to* the number of the lords of the Philistines. For the same plague *was* on all of you and on your lords. Therefore you shall make images of your tumors and images of your rats that ravage the land, and you shall give glory to the God of Israel; perhaps He will lighten His hand from you, from your gods, and from your land. Why then do you harden your hearts as the Egyptians and Pharaoh hardened their hearts? When He did mighty things among them, did they not let the people go, that they might depart?"

a. **What shall we do with the ark of the LORD?** When the Philistines first captured the Ark of the Covenant, they thought it was a great victory but as time went on the Philistines began to regard the ark as a burden, not as a trophy.

i. Why did they keep it **seven months** at all? Because they were reluctant to give up such a wonderful "trophy" of what they at first felt was a great victory over the God of Israel. It can take a long time before we realize the futility of resisting God.

b. **By all means return it with a trespass offering**: The Philistine priests had enough sense to know they offended the LORD God. Therefore, they knew they should do something to express their sorrow and repentance before the LORD.

c. **Five golden tumors and five golden rats**: The specific offering recognizes that it was the LORD who brought the plague upon the Philistines. They said, "We know these plagues were not accidents. We know the LORD God of Israel has caused them. We apologize to the LORD God and ask Him to turn away His anger."

i. We know the plague involved **tumors** (1 Samuel 5:6, 9, 12). We were not told in 1 Samuel 5 that the plague involved **rats**. Some think the **tumors** were the result of bubonic plague, carried by **rats**. Others think the **rats** were part of another plague or calamity mentioned in 1 Samuel 5:11: *For there was a deadly destruction throughout all the city; the hand of God was very heavy there.*

d. **And you shall give glory to the God of Israel**: Acknowledging God's judgment is one way to **give glory to the God of Israel**. We often fail to give God this glory because we ignore His judgment or write it off as fate or bad luck.

e. **Perhaps He will lighten His hand from you, from your gods, and from your land**: The Philistines admitted that the God of Israel judged their gods and had jurisdiction over their lands. They confessed that He was Almighty God, yet they did not worship Him instead of their gods.

f. **Why then do you harden your hearts as the Egyptians and Pharaoh hardened their hearts?** Aware of the Exodus account, the Philistines rightly remembered that no good comes when anyone hardens their heart against the LORD. Even in a purely self-interested sense, it isn't smart to harden your heart against the LORD.

2. (7-9) The Philistines decide *how* to return the ark, including a test to see if the judgment was from God or by chance.

"Now therefore, make a new cart, take two milk cows which have never been yoked, and hitch the cows to the cart; and take their calves home, away from them. Then take the ark of the LORD and set it on the cart; and put the articles of gold which you are returning to Him *as* a trespass offering in a chest by its side. Then send it away, and let it go. And watch: if it goes up the road to its own territory, to Beth Shemesh, *then* He has done us this great evil. But if not, then we shall know that *it is* not His hand *that* struck us; it happened to us by chance."

a. **Take two milk cows which have never been yoked**: Here, the Philistines conducted an experiment. They *thought* all the calamity of the plagues was from the LORD God of Israel but they were not 100% sure. So, they devised another test. Men are almost always reluctant to repent and they guard against repenting "unnecessarily."

i. The test was simple, and stacked against God. By nature, **two milk cows which have never been yoked** should not pull a cart at all, instead they should have resisted their yokes. Additionally, they decided to **take their calves home, away from them**. The "maternal instinct" of the cows would draw them not towards the land of Israel, but back home to their own calves. The Philistines devised a test that "forced" the God of Israel to do something miraculous to demonstrate He really was the cause of the plagues.

b. **Take the ark of the LORD and set it on the cart**. God never wanted the ark to be transported by a cart. He wanted it to be carried by poles set in rings on the side of the ark (Numbers 4:15).

i. The ark didn't have "handles" and was not to be carried by lifting it directly in one's hands. Instead, it was to be carried by inserting gold-overlaid wood poles into gold rings at each corner of the ark. The poles were to remain inserted in the rings, and to be the source of contact with the ark. Apart from touching the poles, it was forbidden to touch the Ark of the Covenant (Exodus 25:12-15).

ii. Though this way of transporting the ark was prohibited by the law, God excused them because of their ignorance of His law. "God winked at it in them, both because they were ignorant of God's law to the contrary, and because they had no Levites to carry it upon their shoulders." (Poole)

c. **Put the articles of gold which you are returning to Him as a trespass offering in a chest by its side**: The Philistines were wise enough to not open the Ark of the Covenant, and set the **articles of gold** in the ark itself. Certainly, they were curious about what was in the ark, but they didn't let their curiosity lead them into sin.

d. **If not, then we shall know that it is not His hand that struck us; it was by chance that it happened to us**: Is it possible that the tumors and other judgments came **by chance**?

i. Many people think things happen **by chance**. Some say the world was created **by chance**. People who are otherwise intelligent often fall into this delusion. Jacques Monod, a biochemist, wrote: "Chance *alone* is at the source of every innovation, of all creation in the biosphere. Pure chance, absolutely free but blind, at the very root of the stupendous edifice of evolution."

ii. Assigning such power to "chance" is crazy because chance has no power. For example, when a coin is flipped, the chance that it will land "heads" is 50%. However, "chance" does not make it land heads. Whether or not it lands heads or tails is due to the strength of the flip, the force of air currents and air pressure as it flies through the air, where it is caught, and if it is flipped over once caught. *Chance* doesn't "do" anything other than describe a probability. We live in a cause and effect world, and *chance* is not a cause, but God is the great cause.

iii. When Carl Sagan petitioned the federal government for a grant to search for intelligent life in outer space, he hoped to find it by using a super sensitive instrument to pick up radio signals from distant space. When he received those radio signals, he looked for order and pattern - which would demonstrate that the signals were transmitted by intelligent life. In the same way, the order and pattern of the whole universe demonstrates that it was fashioned by intelligent life, not by "chance." Scientists detect "chance" in the radio signals constantly (in the form of unpatterned static), but it tells them *nothing*.

iv. Realizing that nothing happens by chance should not make us think every event is full of important meaning from God. Some things just happen and have no great eternal purpose that we can discern. Christians can get off track by trying to see a message from God in everything. But *nothing* happens by chance. We live in a cause and effect world. "But wicked men will sooner believe the most uncertain and ridiculous things, than own the visible demonstrations of God's power and providence." (Poole)

3. (10-12) Against all expectation, the cows go the land of Israel.

Then the men did so; they took two milk cows and hitched them to the cart, and shut up their calves at home. And they set the ark of the Lord on the cart, and the chest with the gold rats and the images of their tumors. Then the cows headed straight for the road to Beth Shemesh, *and* went along the highway, lowing as they went, and did not turn aside to the right hand or the left. And the lords of the Philistines went after them to the border of Beth Shemesh.

a. **Then the cows headed straight for the road to Beth Shemesh**: They should not have done this. The cows should resist the yoke, because they were never harnessed before. They should head back for their Philistine homes out of concern for their young calves. But they **headed straight for the road to Beth Shemesh**. God didn't leave this up to chance.

i. Not only were they **headed straight for the road**, they **did not turn aside to the right hand or the left**. They didn't meander around the way; they went straight where they were supposed to go.

ii. This was a remarkable miracle. Two cows who never pulled a cart before, either alone or together. No driver led them, yet they left home, and marched the ten miles or so to a city they had never been to. They left their own calves behind and went straight on a certain road, with never a wrong turn, never a stop, never turning aside into the fields to feed themselves, never turning back to feed their own calves.

iii. As the cows went on the road back to Israel, we can imagine the Israelites mourning over the loss of the ark. Perhaps at that very moment they cried out to God, grieving because they thought the glory had departed. God's glory had not left *anywhere*! The Israelites and the Philistines both resisted Him, so the LORD found a few cows to show His glory through.

b. **Lowing as they went**: This means the cows were not especially happy. They longed for their calves at home, yet they still did the will of God.

i. The *Theological Wordbook of the Old Testament* on the ancient Hebrew word *ga-ah*, translated **lowing**: "This root indicates an intense aversion which is expressed often in punitive or adverse action."

ii. When people don't believe there is a loving God who sits enthroned in the heavens and has a good plan for our lives, you can't blame them for being *afraid*, for being *proud*, for being *miserable*. But for those who believe in the God of the Bible, there is no excuse for fear, pride, or misery. God is still on His throne! "As we go forth into the world, let us believe that the movement of all things is towards the accomplishment of God's purpose." (Meyer)

B. The Ark at Beth Shemesh.

1. (13-15) The ark is received with honor and joy at Beth Shemesh.

Now *the people of* Beth Shemesh *were* reaping their wheat harvest in the valley; and they lifted their eyes and saw the ark, and rejoiced to see *it*. Then the cart came into the field of Joshua of Beth Shemesh, and stood there; a large stone *was* there. So they split the wood of the cart and offered the cows as a burnt offering to the LORD. The Levites took down the ark of the LORD and the chest that *was* with it, in which *were* the articles of gold, and put *them* on the large stone. Then the men of Beth Shemesh offered burnt offerings and made sacrifices the same day to the LORD.

a. **Rejoiced to see it**: They felt something like the disciples felt on the day they saw the resurrected Jesus, because they felt they received God back to them from the dead. On this day as they were **reaping their wheat harvest** (between May and June), they knew the God of Israel was alive.

i. Of course, God was never dead and never left them. But the Israelites *felt* as though God was dead, and they were as desperate, discouraged, and hopeless as if He really were dead. According to their feelings, it was as if the LORD God of Israel had risen from the dead.

b. **The cart came into the field of Joshua of Beth Shemesh, and stood there**: After being guided for some ten miles from the Philistine city, without stopping or going to one side or the other, the ark then stopped in Israelite land, at the exact field of one chosen man.

c. **They split the wood of the cart and offered the cows as a burnt offering**: They knew this was the right thing to do in honor to God, yet it really cost them something. Cows and carts were expensive property.

i. In a strict sense their offering was against the Mosaic Law. First, they offered female animals to the LORD, which was forbidden (Leviticus 1:3; 22:19). Second, they made a burnt offering to the LORD away from the tabernacle, which violated the command in Deuteronomy 12:5-6. Yet God knew both their hearts and the remarkable circumstances and He was no doubt honored.

d. **The Levites took down the ark of the LORD**: The Israelites were careful to let the Levites handle the ark, as was commanded by the law (Numbers 4:1-6, 15). Beth Shemesh was a priestly city (Joshua 21:16), so priests were on hand.

2. (16-18) The offering from the Philistines included with the ark.

So when the five lords of the Philistines had seen *it*, they returned to Ekron the same day. These *are* the golden tumors which the Philistines returned *as* a trespass offering to the LORD: one for Ashdod, one for Gaza, one for Ashkelon, one for Gath, one for Ekron; and the golden rats, *according to* the number of all the cities of the Philistines *belonging* to the five lords, *both* fortified cities and country villages, even as far as the large *stone of* Abel on which they set the ark of the LORD, *which stone remains* to this day in the field of Joshua of Beth Shemesh.

a. **When the five lords of the Philistines had seen it**: They wondered if all what had happened to them while they had the ark was an accident. So they set up an elaborate and difficult test for God to fulfill, and they personally observed to see if God would indeed meet the test. Their reaction isn't recorded, but they must have been persuaded.

3. (19) The men of Beth Shemesh profane God's holiness.

Then He struck the men of Beth Shemesh, because they had looked into the ark of the LORD. He struck fifty thousand and seventy men of the people, and the people lamented because the LORD had struck the people with a great slaughter.

a. **Then He struck the men of Beth Shemesh, because they had looked into the ark of the LORD**: The Ark of the Covenant was only to be touched and handled by specific Levites from the family of Kohath, and even they were commanded to not touch the ark itself (Numbers 4:15). The men of Beth Shemesh sinned by not only touching the ark, but also looking into it inappropriately.

i. We again notice God dealt with the Israelites more strictly than He dealt with the Philistines, who just transported the ark by a cart. God did this because the Israelites, who had His law, should have and did know better. It is sad to consider that the Philistines showed more honor to the holiness of God than the Israelites.

b. **Because they looked into the ark of the LORD**: Because of the honor and glory of God there are things which He chooses to keep hidden, and it is wrong for men to pry into these secrets of God.

i. Isaiah 55:8-9 shows this thought: *"For My thoughts are not your thoughts, nor are your ways My ways," says the LORD. "For as the heavens are higher than the earth, so are My ways higher than your ways, and My thoughts than your thoughts."* We need to respect the fact that God is God and we are not, and there are some things we just will not, and should not, know.

c. **He struck fifty thousand and seventy men of the people**: The manuscript evidence is pretty clear that the number recorded originally in the text was **seventy**, not **fifty thousand and seventy**. **Seventy** men dead in such an incident is still **a great slaughter**.

i. Basically, the Hebrew grammar can mean that out of fifty thousand men, God struck seventy of them. "We cannot come to any other conclusion than that the number 50,000 is neither correct nor genuine, but a gloss [marginal note] which has crept into the text through some oversight." (Keil and Delitszch)

4. (20-21) The men of Beth Shemesh appeal to the men of Kirjath Jearim to take the ark from them.

And the men of Beth Shemesh said, "Who is able to stand before this holy LORD God? And to whom shall it go up from us?" So they sent messengers to the inhabitants of Kirjath Jearim, saying, "The Philistines have brought back the ark of the LORD; come down *and* take it up with you."

a. **Who is able to stand before this holy LORD God?** In their disrespect for God, the men of Beth Shemesh offended the holiness of the LORD. Now they knew the **LORD** was **holy**, but it didn't make them want to be closer to God. It made them want to distance themselves from God.

i. The primary idea behind holiness is not moral purity (though the idea includes moral purity), but it is the idea of *apartness* - that God is separate, different from His creation, both in His essential nature and in the perfection of His attributes.

ii. When men encounter the holiness of God, they are not necessarily attracted to it. When Peter saw the holy power of Jesus he said, *"Depart from me, for I am a sinful man, O Lord!"* (Luke 5:8). When the disciples on another occasion saw the holy Jesus shining forth at the transfiguration, they were greatly afraid (Matthew 17:6). When we meet the Holy God, we are excited and afraid all at the same time. It's like going up on a roller coaster - you want to be there, but at the same time you don't want to be there. Many of the thrill-seeking pleasures of our modern world are simply weak attempts to imitate the fulfillment we can only find by meeting the Holy God.

b. **Who is able to stand before this holy LORD God?** In one sense, the men of Beth Shemesh showed a bad heart in asking this question. Their question made God seem too harsh instead of showing themselves to be too disobedient.

i. "Here they seem peevishly [angrily] to lay the blame of their sufferings upon God, as over-holy and strict: of their sins, the true cause, they say nothing; but take care to rid their hands of the ark, which they should have retained reverently." (Trapp)

c. **Who is able to stand before this holy LORD God?** In another sense, the men of Beth Shemesh asked a good question. God is in fact holy and **Who is able** indeed?

i. Holiness is not so much achieved through our own efforts, but it is received as we are new men and women in Jesus. Holiness is part of the new man we are in Jesus (Ephesians 4:24), and we are invited to be partakers - sharers of Jesus' holiness (Hebrews 12:10).

ii. Though God is holy, though He is apart from us, instead of building a wall around His *apartness*, God calls us to come to Him and share His *apartness*. As it says in 1 Peter 1:16, God calls us to *be holy, for I am holy*. Holiness is not so much something we have, as much as it is something that has us.

d. **And to whom shall it go up from us?** For the men of Beth Shemesh, the holiness of God was a problem, a problem that could be fixed by putting distance between themselves and God. Their question was not, "How can we be made right with a holy God," but it was "Who can we give this problem to so the holiness of God is no longer a burden to us?"

e. **They sent messengers to the inhabitants of Kirjath Jearim**: We don't know why they picked this village. Perhaps they had good relations with these men and thought they would take good care of the ark. Perhaps they had bad relations with them and wanted the LORD to curse them. Whatever the reason, the men of **Kirjath Jearim** received the ark and it stayed there for many years until King David brought it to the city of Jerusalem (2 Samuel 6).

1 Samuel 7 - Samuel as Judge

A. Samuel leads the nation in repentance.

1. (1-2) The ark at Kirjath Jearim.

Then the men of Kirjath Jearim came and took the ark of the LORD, and brought it into the house of Abinadab on the hill, and consecrated Eleazar his son to keep the ark of the LORD. So it was that the ark remained in Kirjath Jearim a long time; it was there twenty years. And all the house of Israel lamented after the LORD.

a. **The men of Kirjath Jearim**: They treated the Ark of the Covenant with respect and honor, yet they did not take it to the tabernacle. Instead of resting at the house of God, it was brought **into the house of Abinadab**.

b. **Consecrated Eleazar his son**: We don't know if Eleazar was of the proper priestly lineage, or if his consecration ceremony was legitimate according to Exodus 29. At least this reflected a *desire* to do the right thing.

c. **A long time**: Israel had the ark back but things were not really set right. Israel found they were no more right with God just because they had the Ark of the Covenant again. Instead, **all the house of Israel lamented after the LORD.**

i. They had good reason to lament. Their cities were in ruins, their armies were defeated, and they were under Philistine domination - all because they were not right with God.

ii. "It may very naturally be asked, 'Where was Samuel all that time?' I know not what he was doing during those twenty years; but I have a suspicion, I may say, I have a firm persuasion, that he was going from place to place, preaching in quiet spots wherever he could gather an audience; warning the people of their sin, and stirring them up to seek Jehovah, thus endeavouring to infuse some spirituality into their national life." (Spurgeon)

2. (3-4) Samuel preaches repentance, both outward and inward.

Then Samuel spoke to all the house of Israel, saying, "If you return to the LORD with all your hearts, *then* put away the foreign gods and the Ashtoreths from among you, and prepare your hearts for the LORD, and serve Him only; and He will deliver you from the hand of the Philistines." So the children of Israel put away the Baals and the Ashtoreths, and served the LORD only.

a. **Then Samuel spoke to all the house of Israel**: God raised up Samuel as a prophet and a judge (1 Samuel 4:1). Yet Samuel was strangely absent from the whole Ark of the Covenant fiasco. 1 Samuel 4:1 is the last place Samuel was mentioned, right before Israel schemed to use the ark as a good luck charm in battle.

b. **If you return with all your hearts, then put away the foreign gods**: Samuel called the nation to repentance. The repentance had to be *inward* (**with all your hearts**) and *outward* (**put away the foreign gods**).

i. The inward was more important than the outward, and it had to come first. That is why Samuel *first* called Israel to **return with all your hearts**, then told them to **put away the foreign gods**.

ii. However, inward repentance is a secret thing. It is hidden. No one can really "see" the heart of another. Yet the inward was proved by the outward. We can know if Israel did **return with all your hearts** by seeing if they really did **put away the foreign gods**. No one could see their heart, but they *could* see if they **put away the foreign gods**.

c. **And serve Him only**: Israel did not feel they rejected the LORD; they felt they only *added* the worship of other gods to their worship of the LORD. Samuel called on Israel to turn their backs on these other gods **and serve Him only**.

i. "A worse enemy than the Philistines held sway over the land . . . the people were thus in double bondage; the heavy yoke of the Philistines was upon them, because the heavier burden of a false worship crushed out the life of their hearts." (Spurgeon)

d. **So the children of Israel put away the Baals and the Ashtoreths, and served the LORD only**: The local gods of *Baal* and *Ashtoreth* were popular idols among the people of Israel. *Baal* was attractive because he was thought to be the god of weather, bringing good crops and financial success. *Ashtoreth* was attractive because she was thought to be the goddess of fertility, thus connected to love and sex.

i. "Ashtoreth was worshipped over a wide area as the goddess of fertility, love and war, and plaques of naked female figures from the Bronze and Iron Ages in Palestine are numerous. The *Baals* were the corresponding male deities." (Baldwin)

ii. "Baal, god of fertility and the storm, was believed to be the son of Dagon, god of grain. Ashtoreth, goddess of love and fertility, vied for supremacy with Asherah, mother-goddess and consort of El . . . The association of Baal, Asherah, and Ashtoreth with fertility, particularly as expressed in depraved sexual ritual at Canaanite shrines, made them especially abominable in the Lord's eyes." (Youngblood)

2. (5-6) The nation repents at Mizpah.

And Samuel said, "Gather all Israel to Mizpah, and I will pray to the LORD for you." So they gathered together at Mizpah, drew water, and poured *it* out before the LORD. And they fasted that day, and said there, "We have sinned against the LORD." And Samuel judged the children of Israel at Mizpah.

a. **Gather all Israel to Mizpah**: This is where Jacob separated from Laban (Genesis 31:49), and was the gathering place for a repentant Israel in Judges 20:1. This was a place remembered for separation and repentance.

b. **I will pray to the LORD for you**: Samuel already called the nation to repentance, and they made a start at it. Samuel knew God's work in them could only be completed through prayer.

c. **So they gathered together at Mizpah**: This showed the *spiritual* need Israel felt at the time. They expressed their repentance both by putting away the bad and by pursuing the good.

i. The *experience* of conviction of sin proves nothing. It is our response to conviction that demonstrates repentance.

d. **Drew water, and poured it out before the LORD**: In this context a ceremonial pouring of water demonstrated the soul poured out before the LORD. It was an expression of emptiness and need.

i. The Chaldean translation of this passage gives this sense well: "They poured out their hearts like water in penance before the Lord." "They seemed to say in effect, We could wish to shed as many tears for our sins as there are drops of water in this bucket; but because we cannot do this, behold, we do what we can." (Trapp)

ii. They expressed the same heart as Lamentations 2:19: *Arise, cry out in the night, at the beginning of the watches; pour out your heart like water before the face of the Lord.*

e. **And they fasted that day, and said there, "We have sinned against the LORD."** Israel also expressed their sorrow over their sin by *fasting* (a message that nothing else really mattered except getting right with God) and by *confession* (a straightforward claim of guilt and responsibility).

i. 1 John 1:5-10 makes it clear that confession is vital to maintain *relationship* with God. As God convicts us of sin or sins that hinder fellowship with Him, we must confess it and receive forgiveness and cleansing for our relationship with God to continue without hindrance.

ii. If it is meant from the heart, it is hard to make a better statement of confession than **"We have sinned against the LORD."** This is almost exactly what David said when he was confronted with his sin in 2 Samuel 12:13.

e. **And Samuel judged the children of Israel**: Samuel was the last judge and he was a judge over Israel as were the leaders in the days of the Book of Judges. But his leadership was more spiritual than military.

B. Samuel leads the nation to victory.

1. (7) The Philistine threat.

Now when the Philistines heard that the children of Israel had gathered together at Mizpah, the lords of the Philistines went up against Israel. And when the children of Israel heard *of it*, they were afraid of the Philistines.

a. **When the Philistines heard**: The Philistines were right to be afraid of a repentant, God-seeking Israel, because with God fighting for them Israel was invincible.

i. When the Philistines looked at a humble and repentant Israel they probably saw *weakness*. They may have said, "Look at those weakling Israelites. They are such wimps, crying out before their God like this." If the Philistines thought this way, they were dead wrong.

b. **When the children of Israel heard of it, they were afraid of the Philistines**: The Israelites didn't have much more spiritual understanding than the Philistines. They should have been more confident in the LORD.

i. Our feelings of confidence can deceive us. In 1 Samuel 4:5 Israel was completely confident against the Philistines but their confidence was false and they were soon defeated. Here, Israel is fearful and sure of defeat and they have no confidence at all. They seemed to have more faith when they trusted in the ark than when they are humble and repentant before the LORD. But small faith in the true and living God is more powerful than strong faith in a lie.

2. (8-9) Samuel prays for the nation.

So the children of Israel said to Samuel, "Do not cease to cry out to the LORD our God for us, that He may save us from the hand of the Philistines." And Samuel took a suckling lamb and offered *it as* a whole burnt offering to the LORD. Then Samuel cried out to the LORD for Israel, and the LORD answered him.

a. **Do not cease to cry out to the LORD our God for us**: The last time Israel was in this kind of situation they said, "Let's get the Ark of the Covenant and take it into battle with us. Then we can't lose!" Now they are much wiser before the LORD, and instead of trusting in the ark they did the right thing and asked Samuel to **cry out to the LORD our God for us**.

b. **Samuel took a sucking lamb and offered it as whole burnt offering to the LORD. Then Samuel cried out**: Samuel took time for a sacrifice at such a critical time because he knew he could only effectively pray in light of God's atoning sacrifice.

i. Think of that poor lamb - **a suckling lamb** - who never hurt anyone or who never sinned itself, yet its throat was slit, its blood poured out, its body cut up, and its carcass burned. Why? Because Samuel and Israel had to say, "This is what we deserve. This is the punishment that should come upon us. We thank you God for accepting the punishment of this innocent lamb instead." When we trust in *the Lamb of God who takes away the sin of the world* (John 1:29), we say the same thing.

c. **And the LORD answered him**: The battle has not yet been fought and a hostile Philistine army approached. Yet in a real way the battle was over and already won, because **the LORD answered him**.

i. The Bible speaks of Samuel as a mighty man of prayer: *Samuel was among those who called upon His name; they called upon the LORD, and He answered them.* (Psalm 99:6)

3. (10-12) The LORD fights for Israel.

Now as Samuel was offering up the burnt offering, the Philistines drew near to battle against Israel. But the LORD thundered with a loud thunder upon the Philistines that day, and so confused them that they were overcome before Israel. And the men of Israel went out of Mizpah and pursued the Philistines, and drove them back as far as below Beth Car. Then Samuel took a stone and set *it* up between Mizpah and Shen, and called its name Ebenezer, saying, "Thus far the LORD has helped us."

a. **The LORD thundered with a loud thunder**: God fought from heaven on behalf of Israel and defeated the Philistines. This was a special work of God because the Israelites heard the same thunder, but only the Philistines became **so confused . . . that they were overcome**. God not only sent thunder, He also sent *confusion* to the Philistines and *confidence* to Israel.

i. This was the kind of victory Israel hoped for in 1 Samuel 4 when they brought the Ark of the Covenant into battle. If they had only repented and sought the LORD as they did here, they could have had this kind of victory long ago.

b. **Called its name Ebenezer, saying "Thus far the LORD has helped us."** Samuel knew the nation needed to remember this amazing victory, which came to a humble and repentant Israel. The LORD won this battle, not Israel - so he named the stone **Ebenezer**, meaning "stone of help."

c. **"Thus far the LORD has helped us."** Samuel knew the LORD did a great work yet he knew there was much more to be accomplished. So he could say, **"Thus far the LORD has helped us."** God helps us **thus far** at a time and His past work is a pledge of future help.

i. **Thus far the LORD has helped us** can either mean "to this point in time" or "to this geographical place." Probably both are in mind; Hebrew writers loved to use double meanings.

4. (13-14) The success of Samuel as a judge over Israel.

So the Philistines were subdued, and they did not come anymore into the territory of Israel. And the hand of the LORD was against the Philistines all the days of Samuel. Then the cities which the Philistines had taken from Israel were restored to Israel, from Ekron to Gath; and Israel recovered its territory from the hands of the Philistines. Also there was peace between Israel and the Amorites.

a. **The hand of the LORD was against the Philistines all the days of Samuel . . . the cities which the Philistines had taken from Israel were restored to Israel**: Samuel was not a military man, but he was just as successful or more successful than Israel's best generals because the LORD fought for Samuel.

b. **Also there was peace between Israel and the Amorites**: Samuel was successful not only as a man of war, but also as a man of peace.

5. (15-17) Samuel's service as a circuit judge.

And Samuel judged Israel all the days of his life. He went from year to year on a circuit to Bethel, Gilgal, and Mizpah, and judged Israel in all those places. But he always returned to Ramah, for his home *was* there. There he judged Israel, and there he built an altar to the LORD.

a. **Judged Israel all the days of his life**: Samuel was used of God all his days. Some judges ended their ministry early or in disgrace, but Samuel finished well.

b. **He went from year to year on a circuit . . . and judged Israel in all those places**: Samuel worked hard in his service of the LORD. Every year, Samuel worked hard to go all about Israel to help settle disputes and promote righteousness.

c. **He always returned to Ramah . . . and there he built an altar to the LORD**: Samuel remained faithful to the LORD. An altar was a place of sacrifice and worship, and Samuel had a consistent relationship with the LORD in sacrifice and worship.

1 Samuel 8 - Israel Demands a King

A. The people of Israel request a king.

1. (1-3) Samuel appoints his sons as judges.

Now it came to pass when Samuel was old that he made his sons judges over Israel. The name of his firstborn was Joel, and the name of his second, Abijah; *they were* judges in Beersheba. But his sons did not walk in his ways; they turned aside after dishonest gain, took bribes, and perverted justice.

a. **When Samuel was old . . . he made his sons judges over Israel**: Samuel was one of the godliest men in the entire Bible. Yet his action here may be a sin on his part. We never have the pattern of **judges** being appointed by men or of the office of judge being passed from father to son. Samuel was not right to appoint **his sons judges over Israel**.

b. **His sons did not walk in his ways**: This is why Samuel was wrong to appoint his **sons as judges over Israel**. Samuel probably could not look objectively at his sons. He excused sins in them that he saw in others.

2. (4-5) Samuel's sons are rejected as leaders over Israel.

Then all the elders of Israel gathered together and came to Samuel at Ramah, and said to him, "Look, you are old, and your sons do not walk in your ways. Now make us a king to judge us like all the nations."

a. **All the elders of Israel gathered**: It was wise for the elders of Israel to do this. They did not have to accept leaders who were obviously ungodly and unfit to lead.

b. **Now make for us a king to judge us like all the nations**: While it was wise for the elders of Israel to reject Samuel's sons as leaders, it was wrong for them to say this.

i. In itself, the desire to have a king was not bad. God knew one day Israel would have a king. 400 years before this God gave instructions to Israel about their future king (Deuteronomy 17:14-20). A king was in God's plan for Israel.

ii. Yet, the *reason* Israel wanted a king was wrong. "**Like all the nations**" is no reason at all. We often get into trouble by wanting to be like the world when we should instead be transformed into the image of Jesus Christ (Romans 12:1-2).

c. **Make for us a king**: There was a difference between a **king** and a judge. A judge was a leader raised up by God, usually to meet a specific need in a time of crisis. When the crisis was over usually the judge went back to doing what he did before. A **king** not only held his office as king as long as he lived, he also passed his throne down to his descendants.

i. Judges did not make a "government." They met a specific need in a time of crisis. Kings establish a standing government with a bureaucracy, which can be both a blessing and a curse to any people.

ii. In Judges 8 Gideon was offered the throne over Israel. He refused it saying, *"I will not rule over you, nor shall my son rule over you; the LORD shall rule over you."* (Judges 8:23) This was the heart of all the judges, and why Israel went some 400 years in the Promised Land without a king.

3. (6-8) Samuel prays about their request and God answers.

But the thing displeased Samuel when they said, "Give us a king to judge us." So Samuel prayed to the LORD. And the LORD said to Samuel, "Heed the voice of the people in all that they say to you; for they have not rejected you, but they have rejected Me, that I should not reign over them. According to all the works which they have done since the day that I brought them up out of Egypt, even to this day; with which they have forsaken Me and served other gods; so they are doing to you also."

a. **The thing displeased Samuel**: No doubt, Samuel was stung by the rejection of his sons. But more than that, Samuel saw the ungodly motive behind the elders' request for a king.

b. **So Samuel prayed to the LORD**: This is the right thing to do whenever we are **displeased**. We should never carry such troubles with us. Instead, we should do what Samuel did when he **prayed to the LORD**.

i. "Surely it is the mistake of our life, that we carry our burdens instead of handing them over; that we worry instead of trusting; that we pray so little." (Meyer)

c. **Heed the voice of the people**: God told Samuel to fulfill the people's request. This was not because their request was good or right, but because God would teach Israel through this. Sometimes when we insist on having something bad God will allow us to have it and then teach through it.

i. In many ways this was a matter of timing. God knew Israel would have a king but He wanted to give the king in His timing. Because

Israel demanded a king out of bad and carnal reasons, God will give them a bad and carnal king. Israel will get what they want, and will hurt because of it!

d. **They have not rejected you, but they have rejected Me, that I should not reign over them**: God had a purpose in not giving Israel a king up to that point. It was because He did not want them to put an ungodly trust in the king instead of the LORD. Now, Israel rejects God's plan and declares they do not want the LORD God to **reign over them**.

i. In the words **they have not rejected you**, we sense God comforting Samuel. It is as if God says, "Samuel, don't take it personally. They are not rejecting you, but Me."

e. **They have forsaken Me . . . so they are doing to you also**: In fact, Israel forsook God by asking for a king. When the elders of Israel asked for a king, they thought that better politics or government could meet their needs. But if they had just been faithful to their King in heaven, they would not need a king on earth.

i. This strikes us as simply *unfair*. Didn't God show Himself to be a worthy King? Didn't He demonstrate His ability to lead the nation, and demonstrate it over and over again?

ii. There is a sense in which their rejection of God as their king is prophetic. When Jesus stood before Pilate the Jewish mob declared, *we have no king but Caesar* (John 19:15). Jesus was a rejected King.

4. (9) God tells Samuel to warn the nation.

"Now therefore, heed their voice. However, you shall solemnly forewarn them, and show them the behavior of the king who will reign over them."

a. **You shall solemnly forewarn them**: The sense is that Israel will not change their mind, so Samuel's goal is to simply **forewarn them**. If Israel chose this course God wanted them to make an informed choice. So, the LORD told Samuel to **show them the behavior of the king who will reign over them**.

b. **Forewarn them**: Information creates responsibility. In telling Israel this, Samuel did not only help them make an informed choice; he increased their accountability for making the right choice. They couldn't say, "We didn't know."

B. Samuel speaks to the people of Israel about their desire for a king.

1. (10-18) Samuel warns the nation of the responsibilities of having a king.

So Samuel told all the words of the LORD to the people who asked him for a king. And he said, "This will be the behavior of the king who will reign over you: He

will take your sons and appoint *them* for his own chariots and *to be* his horsemen, and *some* will run before his chariots. He will appoint captains over his thousands and captains over his fifties, *will set some* to plow his ground and reap his harvest, and *some* to make his weapons of war and equipment for his chariots. He will take your daughters *to be* perfumers, cooks, and bakers. And he will take the best of your fields, your vineyards, and your olive groves, and give *them* to his servants. He will take a tenth of your grain and your vintage, and give it to his officers and servants. And he will take your male servants, your female servants, your finest young men, and your donkeys, and put *them* to his work. He will take a tenth of your sheep. And you will be his servants. And you will cry out in that day because of your king whom you have chosen for yourselves, and the LORD will not hear you in that day."

a. **This will be the behavior of the king who will reign over you**: God wanted Israel to know there would be problems connected with having a king. In Israel's view, they had problems that would be solved by having a king. While those problems may have been solved, God wanted them to know a king would also *bring* other problems. They should carefully weigh the *benefits* against the *problems*.

b. **He will take . . . He will take . . . he will take . . . He will take . . . he will take . . . He will take . . . And you will be his servants**: The LORD gives fair warning. Most kings are *takers*, not *givers* and they come to be served, not to serve. If Israel wants a king they must realize he will be a taker not a giver, and they **will be his servants**.

i. Not every king is a "taking" king. The King of Kings is a giving king. Jesus said of Himself, *the Son of Man did not come to be served, but to serve* (Matthew 20:28).

c. **And you will cry out in that day because of your king whom you have chosen**: Israel would later **cry out** because they wanted a king for unspiritual and ungodly reasons. So God will call this coming king **your king**, and make it clear that he is the king **whom you have chosen**. If Israel waited for God's king they would not need to **cry out**.

2. (19-22) Israel demands a king despite God's warning.

Nevertheless the people refused to obey the voice of Samuel; and they said, "No, but we will have a king over us, that we also may be like all the nations, and that our king may judge us and go out before us and fight our battles." And Samuel heard all the words of the people, and he repeated them in the hearing of the LORD. So the LORD said to Samuel, "Heed their voice, and make them a king." And Samuel said to the men of Israel, "Every man go to his city."

a. **No, but we will have a king over us**: God will give Israel "their king" - Saul. Later, after "their king" fails, God will give Israel "His king" - David.

Because we suppose that God ultimately wanted Israel to be a monarchy (based on Deuteronomy 17:14-20). we might even guess that if Israel did not forsake the LORD here, God would have made David the first human king of Israel.

b. **That we also may be like all the nations**: This was never God's goal for Israel. God wanted to make them *a special treasure to Me above all people . . . a kingdom of priests and a holy nation* (Exodus 19:6). God wanted to make Israel something special, and they wanted to be just like everyone else.

i. **And that our king may judge us and go out before us and fight our battles**: God just won a spectacular battle for Israel in 1 Samuel 7. Israel did not lack a *king* - they had a king in the LORD God. What they wanted was the *image* of a king. Their desire for a king was really the desire for someone who *looked like* what they thought a king should look like.

c. **So the LORD said to Samuel, "Heed their voice, and make them a king."** This is almost funny. Israel rejects the rule of God yet they cannot escape it, because God will appoint their king. God will never step off His throne, even if man asks Him to. Yet if we resist the rule of God, we will find that we do not benefit from it the way that we might. When we resist God, we only hurt ourselves.

1 Samuel 9 - God Leads Saul to Samuel

A. Saul searches for his father's donkeys.

1. (1-2) Kish, the father of Saul, and his son Saul.

There was a man of Benjamin whose name *was* Kish the son of Abiel, the son of Zeror, the son of Bechorath, the son of Aphiah, a Benjamite, a mighty man of power. And he had a choice and handsome son whose name *was* Saul. *There was* not a more handsome person than he among the children of Israel. From his shoulders upward *he was* taller than any of the people.

a. **A mighty man of power**: Kish, the father of Saul, was a wealthy and influential man in Israel. Saul came from a prestigious family and was born to wealth and influence.

b. **A choice and handsome young man**: Saul was noted for both his family and his appearance. He was tall (**taller than any of his people**) and good looking. In fact, there **was not a more handsome person than he among the children of Israel**. Saul *looked* like a great king. If being king over Israel was all about image and appearances, Saul was the man - the king from central casting.

i. The name "**Saul**" means, "asked of God." Israel asked for a king and Saul was indeed the one "asked of God."

c. **From his shoulders upward he was taller than any of the people** does not mean Saul had an extremely long neck and head. It means he was "head and shoulders" taller than anyone else.

i. What is not mentioned in these first two verses is *God*. Saul came from a wealthy, influential family and was good looking. But nothing is said about his relationship with the God of Israel. There is nothing said because there was nothing to say.

ii. Saul reflected the spiritual state of the whole nation of Israel. There may have been some spiritual image present, but the heart was far from where God wanted it to be.

2. (3-14) Saul and his servant search for his father's donkeys and meet Samuel the prophet.

Now the donkeys of Kish, Saul's father, were lost. And Kish said to his son Saul, "Please, take one of the servants with you, and arise, go and look for the donkeys." So he passed through the mountains of Ephraim and through the land of Shalisha, but they did not find *them*. Then they passed through the land of Shaalim, and *they were* not *there*. Then he passed through the land of the Benjamites, but they did not find *them*. When they had come to the land of Zuph, Saul said to his servant who *was* with him, "Come, let us return, lest my father cease *caring* about the donkeys and become worried about us." And he said to him, "Look now, *there is* in this city a man of God, and *he is* an honorable man; all that he says surely comes to pass. So let us go there; perhaps he can show us the way that we should go." Then Saul said to his servant, "But look, *if* we go, what shall we bring the man? For the bread in our vessels is all gone, and *there is* no present to bring to the man of God. What do we have?" And the servant answered Saul again and said, "Look, I have here at hand one fourth of a shekel of silver. I will give *that* to the man of God, to tell us our way." (Formerly in Israel, when a man went to inquire of God, he spoke thus: "Come, let us go to the seer"; for *he who is* now *called* a prophet was formerly called a seer.) Then Saul said to his servant, "Well said; come, let us go." So they went to the city where the man of God *was*. As they went up the hill to the city, they met some young women going out to draw water, and said to them, "Is the seer here?" And they answered them and said, "Yes, there he is, just ahead of you. Hurry now; for today he came to this city, because there is a sacrifice of the people today on the high place. As soon as you come into the city, you will surely find him before he goes up to the high place to eat. For the people will not eat until he comes, because he must bless the sacrifice; afterward those who are invited will eat. Now therefore, go up, for about this time you will find him." So they went up to the city. As they were coming into the city, there was Samuel, coming out toward them on his way up to the high place.

a. **Now the donkeys of Kish, Saul's father, were lost**: Israel's first king will be led to the throne by three lost donkeys. We have no idea how God will use the seemingly normal and annoying circumstances of life.

i. There are two mistakes people make regarding God's guidance through circumstances. One mistake is to think *every* event of life is heavy with meaning from God. This is wrong, because though nothing happens by accident, not everything happens for a great purpose. The second mistake is to *ignore* the moving of God in our lives through circumstances. God wanted to use this situation to guide Saul, and God will often use circumstances in our lives the same way. We need to trust in God's goodness and in His ability to make *all things work together for good* (Romans 8:28).

b. **They did not find them . . . they were not there . . . did not find them**: This frustrated Saul. Yet God worked out His plan through the lost donkeys in a way Saul couldn't even imagine.

i. Those donkeys could have gone anywhere, but they went exactly where God wanted them to go. They submitted themselves to what God wanted. We often speak of "dumb animals," but these donkeys were smart enough to submit to God.

c. **Look now, there is in this city a man of God . . . perhaps he can show us the way we should go**: The suggestion of Saul's servant shows something about these two men - they weren't men of much spiritual character. They seem to be men who wouldn't think to come to the prophet Samuel for real spiritual guidance, but they did think, "Hey! Maybe he can help us find the donkeys!"

i. Yet, their words are a great credit to Samuel. His reputation was well known: **A man of God . . . an honorable man . . . all that he says surely comes to pass**. Every believer should have such a reputation.

d. **There is no present to bring the man of God**: Out of respect for Samuel, Saul did not want to approach him empty handed. But it is wrong to think that Samuel charged a fee for his "prophetic services." Samuel was a great prophet of the living God, not a fortune-teller.

i. "The word *seer*, *roeh*, occurs for the first time in this place; it literally signifies a *person who* SEES; particularly *preternatural* [supernatural] sights. A *seer* and a *prophet* were the same in most cases; only with this difference, the seer was always a *prophet*, but the prophet was not always a *seer*." (Clarke)

ii. "When consulting a prophet, it was common courtesy to bring a gift (Amos 7:12), whether modest (1 Kings 14:3) or lavish (2 Kings 8:8-9)." (Youngblood)

e. **Hurry now; for today he came to this city**: It "just happened" that Saul and his servant came looking for their donkeys on the same day Samuel was in town. God is guiding through these circumstances.

i. Jewish legends say that it was because Saul was so good looking that the **young women** wanted to talk to him.

B. Samuel and Saul meet.

1. (15-17) God tells Samuel that Saul is the man who will be king.

Now the LORD had told Samuel in his ear the day before Saul came, saying, "Tomorrow about this time I will send you a man from the land of Benjamin, and you shall anoint him commander over My people Israel, that he may save My people from the hand of the Philistines; for I have looked upon My people,

because their cry has come to Me." And when Samuel saw Saul, the LORD said to him, "There he is, the man of whom I spoke to you. This one shall reign over My people."

a. **Now the LORD had told Samuel in his ear the day before**: Saul had no relationship with the LORD, so God spoke to Saul through lost donkeys. But Samuel knew and loved the LORD, so God spoke to **Samuel in his ear**.

i. **The LORD had told Samuel in his ear** is literally, "had uncovered his ear." The same phrase is used in Ruth 4:4. "The phrase is taken from the pushing aside of the headdress in order to whisper, and therefore means that Jehovah had secretly told Samuel." (Smith, *Pulpit Commentary*) It doesn't mean Samuel heard an audible voice from God.

b. **Tomorrow about this time**: God gave the prophet Samuel specific guidance regarding future events. Samuel received this guidance wisely and looked for the fulfillment of the words to confirm God's choice of a king. But Samuel also wisely refused to manipulate circumstances to "make" what God said come to pass. Samuel felt that if this was God's word, He was able to make it happen.

c. **I will send you**: Even though Israel rejected the LORD as their king (1 Samuel 8:7), God was still in control. He didn't step off His throne just because Israel asked Him to. He would indeed give them a king, but He sent a flawed king to a flawed Israel.

d. **That he may save My people from the hand of the Philistines**: Though there were many problems with the reign of Saul, no one should think it was a total disaster. Saul led Israel to many military victories and greater independence from the Philistines.

e. **And when Samuel saw Saul, the LORD said to him**: The day after God told Samuel about the coming of the new king, God specifically identified the man to Samuel. God's speaking one day will be confirmed by His speaking another day.

2. (18-21) Samuel and Saul meet.

Then Saul drew near to Samuel in the gate, and said, "Please tell me, where *is* the seer's house?" And Samuel answered Saul and said, "I *am* the seer. Go up before me to the high place, for you shall eat with me today; and tomorrow I will let you go and will tell you all that *is* in your heart. "But as for your donkeys that were lost three days ago, do not be anxious about them, for they have been found. And on whom *is* all the desire of Israel? *Is it* not on you and on all your father's house?" And Saul answered and said, "*Am* I not a Benjamite, of the smallest of the tribes of Israel, and my family the least of all the families of the tribe of Benjamin? Why then do you speak like this to me?"

a. **You shall eat with me today**: Saul must have been amazed. He looked for a noted prophet, and the first man he asked about the prophet *was* the prophet. Then, the man of God invited Saul to dinner. Finally, he heard the words many fear to hear from a prophet: **tomorrow I will let you go and will tell you all that is in your heart**.

b. **As for your donkeys that were lost three days ago**: With this Samuel proved to Saul that he was a true prophet from God. He showed Saul he knew things that he probably could not have known unless it was revealed to him supernaturally.

c. **On whom is all the desire of Israel? Is it not on you?** With this, Samuel hinted at Saul's destiny. All Israel desired a king, and Saul will become the answer to that desire.

d. **Why then do you speak like this to me?** This was a genuinely humble response from Saul, even if it wasn't completely honest. Saul could not figure out why the prophet said God wanted *him* to be king.

i. Saul's statement **and my family the least of all the families of the tribe of Benjamin** is more an example of his modesty than his truthfulness. Saul's father and family were prominent (1 Samuel 9:1).

ii. "This speech of Saul is exceedingly *modest*; he was now becomingly humble; but who can bear *elevation* and *prosperity?*" (Clarke)

3. (22-24) Samuel makes certain that Saul is honored at the feast.

Now Samuel took Saul and his servant and brought them into the hall, and had them sit in the place of honor among those who were invited; there *were* about thirty persons. And Samuel said to the cook, "Bring the portion which I gave you, of which I said to you, 'Set it apart.'" So the cook took up the thigh with its upper part and set *it* before Saul. And *Samuel* said, "Here it is, what was kept back. *It* was set apart for you. Eat; for until this time it has been kept for you, since I said I invited the people." So Saul ate with Samuel that day.

a. **Had them sit in the place of honor**: In that culture the seating arrangement at dinner had a special protocol. The seat of honor was always on a particular side next to the host. It was a great honor to be seated in this place next to the prophet Samuel.

b. **It was set apart for you**: Saul was also given the special portion. In that culture every meal had a special portion to be given to the one the host wanted to honor. Saul was specially honored at this meal.

i. We may speculate that Samuel was interested to see how Saul reacted when honored. This often shows what kind of person we really are. If we receive honor humbly, without regarding it too much or becoming proud about it, it says something good about us. If we show a false humility or a proud heart in the way we receive honor, it shows something bad in our character.

4. (25-27) Samuel and Saul talk together through the night.

When they had come down from the high place into the city, *Samuel* spoke with Saul on the top of the house. They arose early; and it was about the dawning of the day that Samuel called to Saul on the top of the house, saying, "Get up, that I may send you on your way." And Saul arose, and both of them went outside, he and Samuel. As they were going down to the outskirts of the city, Samuel said to Saul, "Tell the servant to go on ahead of us." And he went on. "But you stand here awhile, that I may announce to you the word of God."

a. **Samuel spoke with Saul on the top of the house**: No doubt, Samuel told Saul all about Israel's desire for a king and how he had to be a good king for Israel.

i. We can imagine Samuel saying: "Look Saul, you have a lot going for you. You have the image, you are a humble man, and you will have the support of the people. But if you don't give your heart to serving God, and submit to Him as your king, you will never be a fit king for Israel."

ii. Queen Victoria reigned over Great Britain for 64 years. When she was 11 years old, her governess showed her a list of the kings and queens of England with her name added at the end. When she understood what it meant she burst into tears. Then she controlled herself and said solemnly, "I will be good." Here, Samuel gave Saul the opportunity to say with his heart, "I will be good."

b. **That I may announce to you the word of God**: Samuel dramatically introduced the official anointing as king he will give to Saul.

1 Samuel 10 - Saul Anointed and Proclaimed King

A. Saul is anointed as king over Israel.

1. (1) Samuel anoints Saul.

Then Samuel took a flask of oil and poured *it* on his head, and kissed him and said: "*Is it* not because the LORD has anointed you commander over His inheritance?"

a. **Samuel took a flask of oil and poured it on his head**: This was a literal *anointing* of Saul. The word "anoint" means *to rub or sprinkle on; apply an ointment or oily liquid to*. When Samuel **poured it on his head**, Saul was **anointed** with oil.

i. But the *idea* of anointing is much bigger. What happened to Saul's head and body was a picture of what God did in him spiritually. The Holy Spirit was poured out on him, equipping him for the job of ruling as king over Israel.

ii. As Christians under the New Covenant we also have an anointing: *But you have an anointing from the Holy One* (1 John 2:20). In the New Testament sense, *anointing* has the idea of being filled with and blessed by the Holy Spirit. This is something that is the common property of *all* Christians, but something we can and should become more submitted to and responsive to.

b. **And kissed him**: This was not only a greeting; it was also a sign of Samuel's personal support of Saul. It was important that the king of Israel feel the support of the man of God.

c. **Is it not because the LORD has anointed you**: God anointed Saul and there were many aspects to this anointing which were especially memorable to Saul.

i. It was a *secret* anointing, because it was not yet time to reveal Saul as king to the nation. As Christians, our anointing often comes in just such a private way, not in a flashy or public ceremony.

ii. It was a *memorable* and *evident* anointing, because Saul's head was drenched with oil. Psalm 133:2 describes how messy an anointing could be: *It is like the precious oil upon the head, running down the beard . . . running down on the edge of his garments.* As Christians our filling and empowering of the Holy Spirit should be memorable and evident. Saul could look back on this event and know God called him to something special as the king of Israel.

d. **Commander over His inheritance**: Samuel reminded Saul that Israel belonged to the LORD, that they were **His inheritance**. At the same time, Saul had an important job to do, because God placed him as **commander over His inheritance**. Saul should try to be the best king he could, because he had care of a people who belonged to the LORD God.

2. (2) Samuel tells Saul of a sign to confirm the anointing as king.

"When you have departed from me today, you will find two men by Rachel's tomb in the territory of Benjamin at Zelzah; and they will say to you, 'The donkeys which you went to look for have been found. And now your father has ceased caring about the donkeys and is worrying about you, saying, "What shall I do about my son?" ' "

a. **You will find two men by Rachel's tomb**: Samuel gave Saul a specific prophetic word, by which Saul could have confidence that his anointing was really from God. If there were no men **by Rachel's tomb**, or if there was only one man and not **two**, then Saul would know that Samuel did not really speak from God.

i. However, speaking purely theoretically, there could have been *three men* **by Rachel's tomb** and the prophecy would still be exactly correct. You can say there are **two men** if there are three or four or five; but you cannot say there are **two men** if there is only one. When a word is from God, it is always fulfilled exactly as God says, but not always exactly as we expect.

b. **They will say to you**: If the men by **Rachel's tomb** didn't tell Saul about finding the donkeys, Saul could know Samuel was not a true prophet. God gave Saul this sign to build confidence in the work of the LORD.

i. We need to trust God's *confirmation* along the way. God did not want Saul to doubt his calling later so he gave him a lot of confirmation.

3. (3-4) Samuel tells Saul of another sign to confirm what God has done.

"Then you shall go on forward from there and come to the terebinth tree of Tabor. There three men going up to God at Bethel will meet you, one carrying three young goats, another carrying three loaves of bread, and another carrying a skin of wine. And they will greet you and give you two *loaves* of bread, which you shall receive from their hands."

a. **The terebinth tree of Tabor . . . three men . . . three young goats . . . three loaves of bread . . . a skin of wine . . . they will greet you and give you**. Again, Samuel gave Saul specific predictions so they could be exactly verified. God may have a place for vague, broad words (such as saying to an audience of 500 people, "There is someone here with a headache"), but they are not remarkable evidence of prophecy.

b. **Which you shall receive**: It would be unusual for men to simply give a stranger like Saul **loaves of bread**. But as king, Saul will often receive gifts, so this was a good way to confirm his anointing as king.

i. **Two loaves of bread** were a strange present, but "The more strange the present was, the more fit it was for a sign of God's extraordinary providence in Saul's affairs." (Poole)

4. (5-7) Samuel tells Saul of a third sign to confirm what God has done.

"After that you shall come to the hill of God where the Philistine garrison *is*. And it will happen, when you have come there to the city, that you will meet a group of prophets coming down from the high place with a stringed instrument, a tambourine, a flute, and a harp before them; and they will be prophesying. Then the Spirit of the LORD will come upon you, and you will prophesy with them and be turned into another man. And let it be, when these signs come to you, *that* you do as the occasion demands; for God *is* with you."

a. **A group of prophets**: They were apparently seeking the LORD and worshipping Him at the place of worship (**the high place**). **They will be prophesying** isn't necessarily saying that they were all predicting the future, but that they all spoke under the inspiration of the Holy Spirit.

i. "Members of prophetic bands were often young (2 Kings 5:22; 9:4); they frequently lived together (2 Kings 6:1-2), ate together (2 Kings 4:38), and were supported by the generosity of their fellow Israelites (2 Kings 4:42-43) . . . Samuel provided guidance and direction for the movement in its early stages, as Elijah and Elisha did later." (Youngblood)

b. **Then the Spirit of the LORD will come upon you**: This reception of the Holy Spirit was the real anointing. The oil poured out on Saul's head was just a picture of this. A gallon of oil could go on his head, but if **the Spirit of the LORD** did not **come upon** him, it would mean nothing.

i. Poole observed **will come upon you** is literally "*will leap* or *rush upon thee*, to wit [namely], for a season. So it may be opposed to the *Spirit's resting* upon a man, as in Numbers 11:25; Isaiah 11:2."

c. **And you will prophesy with them and be turned into another man**: Before this Saul never was a particularly spiritual man. So for him to **prophesy** - that is, speak as inspired from the LORD, whether predicting the future, exhorting others, or speaking unto God - was real evidence that he was **turned into another man**.

i. For God to use Saul to the fullest, he had to be **turned into another man** by the filling of **the Spirit of the LORD**.

d. **When these signs come to you**: God arranged for each one of these three events to be a sign to Saul. God *always* confirms His anointing.

5. (8) Saul is commanded to wait for Samuel at Gilgal.

"You shall go down before me to Gilgal; and surely I will come down to you to offer burnt offerings *and* make sacrifices of peace offerings. Seven days you shall wait, till I come to you and show you what you should do."

a. **Seven days you shall wait**: This was an important command. By the nature of their office, kings do not wait for anybody - others wait for them. But Samuel commanded Saul to wait for him, because the prophet of God had more *real* authority than this king over Israel. Saul had to show that even though he was a king he was submitted to the LORD and the LORD's prophet. Failing to **wait** for Samuel will get Saul into trouble on a future occasion.

6. (9-13) The signs come to pass.

So it was, when he had turned his back to go from Samuel, that God gave him another heart; and all those signs came to pass that day. When they came there to the hill, there was a group of prophets to meet him; then the Spirit of God came upon him, and he prophesied among them. And it happened, when all who knew him formerly saw that he indeed prophesied among the prophets, that the people said to one another, "What is this *that* has come upon the son of Kish? *Is* Saul also among the prophets?" Then a man from there answered and said, "But who *is* their father?" Therefore it became a proverb: "*Is* Saul also among the prophets?" And when he had finished prophesying, he went to the high place.

a. **When he had turned his back to go from Samuel, that God gave him another heart**. Samuel could not give Saul another heart. Only the Spirit of the LORD could do it. To demonstrate this, God did not grant this change of heart to Saul until he left the presence of Samuel. God wanted Saul to honor and respect Samuel but to never look to him in the place of the LORD.

i. **God gave him another heart**: Samuel did not give it. Saul did not even give it to himself. The new **heart** was a gift from God. We also can have **another heart** from the LORD but we must receive it from *Him*. We can't receive a new heart from anyone except from God, and we can never make a new heart in anyone else.

b. **Is Saul also among the prophets?** This phrase **became a proverb** describing astonishment that someone was now deeply religious. As some used to say, "He got religion?" Saul was an unspiritual man who became very spiritual at the time when the Spirit of the LORD came upon him.

c. **But who is their father?** This question asked, "Who is the source of the inspiration upon the prophets?" If God was their inspiration, it wasn't strange that God inspired an unlikely man like Saul.

d. **When he had finished prophesying**. Saul prophesied without ever being recognized as a prophet. This shows us that someone can receive prophecy as a gift from the Holy Spirit without really being a "prophet" in the sense of having that office or title.

7. (14-16) Saul hides his experience from his family.

Then Saul's uncle said to him and his servant, "Where did you go?" So he said, "To look for the donkeys. When we saw that *they were* nowhere *to be found*, we went to Samuel." And Saul's uncle said, "Tell me, please, what Samuel said to you." So Saul said to his uncle, "He told us plainly that the donkeys had been found." But about the matter of the kingdom, he did not tell him what Samuel had said.

a. **Where did you go?** This perhaps was a simple, logical question. Or, **Saul's uncle** may want to know why Saul had very, very oily hair.

b. **About the matter of the kingdom, he did not tell him**: It seems strange that Saul did not tell what he experienced. Perhaps Saul was wise, knowing that the LORD had to reveal him as king over Israel. What point was there in saying, "I'm the king now!" until the LORD declared him king? Or perhaps Saul experienced what many do after a powerful encounter with the LORD: an attack from the enemy, making them fearful and cowardly to tell others what God did.

B. Saul proclaimed as king.

1. (17-19) Samuel's speech to the nation before the appointment of a king.

Then Samuel called the people together to the LORD at Mizpah, and said to the children of Israel, "Thus says the LORD God of Israel: 'I brought up Israel out of Egypt, and delivered you from the hand of the Egyptians *and* from the hand of all kingdoms and from those who oppressed you.' But you have today rejected your God, who Himself saved you from all your adversities and your tribulations; and you have said to Him, 'No, set a king over us!' Now therefore, present yourselves before the LORD by your tribes and by your clans."

a. **I brought Israel out of Egypt**: Before God appointed a king for Israel, God reminded them of all He did for them. God reminded Israel that He was still more than qualified to be their king and their rejection of Him was all because of *them* and not because of the LORD.

b. **But you have rejected your God, who Himself saved you out of all your adversities and your tribulations**: The LORD, speaking through Samuel, showed Israel how their rejection of Him made so little sense. It makes no sense to reject the one **who Himself saved you out of all your adversities and your tribulations**.

2. (20-21a) Saul is selected by lot.

And when Samuel had caused all the tribes of Israel to come near, the tribe of Benjamin was chosen. When he had caused the tribe of Benjamin to come near by their families, the family of Matri was chosen. And Saul the son of Kish was chosen.

a. **And Saul the son of Kish was chosen**: Saul was already anointed king over Israel. But God did this to show the whole nation that Saul was the right man. It showed that *God* chose Saul and not any man.

b. **Was chosen**: It is important to say that Saul did not become king because of the choosing by lot. Instead, he was chosen king because of God's word to the prophet Samuel. The choosing by lot simply confirmed the word of the LORD through Samuel.

3. (21b-24) Saul is revealed to be the king.

But when they sought him, he could not be found. Therefore they inquired of the LORD further, "Has the man come here yet?" And the LORD answered, "There he is, hidden among the equipment." So they ran and brought him from there; and when he stood among the people, he was taller than any of the people from his shoulders upward. And Samuel said to all the people, "Do you see him whom the LORD has chosen, that *there is* no one like him among all the people?" So all the people shouted and said, "Long live the king!"

a. **Hidden among the equipment**: Here Saul showed a healthy embarrassment and humility. He did not look forward to being "center stage" in front of the nation; he seemed to dread it. Saul was not made king because of his personal ambition or to gratify a desire for the limelight.

i. Spurgeon, in his sermon *Hiding Among the Stuff*, showed how both believers and unbelievers hide, avoiding their crown: "There may be some of you here present, who may be doing precisely what Saul did, only you are doing it more foolishly than he did. He did but hide away from an earthly crown, but you hide from a heavenly one." (Spurgeon)

b. **He was taller than any of the people from his shoulders upward**: The physical description of Saul showed he was exactly what the people wanted - a king that looked good to the other nations. God gave them "the king from central casting."

c. **Long live the king!** In their desire for the image and pageantry of a human king, Israel longed to shout these words for a long time. They knew all the other nations got to have royal ceremonies and functions. Now they got to have it all as well.

d. **Do you see him . . . there is no one like him among all the people**: Samuel perhaps said this with a note of sarcasm in his voice. He wanted the nation to **see** the king, and according to what they could **see**, he was a great king. But from his long conversations with Saul (1 Samuel 9:25-26) Samuel probably knew him well enough to mean something else when he said, **there is no one like him among all the people**.

4. (25-27) The monarchy established.

Then Samuel explained to the people the behavior of royalty, and wrote *it* in a book and laid *it* up before the LORD. And Samuel sent all the people away, every man to his house. And Saul also went home to Gibeah; and valiant *men* went with him, whose hearts God had touched. But some rebels said, "How can this man save us?" So they despised him, and brought him no presents. But he held his peace.

a. **Samuel explained to the people the behavior of royalty**: Samuel taught them God's guidelines for both rulers and subjects, probably using Deuteronomy 17:14-20.

b. **Wrote it in a book and laid it up before the LORD**: It doesn't seem that this book Samuel wrote is contained in any of the books of the Bible. This doesn't mean that there is something missing from our Bibles. It simply means God did not want this book preserved in His eternal Word.

c. **Saul also went home to Gibeah**: At the time, there was no palace or capital. So Saul simply walked home with his future leaders, the **valiant men** who **went with him**.

i. God called Saul to be king and lead the nation. Yet, this was not something he could do himself. He needed **valiant men** around him, men **whose hearts God had touched**.

d. **So they despised him . . . But he held his peace**: Not all of Israel supported Saul yet. Because they never had a king before, it was unlikely they could choose any one man the whole nation could immediately support. Saul reacted to this wisely (**he held his peace**). At this point an insecure or unwise leader might feel the need to "crush" any opposition or simply regard them as enemies. Saul did neither, understanding that it might take him some time to win over the doubters.

i. "The Hebrew, as suggested by the margin, is still more striking. 'He was as though he had been deaf' - he pretended not to hear. He did hear; every word had struck deep into his soul, but he made as though he were deaf. It is a great power when a man can act as though he were deaf to slander, deaf to detraction, deaf to unkind and uncharitable speeches, and treat them as though they had not been spoken, turning from man to God, leaving with God his vindication, believing God that sooner or later will give him a chance . . . of vindicating the true prowess and temper of his soul." (Meyer)

ii. From this, we see that Saul started with great promise. He was:

- Chosen and anointed by God
- Filled with the Holy Spirit
- Supported by a great man of God
- Given gifts appropriate to royalty
- Enthusiastically supported by most all the nation
- Surrounded by **valiant men**, men **whose hearts God had touched**
- Wise enough to not regard every doubter or critic as an enemy

iii. Despite all these great advantages, Saul could still end badly. He had to choose to walk in the advantages God gave him, and choose to not go his own way. The rest of the book of 1 Samuel shows how Saul dealt with that choice.

1 Samuel 11 - Saul's Victory at Jabesh Gilead

A. Saul's victory.

1. (1-2) Nahash the Ammonite gives an ultimatum to an Israelite city.

Then Nahash the Ammonite came up and encamped against Jabesh Gilead; and all the men of Jabesh said to Nahash, "Make a covenant with us, and we will serve you." And Nahash the Ammonite answered them, "On this *condition* I will make *a covenant* with you, that I may put out all your right eyes, and bring reproach on all Israel."

a. **Encamped against Jabesh Gilead**: The Ammonite enemy surrounded this Israelite city, and simply by doing so he made his demands clear. They must either surrender or be conquered.

b. **Make a covenant with us, and we will serve you**: The men of Jabesh Gilead felt this was their only hope of survival. Either they must surrender to Nahash (**we will serve you**) under agreed upon terms (**make a covenant with us**), or they will simply be killed and plundered.

i. "Instead of humbling themselves before God and confessing the sins that had brought them into trouble, they put God altogether aside, and basely offered to become the servants of the Ammonites . . . We see here the sad effect of sin and careless living in lowering men's spirits, sapping courage, and discouraging noble effort. Oh, it is pitiable to see men tamely submitting to a vile master! Yet how often is the sight repeated! How often to men virtually say to the devil, 'Make a covenant with us, and we will serve thee'!" (Balike)

c. **That I may put out your right eyes**: When the men of Jabesh Gilead asked Nahash for a covenant, he agreed to settle peacefully with them - *if* all the men of the city had their **right eyes** gouged out. Certainly, Nahash was a serious man.

i. Nahash made this demand for many reasons. First, it was to glorify himself by humiliating the men of this city and all of Israel. Half-blinding the men of this city would **bring reproach on all Israel** by making Israel look weak and unable to prevent such an atrocity. Second, it would make the men of Jabesh Gilead unable to fight effectively in battle. In hand-to-hand combat the man with one eye has less depth perception and is at a disadvantage to a man with two eyes.

ii. "He who opposes his shield to the enemy with his left hand, thereby hides his left eye, and looks at his enemy with his right eye; he therefore who plucks out that right eye makes men useless in war." (Theodoret, cited in Clarke)

iii. We can see in this account a similarity between Satan, our spiritual enemy, and Nahash, the enemy of Israel.

- Satan attacks us but cannot do anything against us without our agreement. He asks for, and requires our *surrender*
- Satan wants us to serve him and will attempt to intimidate us into giving in to him
- Satan wants to humiliate us and exalt himself over us. Through humiliating one saint, Satan wants **to bring reproach** on all God's people
- Satan wants to take away our ability to effectively fight against him
- Satan wants to blind us and if he cannot blind us completely, he will blind us partially
- The name **Nahash** means *serpent* or *snake*

2. (3) The elders of Jabesh Gilead answer Nahash.

Then the elders of Jabesh said to him, "Hold off for seven days, that we may send messengers to all the territory of Israel. And then, if *there is* no one to save us, we will come out to you."

a. **Hold off for seven days . . . if there is no one to save us, we will come out to you**: The men of Jabesh Gilead were in a difficult spot. They were horrified at the demand of Nahash but they also knew they had no other choice. **If there is no one to save** them Nahash could do to them as he pleased, and losing an eye seemed better to them than losing their lives.

b. **If there is no one to save us**: Was there **no one to save** them? The men of Jabesh didn't know for certain. But they knew there was no hope in and of themselves. They knew that they must have a savior.

c. **That we may send messengers**: Nahash let the messengers go for two reasons. First he was confident of Israel's disunity and figured they couldn't find anyone to save them. Second, by allowing the messengers to go through all Israel he made his name big and his reputation feared throughout the whole nation.

3. (4-5) Saul hears of the plight of Jabesh Gilead.

So the messengers came to Gibeah of Saul and told the news in the hearing of the people. And all the people lifted up their voices and wept. Now there was Saul, coming behind the herd from the field; and Saul said, "What *troubles* the people, that they weep?" And they told him the words of the men of Jabesh.

a. **So the messengers came**: As the messengers spread out over all Israel, they came to Gibeah, Saul's home city. Upon hearing of the plight of Jabesh Gilead, **all the people lifted up their voices and wept**. This was exactly the reaction Nahash hoped for.

b. **Coming behind the herd from the field**: This is the humility of the king of Israel. Saul was already anointed and recognized as king, yet in a sense there was nothing for him to do. He really didn't know where to begin when it came to setting up a royal court and a bureaucracy and Israel never had one before. So, he just went back home, went to work in **the field** and figured God would tell him what to do when the time was right.

i. Saul was wise in going back to the farm. He knew it was the LORD's job to raise him up as king over the nation, and he knew the LORD would do it in the right way at the right time. He didn't have to promote himself, or scheme on his own behalf. The LORD would do it.

c. **They told him the words of the men of Jabesh**: This also shows there was no established system of government in Israel. Otherwise, the king would be the first to know of the threat against Jabesh instead of hearing the news second or third hand.

4. (6-8) Zealous for Israel's cause, Saul angrily gathers an army.

Then the Spirit of God came upon Saul when he heard this news, and his anger was greatly aroused. So he took a yoke of oxen and cut them in pieces, and sent *them* throughout all the territory of Israel by the hands of messengers, saying, "Whoever does not go out with Saul and Samuel to battle, so it shall be done to his oxen." And the fear of the LORD fell on the people, and they came out with one consent. When he numbered them in Bezek, the children of Israel were three hundred thousand, and the men of Judah thirty thousand.

a. **Then the Spirit of God came upon Saul**: It was time for Saul to act and God was with him. **The Spirit of God came upon Saul** but it did not come to entertain him or to thrill him. It came to equip him for service so that he could *do* something for the LORD.

i. This is always God's pattern. He doesn't want us to seek the Spirit selfishly, but to be empowered and used by Him to touch others.

b. **And his anger was greatly aroused**: This was good and Spirit-led anger within Saul. The Bible says we can *be angry, and do not sin* (Ephesians

4:26), but most of our anger is selfish. Saul's anger was not out of a personal sense of hurt or offense, but out of a righteous concern for the cause of the LORD among His people.

c. **So he took a yoke of oxen and cut them in pieces**: In doing this, Saul delivered a clear threat to the people of Israel. The manner of the threat seemed more from the Mafia than from the people of God, but Saul wanted it clear that failure to step up and defend the cause of God at this time was sin and it would be punished as sin.

i. When the cause is right and the need desperate, it is wrong to do nothing. Doing nothing in such cases is sin, and when it comes to the sin of doing nothing, *be sure your sin will find you out* (Numbers 32:23).

d. **Whoever does not go out with Saul and Samuel to the battle**: "Saul's inclusion of Samuel implies that he expects the prophet to accompany him into battle in view of the fact that Saul is responding to the Spirit of God." (Baldwin)

e. **And the fear of the LORD fell on the people, and they came out with one consent**: Saul's bloody threat worked. When those hunks of ox-flesh came special delivery, all Israel knew there was a leader in Israel who was serious. They knew **the LORD** called them to do something about the crisis at Jabesh Gilead.

5. (9-11) The defeat of Nahash the Ammonite.

And they said to the messengers who came, "Thus you shall say to the men of Jabesh Gilead: 'Tomorrow, by *the time* the sun is hot, you shall have help.' " Then the messengers came and reported *it* to the men of Jabesh, and they were glad. Therefore the men of Jabesh said, "Tomorrow we will come out to you, and you may do with us whatever seems good to you." So it was, on the next day, that Saul put the people in three companies; and they came into the midst of the camp in the morning watch, and killed Ammonites until the heat of the day. And it happened that those who survived were scattered, so that no two of them were left together.

a. **The messengers came and reported it to the men of Jabesh, and they were glad**: Before they did not know if there was anyone to save them. Now they knew they had someone to save them. Knowing we have a savior should make us **glad**.

b. **Tomorrow we will come out to you, and you may do with us whatever seems good to you**: Here they deceived Nahash. They spoke as if they would surrender to Nahash, so that his army would be unprepared for battle.

i. "The message contained a clever ambiguity, while giving the impression that surrender was intended." (Baldwin)

c. **Saul put the men into three companies**: Saul was a man of good military strategy. He thought out the attack before the battle started.

d. **Killed Ammonites until the heat of the day . . . no two of them were left together**: Through Saul's action and by God's blessing the victory was total. Nahash and his army were utterly routed, and the city of Jabesh Gilead was saved.

B. Saul's coronation.

1. (12-13) Saul shows mercy to his former opponents.

Then the people said to Samuel, "Who *is* he who said, 'Shall Saul reign over us?' Bring the men, that we may put them to death." But Saul said, "Not a man shall be put to death this day, for today the LORD has accomplished salvation in Israel."

a. **Who is he who said, "Shall Saul reign over us?"** At this moment of great victory, the supporters of Saul wanted to expose and kill those who didn't support him as king before (as described in 1 Samuel 10:27).

b. **Not a man shall be put to death this day**: Saul wisely knew this was no time to take revenge on his opponents. Satan, having failed in the attack through Nahash now tried to attack Israel - even in victory - by dividing the nation against each other. Satan will attack us anyway he can, and he often uses times of victory to attack.

c. **Today the LORD has accomplished salvation in Israel**: In 1 Samuel 11:3, the men of Jabesh Gilead wondered if there was *one to save us*. Saul was the man the LORD raised up to bring the victory, yet Saul himself knew that the **LORD has accomplished salvation in Israel**. It was the LORD who did the saving and Saul was humble enough to know it. At this moment of victory, it was all the more tempting to take the credit for himself.

2. (14-15) Saul is accepted as king by the entire nation.

Then Samuel said to the people, "Come, let us go to Gilgal and renew the kingdom there." So all the people went to Gilgal, and there they made Saul king before the LORD in Gilgal. There they made sacrifices of peace offerings before the LORD, and there Saul and all the men of Israel rejoiced greatly.

a. **Samuel said to the people**: As well as anyone, Samuel knew that the people were not entirely behind Saul when he was proclaimed as king in Gilgal (1 Samuel 10:24, 27). So Samuel wisely sees this time of victory as a strategic opportunity to **renew the kingdom** at Gilgal.

i. Saul had to *prove himself* before many would accept his reign as king. This is not necessarily a bad thing. It is one thing for a person to be "anointed" or "appointed," but the evidence must be in the *doing*. It was understandable for some to say, "Let's see what kind of man this Saul is." But once it was demonstrated (as it was in this chapter) it would have been wrong for them to fail to support Saul. "Unwittingly, the Ammonites provided just the opportunity Saul needed to take an initiative, and to prove himself as well to Israel at large that he could 'save' his people from oppressors." (Baldwin)

b. **They made Saul king before the LORD in Gilgal**: It wasn't that Saul *was not* king before this. He was anointed as king by Samuel (1 Samuel 10:1) and recognized by king by much of the nation of Israel (1 Samuel 10:24). Yet there was a sense in which Saul was not king until virtually all the nation recognized him as king, and here that recognition was given.

i. "Jesus is our King. The Father hath anointed Him, and set Him on his holy hill; and we have gladly assented to the appointment, and made Him King. But sometimes our sense of loyalty and devotion wanes. Insensibly we drift from our strenuous endeavour to act always as his devoted subjects. Therefore we need, from time to time, to renew the kingdom, and reverently make Him King before the Lord . . . There is a sense in which we can consecrate ourselves only once; but we can renew our vows often." (Meyer)

c. **There Saul and all the men of Israel rejoiced greatly**: They certainly did. After all, now they felt they had a king, and a good king. It is a great blessing to be under a great, victorious king.

i. Saul won the battle that day, but it was more than one battle he won. This chapter records Saul's *inward* and *outward* battles. The outward victory was obvious, but inwardly Saul defeated the strong and subtle temptations to pride, insecurity, and revenge. But he must continue to fight and win the inward battle, and he could only do so as he was filled with the Spirit of the LORD and walking in the Spirit, under the leadership of the King of Kings over Israel.

ii. "O Saul, Saul, how well for thee it would have been hadst thou maintained this spirit! For then God would not have had to reject thee from being king." (Blaikie)

1 Samuel 12 - Samuel's Speech at Saul's Coronation

A. Testimony to Samuel's integrity.

1. (1-3) Samuel talks about his leadership over Israel.

Now Samuel said to all Israel: "Indeed I have heeded your voice in all that you said to me, and have made a king over you. And now here is the king, walking before you; and I am old and grayheaded, and look, my sons *are* with you. I have walked before you from my childhood to this day. Here I am. Witness against me before the LORD and before His anointed: Whose ox have I taken, or whose donkey have I taken, or whom have I cheated? Whom have I oppressed, or from whose hand have I received *any* bribe with which to blind my eyes? I will restore *it* to you."

a. **Samuel said to all Israel**: After the victory of Saul over the Ammonites in 1 Samuel 11, Samuel knew the nation would now begin to look to this king for leadership. Here he helped Israel make the transition from Samuel's leadership to Saul's leadership. Samuel made this clear when he said, "**now here is the king**" and "**I am old and gray headed**." Samuel told Israel that his day was over, and Saul's day was beginning.

i. It is true that *Samuel judged Israel all the days of his life* (1 Samuel 7:15), but now that a king was raised up, his role would change and diminish. Samuel never officially "stepped down" from leading Israel as a judge, but didn't allow his shadow to eclipse Saul. Perhaps he knew Saul would have enough trouble on his own and Samuel didn't want to be accused of subverting Saul's reign as king.

ii. In this, Samuel showed himself as a truly godly man. He was willing to pass from the scene when God brought up another leader. Samuel did not grasp onto a position when God wanted to change it.

b. **Indeed I have heeded your voice in all that you have said to me**: Samuel wanted it clearly known that it was not *his* idea to appoint a king over Israel. This idea began in the hearts of Israel, not in the heart and mind of God. God allowed it and directed its execution, but it was the **voice** of the people that prompted it.

c. **My sons are with you**: In 1 Samuel 8:1-5, Samuel was challenged to take his sons out of leadership in Israel because they were not godly men. Though it must have been difficult, he did it. The words **my sons are with you** are proof; Samuel's sons were simply a part of the assembly of Israel and not "up on the platform" with Samuel.

i. "It is generally agreed that these words intimate [imply] that Samuel had deprived them of their public employ, and reduced them to a level with the common people." (Clarke)

d. **I have walked before you from my childhood to this day**: Samuel remembered his humble beginnings as a child, dedicated to the LORD and serving Israel and the LORD at the tabernacle (1 Samuel 2:18, 3:1).

i. **I have walked before you** is not the idea "I have been on display before you." Instead, it is the idea of a shepherd walking before his flock, leading it on. Samuel was a godly leader and shepherd for Israel these many years.

e. **Witness against me before the LORD**: Samuel reminded them that he had not **defrauded** or **oppressed** or been corrupt in anyway. He simply challenged the nation: "If I have wronged you or been corrupt, come forward now and declare it."

i. Samuel wanted the nation to know that he passed a good legacy of leadership to the new king Saul. He wanted Israel to recognize that he didn't hand Saul a mess to clean up. If Saul proved to be a poor leader no one could say it was because of Samuel's bad example.

f. **I will restore it**: It seems as if Samuel meant, "I may have wronged someone without knowing it. If that is the case, state it now, so I can make it right. I don't want to leave any unfinished business." This testified to Samuel's humble heart.

2. (4-5) Israel affirms the blameless leadership of Samuel.

And they said, "You have not cheated us or oppressed us, nor have you taken anything from any man's hand." Then he said to them, "The LORD *is* witness against you, and His anointed *is* witness this day, that you have not found anything in my hand." And they answered, "*He is* witness."

a. **You have not defrauded us or oppressed us**: Israel knew Samuel was a good, godly leader. He did not lead them for what he could *get* from them, but for what he could *give* to them.

b. **The LORD is witness against you, and His anointed is witness this day**: Samuel settled the matter. All parties agreed that he led Israel well.

This is the second time Samuel mentioned **His anointed** in this passage, and the phrase refers to Saul, because he was anointed as king (1 Samuel 10:1). Samuel deliberately included Saul in all this to make the idea of a transition between his leadership and Saul's clear.

i. In what sense was the LORD **witness against** them? If Israel were to later accuse Samuel of wrong, he could call them back to what they said here as a **witness against** them. As well, if Israel ever tried to blame Saul's problems on Samuel, what they said here would be a **witness against** them.

B. Samuel challenges Israel to serve God under their new king.

1. (6-12) Samuel gives a brief history lesson.

Then Samuel said to the people, "*It is* the LORD who raised up Moses and Aaron, and who brought your fathers up from the land of Egypt. Now therefore, stand still, that I may reason with you before the LORD concerning all the righteous acts of the LORD which He did to you and your fathers: When Jacob had gone into Egypt, and your fathers cried out to the LORD, then the LORD sent Moses and Aaron, who brought your fathers out of Egypt and made them dwell in this place. And when they forgot the LORD their God, He sold them into the hand of Sisera, commander of the army of Hazor, into the hand of the Philistines, and into the hand of the king of Moab; and they fought against them. Then they cried out to the LORD, and said, 'We have sinned, because we have forsaken the LORD and served the Baals and Ashtoreths; but now deliver us from the hand of our enemies, and we will serve You.' And the LORD sent Jerubbaal, Bedan, Jephthah, and Samuel, and delivered you out of the hand of your enemies on every side; and you dwelt in safety. And when you saw that Nahash king of the Ammonites came against you, you said to me, 'No, but a king shall reign over us,' when the LORD your God *was* your king."

a. **The righteous acts of the LORD**: In this remembrance of God's work from the time of the Exodus until his day Samuel focused not on the history of Israel, but on the history of **the righteous acts of the LORD**.

b. **Who brought your fathers out of Egypt and made them dwell in this place**: Israel should remember their salvation from slavery and the new life God gave them in the Promised Land. This was one of **the righteous acts of the LORD**.

c. **He sold them into the hand of Sisera**: Israel should remember how God allowed a disobedient Israel to be dominated by their enemies, as a chastisement intending to bring them to repentance. This was one of **the righteous acts of the LORD**.

i. We should recognize chastisement as one of **the righteous acts of the LORD**. His discipline is just as **righteous** as His deliverance.

d. **They cried out to the LORD . . . now deliver us from the hand of our enemies, and we will serve You . . . And the LORD sent . . . and delivered you**: Israel should remember when they **cried out** to God, confessed their sin and humbled themselves in repentance before Him, that He **delivered** them. This was one of **the righteous acts of the LORD**.

i. **Jerubbaal** was another name for Gideon (Judges 6:32). There is no mention of **Bedan** in the Book of Judges. Perhaps he was a deliverer known in their history, but not recorded in the Book of Judges. Or, **Bedan** may be a variant spelling or name for *Barak*, mentioned in Judges 4:6. The Septuagint, an ancient translation of the Old Testament, translates the name as *Barak*. Other ancient translations have *Samson*, and some commentators believe *Jair* is intended.

e. **Nahash the king of the Ammonites came against you**: Samuel remembered the most recent example of God's deliverance for Israel (recorded in 1 Samuel 11). Samuel linked together the story of God's deliverance for Israel from the time of the Exodus to the present day. Each of these was an example of **the righteous acts of the LORD**.

i. As Israel made the transition into monarchy, they must remember **the righteous acts of the LORD**. Everything the LORD will do is in the setting of what He has already done in our lives.

f. **You said to me, "No, but a king shall reign over us," when the LORD your God was your king**: As they began to live under the king, Samuel reminded the nation of their disobedient desire for a king. The LORD was a good king for Israel, but they wanted a king for carnal and fleshly reasons.

2. (13-15) **If you fear the LORD**: a choice for Israel.

"Now therefore, here is the king whom you have chosen *and* whom you have desired. And take note, the LORD has set a king over you. If you fear the LORD and serve Him and obey His voice, and do not rebel against the commandment of the LORD, then both you and the king who reigns over you will continue following the LORD your God. However, if you do not obey the voice of the LORD, but rebel against the commandment of the LORD, then the hand of the LORD will be against you, as *it was* against your fathers."

a. **Here is the king whom you have chosen and whom you have desired**: Samuel probably had the feeling, "Here is the king you wanted. You will find that he isn't quite the king you need, but he is the king you wanted."

b. **If you fear the LORD and serve Him and obey His voice**: Samuel presents Israel with an important choice. They were disobedient in wanting a king, yet God gave them one. Even so, if they would **fear the LORD and serve Him**, God could still bless them.

i. One wrong turn did not put them out of God's plan forever. Israel should have never sought a human king. But now they had one, and Samuel simply called them to serve the LORD where they were at now.

c. **However, if you do not obey the voice of the LORD . . . then the hand of the LORD will be against you**: Samuel put the choice before Israel. They made a wrong turn, yet God put them at a fork in the road. On one side is submission to God and obedience; on the other is rebellion and disobedience. If they chose the wrong path, they can trust God will not bless it.

d. **As it was against your fathers**: Every individual generation is tempted to think of itself as a special exception. They know of *the righteous acts of the LORD* in previous generations, yet somehow feel they are and exception regarding God's correction or judgment. Samuel reminded Israel they were not any different from their fathers, and God would not deal with them any differently than He did with their fathers.

3. (16-18) God confirms Samuel's word with a sign.

"Now therefore, stand and see this great thing which the LORD will do before your eyes: *Is* today not the wheat harvest? I will call to the LORD, and He will send thunder and rain, that you may perceive and see that your wickedness *is* great, which you have done in the sight of the LORD, in asking a king for yourselves." So Samuel called to the LORD, and the LORD sent thunder and rain that day; and all the people greatly feared the LORD and Samuel.

a. **Now therefore, stand and see this great thing which the LORD will do**: Samuel will pray and ask God to send a sign to confirm His word. This is a concession to the wicked hearts of the people, because Samuel knew only a sign from God will impress them.

b. **That you may perceive and see that your wickedness is great, which you have done in the sight of the LORD, in asking a king for yourselves**: Why would Samuel and the LORD wait until now for such a dramatic sign? Why not do it when Israel first asked for a king, so they would have known their sin and take back their request for a king?

- Because God had a purpose in allowing the "people's king," Saul, to come first
- Because if it had happened in the first days of Saul's reign, the people would have cast him off just as quickly and just as wrongly as they asked for him. Now, that his reign has been confirmed by the victory of 1 Samuel 11 and accepted by the people, they can be more directly confronted with their sin
- Because Samuel might have been accused of reproving the people out of a personal sense of hurt. By waiting until now,

everyone knew that Samuel wasn't saying, "Get rid of Saul so I can lead the nation again"

• Because now, *Israel rejoiced greatly* (1 Samuel 11:15). They were perhaps a little too excited about their new king, and Samuel wants them to have a more spiritual perspective

c. **The Lord sent thunder and rain that day**: Thunder and rain were unusual during **the wheat harvest**. This was a remarkable sign from God.

i. Because it was **the wheat harvest**, the sign displayed not only God's power, but also His judgment. Heavy rain during the harvest could destroy all their crops. The sign was a warning. "In that part of the world not only is 'rain in harvest . . . not fitting' (Prov. 26:1), it is so totally unexpected that it could easily be interpreted as a sign of divine displeasure." (Youngblood)

d. **The people greatly feared the Lord and Samuel**: The result was good, but it showed something weak and carnal in the hearts of the people. Didn't they know God was this powerful before? Perhaps their knowledge was only *intellectual* knowledge. They *could* have known the power and majesty and sovereignty of God in their hearts before this, and then it would have been unnecessary to bring a sign before **the people greatly feared the Lord and Samuel**.

e. **I will call to the Lord, and He will send thunder . . . So Samuel called to the Lord**: This is an impressive example of power in prayer. Samuel is known in the Bible as a mighty man of prayer (Psalm 99:6, Jeremiah 15:1).

4. (19) Israel sees their sin of desiring a king.

And all the people said to Samuel, "Pray for your servants to the Lord your God, that we may not die; for we have added to all our sins the evil of asking a king for ourselves."

a. **Pray for your servants**: Samuel just proved he was a mighty man of prayer, and Israel now knew how much they needed prayer. It made sense to ask Samuel to pray for them!

b. **We have added to all our sins the evil of asking a king for ourselves**: Finally, Israel saw their sin of wanting a king. They saw it too late; if only they had realized it in 1 Samuel 8, when Samuel first warned them! Now they are stuck with a king, yet God can still turn it for good if Israel will repent and seek the Lord.

5. (20-25) Samuel exhorts Israel to walk right with the Lord today.

Then Samuel said to the people, "Do not fear. You have done all this wickedness; yet do not turn aside from following the Lord, but serve the Lord with all

your heart. And do not turn aside; for *then you would go* after empty things which cannot profit or deliver, for they *are* nothing. For the LORD will not forsake His people, for His great name's sake, because it has pleased the LORD to make you His people. Moreover, as for me, far be it from me that I should sin against the LORD in ceasing to pray for you; but I will teach you the good and the right way. Only fear the LORD, and serve Him in truth with all your heart; for consider what great things He has done for you. But if you still do wickedly, you shall be swept away, both you and your king."

a. **You have done all this wickedness; yet do not turn aside from following the LORD, but serve the LORD with all your heart**: Samuel would not minimize Israel's sin. Yet, he did not want them to dwell on the sin of the past, but to go on walking with the LORD today.

i. The Living Bible puts the thought well: *Make sure now that you worship the Lord with true enthusiasm, and that you don't turn your back on Him in any way.* We can't do anything about yesterday, and at the present moment we can't serve God tomorrow. At the present moment all we can do is **not turn aside from following the LORD, but serve the LORD with all your heart**. Satan loves it when we live in the past or in the future, when we do anything but serve the LORD with all we have *right now.*

b. **Do not turn aside; for then you would go after empty things which cannot profit or deliver, for they are nothing**: Samuel wanted Israel to know that rejecting the LORD and turning aside from Him *just doesn't work.* If they would not serve God out of spiritual reasons, then let them do it for simply to succeed because nothing else can **profit or deliver**.

c. **For the LORD will not forsake His people . . . it has pleased the LORD to make you His people**: Samuel wanted Israel to know that *God loves them.* Despite the sin of their past they could get on with serving the LORD and still see His blessing because *God loves them.* His favor towards Israel was not prompted by good they did, were doing, or promised to do. It was **for His great name's sake**, because it **pleased the LORD** to do it. The reasons were in Him, not in Israel.

d. **Far be it for me that I should sin against the LORD in ceasing to pray for you**: Samuel knew the best thing he could do for Israel was to pray for them. His words would make no difference if the LORD did not work in their hearts, and the best way to promote the work of the LORD in their hearts was through prayer.

i. Samuel could have felt hurt that the people rejected him and the LORD as leaders over the nation. He might have been bitter against the people, and refused to pray for them. But Samuel was a more godly man than that.

ii. Many would say, "I promise I will *start* praying for you." For Samuel, *starting* to pray was a non-issue, because he was already praying. For him the issue was **ceasing to pray**. "Samuel had become so rooted in the habit of prayer for the people that he seems to start at the very thought of bringing his intercession to an end." (Spurgeon)

iii. This statement of Samuel makes it plain: it is a sin for a leader of God's people to stop praying for them. It is the most basic of his duties as a leader. If it is sin to *stop* praying, how much worse must it be to even fail to *start* praying!

iv. The blessing of unceasing prayer is not the property of the preacher or leader alone. All can share in it. "Perhaps you will never preach, but you may pray. If you cannot climb the pulpit you may bow before the mercy-seat, and be quite as great a blessing." (Spurgeon)

e. **I will teach you the good and the right way**: Samuel would pray, but he would not *only* pray. There was still a place for teaching, and Samuel would faithfully fulfill that role as well.

i. "Whether a minister shall do more good to others by his prayers or preaching, I will not determine, saith one; but he shall certainly by his prayers reap more comfort to himself." (Trapp)

ii. Samuel wants the people of Israel to know that even as he steps back and allows Saul to emerge as a leader, he will not forsake Israel. He will continue to lead and to serve them, but more in a spiritual way through prayer and teaching.

f. **Only fear the Lord . . . for consider what great things He has done for you**: All our service, all our obedience, all our love for God should be put in this context. We do it because of the **great things He has done for** us. We don't serve God so as to persuade Him to do **great things** for us. He has done the **great things**, and asks us to receive them by faith. Then we serve Him because of the **great things he has done for** us.

i. We can only keep perspective in our Christian lives if we keep focused on **what great things He has done for you**. If we lose perspective, *everything* is distorted. Many people tend to magnify their problems and lose sight of **what great things He has done for you**.

g. **If you still do wickedly, you shall be swept away**: This warning became the sad legacy of Israel when they were conquered and taken from the land in captivity.

i. "Never was a people more fully warned, and never did a people profit less by the warning." (Clarke)

1 Samuel 13 - Saul's Disobedience

A. The Philistine threat.

1. (1-2) Saul assembles Israel's first standing army.

Saul reigned one year; and when he had reigned two years over Israel, Saul chose for himself three thousand *men* of Israel. Two thousand were with Saul in Michmash and in the mountains of Bethel, and a thousand were with Jonathan in Gibeah of Benjamin. The rest of the people he sent away, every man to his tent.

a. **Saul chose for himself three thousand men of Israel**: This was the first "regular" army for Israel. Previously Israel only had a militia that assembled in times of national threat. Now for the first time Israel had a professional army.

b. **A thousand were with Jonathan**: This is the first mention of Saul's son Jonathan. He will be a prominent and wonderful part of 1 Samuel.

i. "This is the first place in which this brave and excellent man appears; a man who bears one of the most amiable characters in the Bible." (Clarke)

2. (3-4) Jonathan initiates conflict with the Philistines.

And Jonathan attacked the garrison of the Philistines that *was* in Geba, and the Philistines heard of *it*. Then Saul blew the trumpet throughout all the land, saying, "Let the Hebrews hear!" Now all Israel heard it said *that* Saul had attacked a garrison of the Philistines, and that Israel had also become an abomination to the Philistines. And the people were called together to Saul at Gilgal.

a. **Jonathan attacked the garrison of the Philistines**: Jonathan was a remarkable military leader. He repeatedly demonstrated the ability to lead a successful attack. Yet this attack merely wakened the Philistines. Israel had enjoyed the "peace" of subjected people: everything will be fine as long as you take your place of subjugation. Through this attack Jonathan proclaimed, "We won't meekly surrender to the Philistines any longer."

i. It clearly says, "**Israel had become an abomination to the Philistines.**" As long as the Israelites stayed in their weak, defeated place, the Philistines thought they were great guys. As soon as the Israelites showed boldness and courage against the LORD's enemies, the Philistines considered the Israelites **an abomination**.

ii. The same principle is true spiritually in our lives. We don't war against armies of Philistines; our enemies are *principalities . . . powers . . . the rulers of the darkness of this age . . . spiritual hosts of wickedness in the heavenly places* (Ephesians 6:12). But our spiritual enemies have the same attitude as the Philistines. As long as we are weak and subjected to our spiritual enemies, they don't mind us at all. They may even kind of like us. But as soon as we show some boldness and courage against the LORD's enemies, our spiritual foes consider us **an abomination**. If peace with the devil is more important to you than victory in the LORD, you will often be defeated and subjected.

b. **In Geba**: Archaeologists have found this Philistine fortress at **Geba** (also known as *Gibeah*). The archaeological evidence shows that it was destroyed but later rebuilt by Saul, and became his palace and fortress.

c. **All Israel heard it said that Saul had attacked a garrison of the Philistines**: Saul plainly took credit for Jonathan's bold attack on the **garrison of the Philistines**. This was a bad sign in the heart and character of Saul. His own sense of insecurity will not allow any of his associates (even his own son) to receive credit. He needed to drink in praise like thirsty men drink water.

3. (5-7) The Philistines prepare their army.

Then the Philistines gathered together to fight with Israel, thirty thousand chariots and six thousand horsemen, and people as the sand which *is* on the seashore in multitude. And they came up and encamped in Michmash, to the east of Beth Aven. When the men of Israel saw that they were in danger (for the people were distressed), then the people hid in caves, in thickets, in rocks, in holes, and in pits. And *some of* the Hebrews crossed over the Jordan to the land of Gad and Gilead. As for Saul, he *was* still in Gilgal, and all the people followed him trembling.

a. **Thirty thousand chariots and six thousand horsemen, and people as the sand which is on the seashore in multitude**: The Philistines, angered by the Israelites, gathered a huge army to crush Israel.

i. **Thirty thousand chariots** is a massive number, and some doubt the accuracy of this number. "This number seems incredible to infidels; to whom it may be sufficient to reply, that it is far more rational to acknowledged a mistake in him that copied out the sacred text in such numeral or historical passages, wherein the doctrine of faith and good life in not directly concerned, than upon such a pretense to question the truth and divinity of the Holy Scriptures, which are so fully attested, and evidently demonstrated. And the mistake is not great in the Hebrew, *schalosh* for *shelishim*; and so indeed those two ancient translators, the Syriac and Arabic, translate it, and are supposed to have read in their Hebrew copies, *three thousand*." (Poole)

b. **When the men of Israel saw that they were in danger**: Jonathan was bold enough to launch the initial attack against the Philistines but the men of Israel were not bold enough to now stand strong against their enemy. In great fear (**the people were distressed**) they hid anywhere they could (**in caves, in thickets, in rocks, in holes, and in pits**) or they fled across the Jordan River (**to the land of Gad and Gilead**). This was a low point for Israel.

i. Probably many of them thought, "What we really need is a king. A king would solve our problems." Now they have a king and the problems are still there. We often think things will "fix" problems when they won't at all. "And hereby God intended to teach them the vanity of all carnal confidence in men; and that they did not one jot less need the help and favour of God now than they did before, when they had no king." (Poole)

c. **As for Saul, he was still in Gilgal**: Saul's position as king was confirmed at Gilgal (1 Samuel 11:15). He was still there many months later (1 Samuel 13:1). It may be that Saul wanted to keep re-living the glorious day when Samuel recognized and confirmed him as king before the entire nation. Now that he was king, the men of Israel expected greater things from him.

d. **The people followed him trembling**: They still honored Saul as king, but they were really frightened. It must be better to have **trembling** followers than no followers at all, but how much better if Israel would have really trusted the LORD here.

B. Saul's unlawful sacrifice.

1. (8-9) Saul offers the burnt offering.

Then he waited seven days, according to the time set by Samuel. But Samuel did not come to Gilgal; and the people were scattered from him. So Saul said, "Bring a burnt offering and peace offerings here to me." And he offered the burnt offering.

a. **He waited seven days**: Saul was in Gilgal for many months. In the press of the current crisis, every day now seemed much more important. He knew the Philistines were assembling a huge army against him, and that once they were organized they would be much harder to beat. Saul probably felt that a quick response gave them the best chance to win the battle.

b. **According to the time set by Samuel**: Samuel told Saul to wait for him at Gilgal. Then Samuel would preside over sacrifices and Israel would be spiritually ready for battle.

c. **But Samuel did not come to Gilgal; and the people were scattered from him**: This added to Saul's anxiety. First the waiting for Samuel was stressful because he felt time was his enemy. Second, **the people were scattered from him** feeling that the battle wouldn't be fought and that the plan wasn't working out.

i. We may imagine that in the early part of the week, Saul explained his thinking in a pep talk to the troops: "Men, we're going into battle against the Philistines. They have more men, more chariots, more horses, and better swords and spears than we have. So we have to trust God and make a quick attack before they can get organized. Soon Samuel will come and lead us in sacrifice before God. Then we'll go out and whip the Philistines!" But it didn't happen like that. The days dragged on and Samuel didn't come. The troops were losing confidence in Saul as a leader, and beginning to scatter. Saul felt he was in a lot of trouble.

d. **And he offered the burnt offering**: This was plainly sinful. First, Saul plainly disobeyed Samuel. Second, Saul was a king, not a priest, and only priests were to offer sacrifices. Saul had no business doing what only a priest should do.

i. History shows how dangerous it is to combine religious and civic authority and God would not allow the kings of Israel to be priests and the priests to be kings. In 2 Chronicles 26 King Uzziah tried to do the work of priest and God struck him with leprosy.

ii. Out of fear, out of panic, out of not knowing what else to do, Saul did something clearly sinful. "If Saul was among the prophets before, will he now be among the priests? Can there be any devotion in disobedience? O vain man! What can it avail to sacrifice to God, against God?" (Trapp)

2. (10-12) Samuel arrives and Saul tries to explain what he did.

Now it happened, as soon as he had finished presenting the burnt offering, that Samuel came; and Saul went out to meet him, that he might greet him. And Samuel said, "What have you done?" And Saul said, "When I saw that the people were scattered from me, and *that* you did not come within the days appointed, and *that* the Philistines gathered together at Michmash, then I said,

'The Philistines will now come down on me at Gilgal, and I have not made supplication to the LORD.' Therefore I felt compelled, and offered a burnt offering."

a. **As soon as he finished offering the burnt offering**: Saul decided to perform the sacrifice not more than an hour before Samuel arrived. If he trusted God and waited one more hour, how different things could have been! The last moments of waiting are usually the most difficult and they powerfully tempt us to take matters into our own hands.

b. **Saul went out to meet him, that he might greet him**: Now Saul really overstepped his bounds. Literally, the Hebrew says that Saul wanted to *bless* Samuel - perhaps as a priest blesses the people. Now Saul *really* saw himself as a priest, first offering sacrifice and then giving a blessing.

i. In wanting to *bless* Samuel, Saul may also be trying to show Samuel how spiritual he is. He is like a child who gets caught with his hand in the cookie jar and then says to his mother, "Let's pray!"

c. **Samuel said, "What have you done?"** Samuel knew Saul did something wrong. He could probably smell the sacrifice in the air. But Samuel did not look for reasons or excuses because there were no valid reasons or excuses. All Samuel wanted to hear was confession and repentance.

d. **And Saul said**: Saul's response is a classic example of excuse making and failure to trust God. Line upon line, Saul made his sin worse with excuses.

i. **I saw that the people were scattered from me**: "I had to do something to impress the people and gain back their support." But if Saul had obeyed and trusted God, God would have seen him to victory over the Philistines with or without the people. Perhaps many Israelites admired Saul for offering the sacrifice. "My, there's a man of action! He gets things done. I never understood why the priests were so special anyway." Saul could have positive response in the polling data but if God were not with him, it would all crumble. He should have been more concerned with pleasing God instead of the people.

ii. **You did not come within the days appointed**: "You see Samuel, it was really your fault. If you came earlier, I wouldn't have done this." But if Saul obeyed and trusted God, God would take care of Samuel and the timing. Even if Samuel was totally in the wrong, it didn't justify Saul's sin. We often try to blame our sin on someone else.

iii. **The Philistines will now come down on me at Gilgal, and I have not made supplication to the LORD**: "We really needed God's help against the Philistines, and we needed it now, so I had to do it." But if Saul would have obeyed and trusted God, the LORD would take care of the Philistines. Saul could have **made supplication to the Lord** in any number of ways. He could have cried out the Lord for the whole nation with a humble heart, but instead he did the *one* thing he must not do: offer a sacrifice.

iv. **Therefore I felt compelled**: "I had to. It just seemed like the right thing to do. I couldn't wait any longer." Even though Saul **felt compelled**, he was not supposed to be ruled by his feelings. He didn't have to sin though he felt like sinning.

d. The whole manner of Saul's explanation makes it clear this was no misunderstanding. He didn't say to Samuel, "Did I do something wrong?" He knew exactly what he did and probably thought of the excuses ahead of time.

3. (13-14) Samuel proclaims God's judgment upon Saul's household.

And Samuel said to Saul, "You have done foolishly. You have not kept the commandment of the Lord your God, which He commanded you. For now the Lord would have established your kingdom over Israel forever. But now your kingdom shall not continue. The Lord has sought for Himself a man after His own heart, and the Lord has commanded him *to be* commander over His people, because you have not kept what the Lord commanded you."

a. **You have done foolishly**: This is a stronger phrase than we might think. Samuel did not mean Saul was unintelligent or silly. The Bible speaks of the *fool* as someone morally and spiritually lacking.

b. **You have not kept the commandment of the Lord your God, which He commanded you**: Despite all the excuses, all the reasons, all the blaming of someone else, the bottom line was still the bottom line. Samuel put it plainly: **you have not kept the commandment of the Lord your God**. God commanded him to do something, and he did the opposite.

c. **For now the Lord would have established your kingdom over Israel forever**: The whole point in being a king was to establish a dynasty, where one's sons sat on the throne afterwards. God told Saul that his descendants would not reign after him. Though he was a king, he would not establish the monarchy in Israel.

d. **But now your kingdom shall not continue**: From these words we might expect Saul to be "impeached" as king right then and there. But Saul would actually reign another 20 years. He will still be on the throne as a king, but it will never be the same, because the end of his kingdom is certain.

i. This was no small sin. "To disobey God in the smallest matter is sin enough: there can be no sin little, because there is no little God to sin against." (Trapp)

ii. Because the actual judgment for this sin was so far off we should regard Samuel's pronouncement of judgment as an invitation to repentance. Many times when God announces judgment, He will relent if His people repent. "Though God threaten Saul with the loss of his kingdom for this sin, yet it is not improbable that there was a tacit condition implied, as is usual in such cases." (Poole)

e. **The LORD has sought for Himself a man after His own heart, and the LORD has commanded him to be commander over His people**: Though God rejected Saul He did not reject Israel. Because God loved Israel He would raise up a king, **a man after His own heart**.

i. Saul was a man after Israel's heart. He was all about image, prestige, and the things men look at. But God will now give Israel a man **after His own heart**, and raise that man up to be the next king.

ii. It would be easy to say that the kingdom was taken from Saul because he sinned and on one level, that was true; but it was more than that. David also sinned yet God never took the kingdom from David and his descendants. The issue was bigger than an incident of sin; the issue was being a man after God's own heart.

f. **A man after His own heart**: What does this mean? We can discover this by looking at the man who was *not* **a man after His own heart** (Saul) and comparing him to the man who *was* **a man after His own heart** (David).

i. *A man after God's heart honors the LORD*. Saul was more concerned with his will than God's will. David knew God's will was most important. Even when David didn't do God's will, he still knew God's will was more important. All sin is a disregard of God, but David sinned more out of weakness and Saul more out of a disregard for God.

ii. *A man after God's heart enthrones God as king*. For Saul, *Saul* was king. For David, the *LORD God* was king. Both David and Saul knew sacrifice before battle was important. But David thought it was important because it pleased and honored God. Saul thought it was important because it might help him win the battle. Saul thought God would help him achieve his goals. David thought that God was the goal.

iii. *A man after God's heart has a soft, repentant heart*. When Saul was confronted with his sin he offered excuses. When David was confronted with his sin he confessed his sin and repented (2 Samuel 12:13).

iv. *A man after God's heart loves other people*. Saul became increasingly bitter against people and lived more and more unto himself, but David loved people. When David was down and out he still loved and served those who were even more down and out (1 Samuel 22:1-2).

g. **The LORD has sought for Himself a man after His own heart**: God was *looking* for this kind of man and God found this man in an unlikely place. In fact at this time, he wasn't a man at all! God is *still looking* for men and women **after His own heart**.

i. If David had some of our sins then we can have his heart. We can love and pursue God with the kind of focus and passion David had.

C. The Philistine threat.

1. (15-18) The Philistines begin their raids.

Then Samuel arose and went up from Gilgal to Gibeah of Benjamin. And Saul numbered the people present with him, about six hundred men. Saul, Jonathan his son, and the people present with them remained in Gibeah of Benjamin. But the Philistines encamped in Michmash. Then raiders came out of the camp of the Philistines in three companies. One company turned to the road to Ophrah, to the land of Shual, another company turned to the road *to* Beth Horon, and another company turned *to* the road of the border that overlooks the Valley of Zeboim toward the wilderness.

a. **Then Samuel arose**: Samuel left probably knowing that the announcement of judgment was an invitation to repentance, and probably knowing that Saul would not repent.

b. **About six hundred men**: Earlier, Saul had about 3,000 in his regular army (1 Samuel 13:2). Now he is down to 600 because many soldiers scattered while Saul waited for Samuel (1 Samuel 13:8). The loss of so many men was probably the reason why Saul offered the sacrifice without Samuel, and it displayed a heart of distrust and disobedience to God.

i. According to 1 Samuel 13:5 the Philistines already had a huge army, easily outmatching Saul's 3,000 men. Saul saw his already mismatched force shrink to one-fifth of its previous size (from 3,000 to 600). God allowed this to test Saul's faith, to see if he believed God was great enough to deliver from so many with so few.

c. **Then raiders came out of the camp of the Philistines**: With so many troops the Philistines could raid at will. They were a fearless and fearsome army against Saul and Israel.

2. (19-23) The technological superiority of the Philistines.

Now there was no blacksmith to be found throughout all the land of Israel, for the Philistines said, "Lest the Hebrews make swords or spears." But all the Israelites would go down to the Philistines to sharpen each man's plowshare, his mattock, his ax, and his sickle; and the charge for a sharpening was a pim for the plowshares, the mattocks, the forks, and the axes, and to set the points of the goads. So it came about, on the day of battle, that there was neither sword nor

spear found in the hand of any of the people who *were* with Saul and Jonathan. But they were found with Saul and Jonathan his son. And the garrison of the Philistines went out to the pass of Michmash.

a. **There was no blacksmith to be found throughout all the land of Israel**: The Philistines had superior military technology and they wanted to keep it that way. Since they were a seafaring people, the Philistines traded with the technologically sophisticated cultures to the west, especially the Greeks. They imported weapons and know how from those distant lands.

i. "For decades archaeologists working at many different sites have unearthed iron artifacts in bewildering number and variety dating from the period of greatest Philistine power and leading to the general consensus that the metal was introduced into Canaan - at least for weapons, agricultural tools, and jewelry - by the Philistines." (Youngblood)

b. **All the Israelites would go down to the Philistines to sharpen each man's plowshare**: By carefully guarding their military technology, the Philistines kept the Israelites in a subservient place.

i. We might imagine that the Philistine blacksmiths, even though they charged each Israelite **a pim** for sharpening, would never put too fine an edge on anything. First, this was because these farm tools were the only weapons the Israelites had, so why make them so sharp? Secondly, if you make it really sharp, it will be longer before they come back with another **pim** to get their ax sharpened.

c. **There was neither sword nor spear found in the hand of any of the people . . . they were found with Saul and Jonathan**: There were so few iron weapons available that only the royal family could be properly equipped. The rest of Israel fought with whatever they could.

i. It was bad enough to be outnumbered so badly. Now, we see God allowed the Philistines to have a huge technological advantage over the Israelites. The only way the Israelites could ever win was to trust in God for everything.

1 Samuel 14 - Victory Over the Philistines

A. Jonathan's adventure in faith.

1. (1-3) Jonathan's proposal.

Now it happened one day that Jonathan the son of Saul said to the young man who bore his armor, "Come, let us go over to the Philistines' garrison that *is* on the other side." But he did not tell his father. And Saul was sitting in the outskirts of Gibeah under a pomegranate tree which *is* in Migron. The people who *were* with him *were* about six hundred men. Ahijah the son of Ahitub, Ichabod's brother, the son of Phinehas, the son of Eli, the Lord's priest in Shiloh, was wearing an ephod. But the people did not know that Jonathan had gone.

a. **It happened one day**: At the beginning, there was nothing in this day to indicate it would be remarkable. But on this day, God would win a great victory through the bold trust of Jonathan.

i. "God is ever on the outlook for believing souls, who will receive his power and grace on the one hand, and transmit them on the other. He chooses them, that by them he should make his mighty power known." (Meyer)

b. **Said to the young man who bore his armor**: Every "officer" in the Israelite army had an "assistant" known as an *armor bearer*. The armor bearer helped the officer in battle and in the administration of the army. They often carried the armor and weapons of the officer, so they were known as *armor bearers*.

i. "Armor-bearers in ancient times had to be unusually brave and loyal, since the lives of their masters often depended on them." (Youngblood)

c. **Come, let us go over to the Philistines garrison**: The Israelites were in a military conflict where victory seemed impossible. They were vastly outnumbered and greatly surpassed in military technology. Yet Jonathan was bold enough to **go over to the Philistine garrison** just to see what the Lord might do.

i. Jonathan perhaps thought of Shamgar and how Judges 3:31 described Shamgar's victory over 600 Philistines with a sharp stick. Jonathan perhaps thought, "Well, if God could do it through Shamgar, He could do it through me!"

ii. Jonathan could strengthen himself in promises such as Leviticus 26:8: *Five of you shall chase a hundred, and a hundred of you shall put ten thousand to flight; your enemies shall fall by the sword before you.*

d. **He did not tell his father**: Perhaps this was just an oversight or something easily and properly explained. Or, it may be that Jonathan *deliberately* **did not tell his father**, because he believed his father would have simply said "no."

e. **Saul was sitting**: This was a big contrast to Jonathan. The bold, brave, king was simply **sitting . . . under a pomegranate tree** while his son boldly went **over to the Philistine garrison**. Saul and the priest with the **ephod** sat back while Jonathan bravely trusted God.

f. **Ahijah the son of Ahitub, Ichabod's brother**: The mention of **Ichabod** seems almost unnecessary. Why would we need to know that the priest with Saul, **Ahijah**, was the nephew of **Ichabod**? Probably, God wants us to associate the meaning of Ichabod's name with where Saul is at spiritually. Saul's royal glory is almost gone, and it is appropriate that he associates with a relative of the man named "The Glory Has Departed."

g. **The people did not know that Jonathan was gone**: This indicates that Jonathan did not **go over to the Philistine garrison** out of a desire for personal glory. If that were his motive he would have told at least a few people that he went.

2. (4-5) Jonathan finds a strategic position.

Between the passes, by which Jonathan sought to go over to the Philistines' garrison, *there was* a sharp rock on one side and a sharp rock on the other side. And the name of one *was* Bozez, and the name of the other Seneh. The front of one faced northward opposite Michmash, and the other southward opposite Gibeah.

a. **Between the passes . . . there was a sharp rock on one side and a sharp rock on the other side**: On his way to the Philistine garrison, Jonathan saw a strategic position - a narrow path through a pass with large, sharp rocks on either side. A few men could easily fight against a much larger number at this strategic place.

b. **Jonathan sought to go over to the Philistines' garrison**: If Jonathan never decided, *Come, let us go over to the Philistines' garrison that is on the other side* (1 Samuel 14:1) he would have never found this strategic place. God guided Jonathan as he boldly trusted God and acted on that bold trust.

3. (6-7) Jonathan's bold proposal.

Then Jonathan said to the young man who bore his armor, "Come, let us go over to the garrison of these uncircumcised; it may be that the LORD will work for us. For nothing restrains the LORD from saving by many or by few." So his armorbearer said to him, "Do all that is in your heart. Go then; here I am with you, according to your heart."

a. **It may be that the LORD will work for us**: For Jonathan, this was more than a reconnaissance expedition. He wanted to see what God might do through two men who trusted Him and stepped out boldly.

i. *Jonathan knew the need was great.* Israel was hopelessly outnumbered and demoralized.

ii. *Jonathan knew God wanted to use someone.* King Saul just wanted to sit under a pomegranate tree. Something had to be done, and Jonathan was willing to let God use him.

iii. *Jonathan knew God wanted to work with someone.* Jonathan could have just *prayed* that God would rain down fire from heaven on the Philistines. But Jonathan knew that God uses the bold action and fighting spirit of His people. "It was not Jonathan that was to work with some help from God; it was the Lord that was to work by Jonathan." (Blaikie)

b. **For nothing restrains the LORD from saving by many or by few**: This is wise courage in God. Many in Israel probably believed this as theological truth but few believed it enough to *do something.* Jonathan's faith was demonstrated by his works.

i. **Nothing restrains the LORD**: The only thing that can be said to restrain God is our *unbelief* (Matthew 13:58). God's *power* is never restrained but His *will* may be restrained by our unbelief. He may choose not to act until we partner with Him in trust. God had a trusting partner in Jonathan.

ii. **By many or few**: The odds were already against Israel. Did it matter if it was a million-to-one or a thousand-to-one? Numbers or odds did not restrain God, but unbelief could. Jonathan never read the New Testament, but he had a Romans 8:31 heart: *If God be for us, who can be against us?*

iii. Jonathan had little faith in himself but great faith in God. It wasn't "I can win a great victory with God's help." It was "God can win a great victory through even me."

c. **Go then; here I am with you**: These words from Jonathan's armor bearer must have cheered Jonathan greatly. When we step out in faith, encouragement can make all the difference for good and discouragement can make all the difference for evil.

i. God was going to use Jonathan, but He wasn't going to use Jonathan *alone*. When God uses a man He almost always calls others around the man to support and help him. They are just as important in getting God's work done as the man God uses.

4. (8-10) Jonathan proposes a test.

Then Jonathan said, "Very well, let us cross over to *these* men, and we will show ourselves to them. If they say thus to us, 'Wait until we come to you,' then we will stand still in our place and not go up to them. But if they say thus, 'Come up to us,' then we will go up. For the LORD has delivered them into our hand, and this *will be* a sign to us."

a. **Very well**: This indicates that Jonathan took the support of his armor bearer as confirmation.

b. **This will be a sign to us**: In his step of faith, Jonathan wanted to know if God was really leading. He proposed a test based on the response of the Philistine guards.

i. Jonathan showed wisdom and not unbelief. To this point, he does not act on a specific, confirmed word from God. Instead, he followed the bold hope and impression of his heart. He was humble enough to know his heart might be wrong on this day, so Jonathan asked God to guide him.

ii. This was not the same as Gideon's setting of a fleece (Judges 6:36-40). Gideon had a confirmed word of God to guide him, and he doubted God's word. Jonathan did not doubt a word from God; he doubted his own heart and mind.

iii. Jonathan was prompted by *faith*. Significantly, he did not demand to know the whole battle plan from God in advance. He was willing to take it one step at a time, and let God plan it out. Faith is willing to let God know the whole plan, and to know our part one step at a time.

5. (11-14) Jonathan and his armor bearer attack the Philistines.

So both of them showed themselves to the garrison of the Philistines. And the Philistines said, "Look, the Hebrews are coming out of the holes where they have hidden." Then the men of the garrison called to Jonathan and his armorbearer, and said, "Come up to us, and we will show you something." Jonathan said to his armorbearer, "Come up after me, for the LORD has delivered them into the hand of Israel." And Jonathan climbed up on his hands and knees with his armorbearer after him; and they fell before Jonathan. And as he came after him, his armorbearer killed them. That first slaughter which Jonathan and his armorbearer made was about twenty men within about half an acre of land.

a. **Look, the Hebrews are coming out of the holes where they have hidden**: At this time of crisis the Israelites hid anywhere they could (1 Samuel 13:6). It was reasonable for the Philistines to think these were Hebrew deserters surrendering to the Philistines because they thought it was better than hiding in a hole.

b. **Come up after me, for the LORD had delivered them into the hand of Israel**: At this exciting moment God confirmed Jonathan's bold trust with this sign, and he knew God would do something great.

c. **Jonathan climbed up on his hands and knees with his armorbearer after him**: This was a difficult climb. Jonathan was not the kind to say, "Well, it would be nice to do this. But the rocks are steep and there are a lot of Philistines up there. Let's just pray instead." If we only want victory or only want to be used by God when it is *easy*, we won't see much victory and we won't be used much.

d. **And they fell before Jonathan**: Jonathan knew that the battle was the LORD's yet he knew God would use him to fight. When Jonathan saw God's confirming sign, he didn't lay down his sword and start praying that God would strike them all down. He prayed, made sure his sword was sharp, and trusted God would use him to strike them all down.

6. (15) God attacks the Philistines.

And there was trembling in the camp, in the field, and among all the people. The garrison and the raiders also trembled; and the earth quaked, so that it was a very great trembling.

a. **There was trembling in the camp, in the field, and among all the people**: It seems that the Philistines were under a divine confusion and they woke that morning thinking "We are attacked by enemies in our midst!" They rushed about thinking their fellow Philistines might be the enemy, and began to fight and kill one another.

i. It didn't matter if the Philistines greatly outnumbered the Israelites and had far better weapons. God was more than able to set the Philistines against each other. If the Israelites had no swords, the LORD would use the swords of the Philistines against the Philistines.

b. **The earth quaked, so that it was a very great trembling**: Jonathan used his heart and sword but God did what Jonathan could not do - send a great earthquake to terrify the Philistines. Often we wait around for God to do what *we* can do. But God will often do miracles - what He alone can do - if we will do what *we* can do.

7. (16-19) Saul learns of the battle.

Now the watchmen of Saul in Gibeah of Benjamin looked, and *there* was the multitude, melting away; and they went here and there. Then Saul said to the

people who *were* with him, "Now call the roll and see who has gone from us." And when they had called the roll, surprisingly, Jonathan and his armorbearer *were* not *there*. And Saul said to Ahijah, "Bring the ark of God here" (for at that time the ark of God was with the children of Israel). Now it happened, while Saul talked to the priest, that the noise which *was* in the camp of the Philistines continued to increase; so Saul said to the priest, "Withdraw your hand."

a. **There was the multitude, melting away**: As the watchmen of Israel kept an eye on the huge army of the Philistines, the army started to melt away as they watched.

b. **Call the roll**: This was useless at the moment. Saul should go and fight the Philistines at this strategic moment. Instead, he was probably worried about who was leading the battle and who would get the credit.

c. **Bring the ark of God here**: This was useless at the moment. Saul is probably trying to look spiritual here, but there was nothing to seek God about. There is a time to go aside and pray, and there is a time to get your sword out and fight. Saul didn't know what time this was.

d. **While Saul talked to the priest . . . the noise which was in the camp of the Philistines continued to increase; so Saul said to the priest, "Withdraw your hand."** Eventually, the noise of God and Jonathan fighting against the Philistines became so loud that Saul knew he had to also fight. So, he told the priest **"Withdraw your hand."** This meant, "Stop seeking an answer from God with the urim and thummin," which were held in a pouch in the priest's breastplate.

8. (20-23) Saul fights in the battle and a great victory is won.

Then Saul and all the people who *were* with him assembled, and they went to the battle; and indeed every man's sword was against his neighbor, *and there was* very great confusion. Moreover the Hebrews *who* were with the Philistines before that time, who went up with them into the camp *from the* surrounding *country*, they also joined the Israelites who *were* with Saul and Jonathan. Likewise all the men of Israel who had hidden in the mountains of Ephraim, *when* they heard that the Philistines fled, they also followed hard after them in the battle. So the LORD saved Israel that day, and the battle shifted to Beth Aven.

a. **They went to the battle**: Saul was the leader of Israel but it took him a long time to start leading. Now he follows God and Jonathan into battle.

b. **Moreover the Hebrews who were with the Philistines before that time . . . also joined the Israelites**: It seems that many in Israel had the insecure heart of Saul. These Hebrew servants of the Philistines probably hated their masters but were afraid to stand free in the LORD. They only came out for Israel when victory was assured.

c. **So the LORD saved Israel that day**: God really used Jonathan but it wasn't Jonathan's victory. It was the LORD's victory. God was just waiting for someone with the bold trust of Jonathan.

B. Saul's foolish oath and its consequences.

1. (24) Saul compels the army of Israel under an oath.

And the men of Israel were distressed that day, for Saul had placed the people under oath, saying, "Cursed *is* the man who eats *any* food until evening, before I have taken vengeance on my enemies." So none of the people tasted food.

a. **Saul had placed the people under an oath**: Jonathan, in his bold trust in the LORD, had just struck a mighty blow against the Philistines. Now it was the job of the army of Israel, under King Saul, to finish the job by striking down the fleeing Philistine army. On this day of battle against the Philistines Saul declared a curse: **"Cursed is the man who eats any food until evening, before I have taken vengeance on my enemies."**

i. On the surface, this sounds *so spiritual*. "Let's set today aside as a special day of fasting unto the LORD. We want God to do a great work, so we should fast today. I will enforce this among the whole army with a curse."

b. **Before I have taken vengeance on my enemies**: This shows that *Saul's focus was wrong*. Saul put the army of Israel under an oath so *he* could take vengeance on *his* enemies. If he regarded it as *his* battle, he should simply fast himself. Saul showed that even in doing something spiritual like fasting his focus is on *himself*, not the LORD.

i. Through this curse, Saul put the focus back on himself. That day, no one would be thinking much about Jonathan because their hunger would always remind them of Saul's curse.

c. **Cursed is the man**: This shows that *Saul's sense of authority was wrong*. He did not have the authority to proclaim such a curse and he was not the spiritual leader of the nation. If any such fast was to be declared and a curse attached to it, Samuel had the spiritual authority to do it, not Saul.

i. This also shows that *Saul's promised punishment was wrong*. It was certainly heavy handed to say, "**Cursed is the man**." If Saul wanted to call for a voluntary fast, that was one thing. He might have said, "I'm fasting today before the LORD. If anyone wants to join me, they are welcome." But instead of leading by example and inviting the army of Israel to follow, he **placed the people under an oath**.

d. **The men of Israel were distressed that day**: This shows that *the result among the army of Israel was wrong*. No matter what Saul's motive was, this was foolish. When the morale and the physical energy of Israel should have been the strongest, the army was weak and discouraged.

i. There is nothing wrong with fasting itself, but this wasn't the right day. It was *Saul's* day to fast, not the LORD's day to fast.

2. (25-30) Jonathan unknowingly breaks the oath and is told of his offense.

Now all *the people* of the land came to a forest; and there was honey on the ground. And when the people had come into the woods, there was the honey, dripping; but no one put his hand to his mouth, for the people feared the oath. But Jonathan had not heard his father charge the people with the oath; therefore he stretched out the end of the rod that *was* in his hand and dipped it in a honeycomb, and put his hand to his mouth; and his countenance brightened. Then one of the people said, "Your father strictly charged the people with an oath, saying, 'Cursed *is* the man who eats food this day.' " And the people were faint. But Jonathan said, "My father has troubled the land. Look now, how my countenance has brightened because I tasted a little of this honey. How much better if the people had eaten freely today of the spoil of their enemies which they found! For now would there not have been a much greater slaughter among the Philistines?"

a. **There was honey on the ground**: This was provision from God. The Israeli army was hot on the pursuit of the fleeing Philistines. They were all tired and hungry. They needed energy to continue the pursuit and finish the battle. And God provided **honey on the ground**.

i. "The mopping-up operations after a rout were all-important if the maximum benefit from the victory was to be reaped, but pursuit of the enemy involved an exhausting, unremitting journey over steep hills for hours on end." (Baldwin)

b. **No one put his hand to his mouth, for the people feared the oath**: This group of soldiers saw the honey **dripping** right in front of their eyes. Yet Saul's foolish oath prevented them from receiving what God put right in front of them.

c. **But Jonathan had not heard his father charge the people with the oath**: Because of this, Jonathan ate some of that honey and immediately, it did the weary soldier well: **his countenance brightened**. He needed the energy to fight, and here it was, provided by God.

d. **My father has troubled the land**: Perhaps Jonathan should not have said this. There was a sense in which he was undercutting his father's authority before the troops. If there were anything to say, it would have been best to say it to his father directly. Despite all that, *Jonathan was exactly right!*

i. King Saul had indeed **troubled the land** with his pseudo-spiritual command to fast. Because of his command, **the people were faint** on a day when they should have been strong. They were weak and distracted and the victory was diminished.

3. (31-35) The soldiers of Israel sin because of Saul's foolish command.

Now they had driven back the Philistines that day from Michmash to Aijalon. So the people were very faint. And the people rushed on the spoil, and took sheep, oxen, and calves, and slaughtered *them* on the ground; and the people ate *them* with the blood. Then they told Saul, saying, "Look, the people are sinning against the LORD by eating with the blood!" So he said, "You have dealt treacherously; roll a large stone to me this day." And Saul said, "Disperse yourselves among the people, and say to them, 'Bring me here every man's ox and every man's sheep, slaughter *them* here, and eat; and do not sin against the LORD by eating with the blood.'" So every one of the people brought his ox with him that night, and slaughtered *it* there. Then Saul built an altar to the LORD. This was the first altar that he built to the LORD.

a. **The people rushed on the spoil . . . and the people ate them with the blood**: God specifically commanded Israel that they should always properly drain the blood from an animal before they butchered it (Deuteronomy 12:23-25). On this day of battle, because of Saul's foolish command, the people were so hungry they broke this command. Their obedience to *Saul's foolish command* led them to disobey *God's clearly declared command.* This is always the result of legalism.

i. We often think that legalistic rules will keep people from sin. Actually the opposite is true. Legalistic rules lead us into sin because they either provoke our rebellion or they lead us into legalistic pride.

b. **You have dealt treacherously**: Saul blamed the people for what was really his own fault. He should have never made such a foolish commandment, and his commandment provoked the people into sin.

c. **Slaughter them here, and eat; and do not sin against the LORD by eating with the blood**: Saul set up a stone to properly butcher the animals, and also **built an altar to the LORD**. At least Saul did some of what was right after he did what was wrong.

4. (36-39) In response to God's silence, Saul makes another foolish oath.

Now Saul said, "Let us go down after the Philistines by night, and plunder them until the morning light; and let us not leave a man of them." And they said, "Do whatever seems good to you." Then the priest said, "Let us draw near to God here." So Saul asked counsel of God, "Shall I go down after the Philistines? Will You deliver them into the hand of Israel?" But He did not answer him that day. And Saul said, "Come over here, all you chiefs of the people, and know and see what this sin was today. For *as* the LORD lives, who saves Israel, though it be in Jonathan my son, he shall surely die." But not a man among all the people answered him.

a. **So Saul asked counsel of God**: This was good. Saul should have sought the **counsel of God**. We shouldn't think that *everything* Saul did was bad before the LORD.

b. **He did not answer him that day**: Saul inquired of the LORD through the priest. It is likely that the priest used the *Urim and Thummim* to inquire of the LORD.

i. The use of the discerning tools of *Urim and Thummim* is described on a few occasions (Exodus 28:30, Numbers 27:21, 1 Samuel 28:6; Ezra 2:63, Nehemiah 7:65) and their use may be implied in other passages where Israel sought God (Judges 1:1 and Judges 20:18, 23).

ii. The names *Urim and Thummim* mean "Lights and Perfections." We aren't sure what they were or how they were used. Most think they were a pair of stones, one light and another dark, and each stone indicated a "yes" or "no" from God. The High Priest would ask God a question, reach into the breastplate, and pull our either a "yes" or a "no."

iii. On this occasion, the priest probably started inquiring of the LORD with this question: "LORD, do you want to speak to us today?" Because we are told **He did not answer him that day**, the stone that indicated "no" kept being drawn out.

c. **For as the LORD lives, who saves Israel, though it be in Jonathan my son, he shall surely die**: This shows how sure Saul was that he was right. He was so sure that he pronounced *another* oath.

i. Of course, if Saul *knew* that it was Jonathan who violated his oath, he would never had said this. But he was so caught up in being "right" that he added this foolish vow to his previous foolish commandment.

ii. Saul was very good at making religious oaths and promises. But that didn't mean very much because he was not good at having a heart after God and he was not good at keeping the oaths he made.

iii. "Strange perverseness! He who was so indulgent as to spare wicked Agag, chapter 15, is now so severe as to destroy his own worthy son." (Poole)

d. **Not a man among all the people answered him**: The people knew Jonathan ate the honey, and Saul's sentence of death on anyone who had eaten must have sent a chill up their back. All the people loved and respected Jonathan and they knew that Saul was in the wrong.

5. (40-44) Jonathan is implicated by the casting of lots.

Then he said to all Israel, "You be on one side, and my son Jonathan and I will be on the other side." And the people said to Saul, "Do what seems good to you." Therefore Saul said to the LORD God of Israel, "Give a perfect *lot*." So Saul and

Jonathan were taken, but the people escaped. And Saul said, "Cast *lots* between my son Jonathan and me." So Jonathan was taken. Then Saul said to Jonathan, "Tell me what you have done." And Jonathan told him, and said, "I only tasted a little honey with the end of the rod that *was* in my hand. So now I must die!" And Saul answered, "God do so and more also; for you shall surely die, Jonathan."

a. **Saul and Jonathan were taken, but the people escaped**: Saul wanted to find the wrong doer by the casting of lots. They separated the people into two groups, and then selected one group by a "low" or "high" roll of something like dice. They continued to narrow the selected group until they found the one. Saul wanted everyone to know that he and his son Jonathan were innocent, so that was the first division. Imagine Saul's shock when the lot indicated that he and Jonathan were the guilty group!

i. "**Perfect lot**" in the Hebrew is very close to the word for *Thummim*. They probably used the *Urim and Thummim* as the way to cast the lot.

b. **So Jonathan was taken**: Saul was shaken. He pronounced a death sentence on whoever ate in violation of his forced vow. Instead of admitting that the commandment and death sentence were foolish, Saul hardened his foolishness and declared **"God do so and more also; for you shall surely die, Jonathan."**

i. Saul was willing to kill his son rather than to humbly admit that *he* was really at fault. Saul started out as a humble man (1 Samuel 10:21), but his once impressive humility was overtaken by pride.

6. (45-46) The people rescue Jonathan from execution.

But the people said to Saul, "Shall Jonathan die, who has accomplished this great deliverance in Israel? Certainly not! *As* the LORD lives, not one hair of his head shall fall to the ground, for he has worked with God this day." So the people rescued Jonathan, and he did not die. Then Saul returned from pursuing the Philistines, and the Philistines went to their own place.

a. **Certainly not! As the LORD lives, not one hair of his head shall fall to the ground, for he has worked with God this day**: Happily, the people finally stood up to Saul's foolishness. They simply would not allow Jonathan to be executed. They knew that Jonathan worked **with** the LORD that day, not *against* the LORD.

i. There are at least three reasons why it was right to spare Jonathan, even though he broke the oath. First, the oath itself and the penalty on the oath breaker were simply bad and foolish laws, and should not have been enforced. Second, Jonathan broke the oath in ignorance. Finally, God's approval was evident from His great blessing on Jonathan (**he has worked with God today**).

ii. Jonathan's bold faith in God had much more to do with the victory on that day than Saul's foolish oath.

b. **And the Philistines went to their own place**: The implication in this phrase is that the victory might have been greater if not for Saul's foolish oath.

7. (47-52) Saul's many wars and his family.

So Saul established his sovereignty over Israel, and fought against all his enemies on every side, against Moab, against the people of Ammon, against Edom, against the kings of Zobah, and against the Philistines. Wherever he turned, he harassed *them*. And he gathered an army and attacked the Amalekites, and delivered Israel from the hands of those who plundered them. The sons of Saul were Jonathan, Jishui and Malchishua. And the names of his two daughters *were these*: the name of the firstborn Merab, and the name of the younger Michal. The name of Saul's wife *was* Ahinoam the daughter of Ahimaaz. And the name of the commander of his army *was* Abner the son of Ner, Saul's uncle. Kish *was* the father of Saul, and Ner the father of Abner *was* the son of Abiel. Now there was fierce war with the Philistines all the days of Saul. And when Saul saw any strong man or any valiant man, he took him for himself.

a. **So Saul established his sovereignty over Israel**: This last passage in the chapter is all about *Saul's strength*, and Saul was strong. He **established his sovereignty over Israel**. He fought many successful wars. He had a large and influential family. The strength of Saul's army grew (**when Saul saw any strong man or any valiant man, he took him for himself**). Saul's strength was broad over many areas.

i. "Ishbosheth, Saul's other son, is here omitted, because he intended to mention only those of his sons who went with him into the battles here mentioned, and who were afterwards slain with him." (Poole)

b. **Wherever he turned, he harassed them**: Saul's strength was broad but shallow. Because Saul was not a man after God's own heart and because his own relationship with God was more about image than substance, his kingdom cannot last. The next chapter will fully expose the weakness of Saul.

1 Samuel 15 - God Rejects Saul as King

A. Battle against the Amalekites.

1. (1-3) A clear, radical command: destroy Amalek.

Samuel also said to Saul, "The LORD sent me to anoint you king over His people, over Israel. Now therefore, heed the voice of the words of the LORD. Thus says the LORD of hosts: 'I will punish Amalek *for* what he did to Israel, how he ambushed him on the way when he came up from Egypt. Now go and attack Amalek, and utterly destroy all that they have, and do not spare them. But kill both man and woman, infant and nursing child, ox and sheep, camel and donkey.' "

a. **Samuel also said to Saul**: This was a message from the spiritual leader of Israel to the political and military leader of Israel. The message was clear: **punish what Amalek did to Israel . . . utterly destroy all that they have, and do not spare them**. God clearly told Samuel to tell Saul to bring a total judgment against the Amalekites.

i. **Utterly destroy**: This Hebrew verb (*heherim*) is used seven times in this account. The idea of total, complete judgment is certainly stressed.

b. **How he laid wait for him on the way when he came up from Egypt**: This explains why the Amalekites should be judged so completely. Centuries before this the Amalekites were the first people to attack Israel after their escape from Egypt (Exodus 17).

i. Hundreds of years before, the LORD said He would bring this kind of judgment against Amalek: *Then the LORD said to Moses, "Write this for a memorial in the book and recount it in the hearing of Joshua, that I will utterly blot out the remembrance of Amalek from under heaven." And Moses built an altar and called its name, The-LORD-Is-My-Banner; for he said, "Because the LORD has sworn: the LORD will have war with Amalek from generation to generation."* (Exodus 17:14-16) Deuteronomy 25:17-19 repeats this idea.

ii. The Amalekites committed a terrible sin against Israel. When the nation was weak and vulnerable the Amalekites attacked the weakest and most vulnerable of the nation (Deuteronomy 25:18). They did this for no reasons except violence and greed. God hates it when the strong take cruel advantage over the weak, especially when the weak are His people.

iii. Though this happened more than 400 years before, God still held it against the Amalekites because *time does not erase sin before God.* Among men time should erase sin and the years should make us more forgiving to one another. But before God, time cannot atone for sin. Only the blood of Jesus Christ can erase sin, not time. In fact, it was time that the Amalekites were mercifully given opportunity to repent and they did not repent. The hundreds of years of hardened unrepentant hearts made them *more* guilty, not less guilty.

c. **Now go and attack Amalek**: God could have judged Amalek directly as He did against the cities of Sodom and Gomorrah. But God had a special purpose in this for His special nation, Israel. He wanted it to be a test of obedience for Saul and all of Israel. Plus, since Amalek's sin against Israel was a military attack, God wanted to make the judgment fit the sin.

i. Would God call His people today to fight such a war of judgment? God has a completely different call for Christians under the New Covenant than He did for Israel under the Old Covenant (John 18:36).

ii. Though God no longer calls His people to take up arms as instruments of His judgment, it does not mean that God has stopped judging the nations. "But we cannot suppose, for a single moment, that the judgment of the nations is to be altogether relegated [appointed] to that final day. Throughout the history of the world the nations have been standing before Christ's bar. Nineveh stood there, Babylon stood there, Greece and Rome stood there, Spain and France stood there, and Great Britain is standing there to-day. One after another has had the solemn word - *depart*, and they have passed into a destruction which has been absolute and terrible." (Meyer)

2. (4-6) Saul prepares for the attack on the Amalekites.

So Saul gathered the people together and numbered them in Telaim, two hundred thousand foot soldiers and ten thousand men of Judah. And Saul came to a city of Amalek, and lay in wait in the valley. Then Saul said to the Kenites, "Go, depart, get down from among the Amalekites, lest I destroy you with them. For you showed kindness to all the children of Israel when they came up out of Egypt." So the Kenites departed from among the Amalekites.

a. **So Saul gathered the people together and numbered them**: Saul was certainly a capable military leader. He could gather and organize a large army. He also knew how to time his attack properly; and he **lay in wait in the valley**.

b. **Saul said to the Kenites, "Go, depart"**: Here, Saul shows wisdom and mercy in letting the Kenites go. God's judgment was not upon them, so he did not want to destroy them with the Amalekites.

3. (7-9) Saul attacks the Amalekites.

And Saul attacked the Amalekites, from Havilah all the way to Shur, which is east of Egypt. He also took Agag king of the Amalekites alive, and utterly destroyed all the people with the edge of the sword. But Saul and the people spared Agag and the best of the sheep, the oxen, the fatlings, the lambs, and all *that was* good, and were unwilling to utterly destroy them. But everything despised and worthless, that they utterly destroyed.

a. **Saul attacked the Amalekites**: This was good and in obedience to the LORD. But it was a selective, incomplete obedience. First, Saul **took Agag king of the Amalekites alive, and utterly destroyed all the people with the edge of the sword**. God commanded Saul to bring His judgment on *all* the people, including the king.

i. Why did Saul take **Agag king of the Amalekites alive**? "Saul spared *Agag*, either out of a foolish pity for the goodliness of his person, which Josephus notes; or for his respect to his royal majesty, in the preservation of which he thought himself concerned; or for the glory of his triumph." (Poole)

ii. "If Saul spare Agag, the people will take liberty to spare the best of the spoil . . . the sins of the great command imitation." (Trapp)

b. **Saul and the people spared Agag and the best of the sheep, the oxen, the fatlings, the lambs, and all that was good, and were unwilling to utterly destroy them**: God clearly commanded in 1 Samuel 15:3 that every *ox and sheep, camel and donkey* was to be destroyed and Saul didn't do this.

i. In a normal war in the ancient world, armies were freely permitted to plunder their conquered foes. This was often how the army was paid. But it was wrong for anyone in Israel to benefit from the war against the Amalekites, because it was an appointed judgment from God. This was just as wrong as a hangman emptying the pockets of the man he just executed for murder.

c. **Everything despised and worthless, that they utterly destroyed**: They were careful to keep the best for themselves. We can imagine they were all pleased with what they gained after the battle.

i. This perhaps was worst of all, because Israel did not show God's heart in judgment. When they came home happy and excited because of what they gained from the battle, they implied there was something joyful or happy about God's judgment. This dishonored God, who brings His judgment reluctantly and without pleasure, longing that men would repent instead.

ii. "Partial obedience is complete disobedience. Saul and his men obeyed as far as suited them; that is to say, they did not obey God at all, but their own inclinations, both in sparing the good and destroying the worthless. What was not worth carrying off was destroyed, - not because of the command, but to save trouble." (Maclaren)

iii. "To spare the best of Amalek is surely equivalent to sparing some root of evil, some plausible indulgence, some favourite sin. For us, Agag must stand for that evil propensity, which exists in all of us, for self-gratification; and to spare Agag is to be merciful to ourselves, to exonerate and palliate [excuse] our failures, and to condone our besetting sin." (Meyer)

4. (10-11) God's word to Samuel.

Now the word of the LORD came to Samuel, saying, "I greatly regret that I have set up Saul *as* king, for he has turned back from following Me, and has not performed My commandments." And it grieved Samuel, and he cried out to the LORD all night.

a. **I greatly regret that I have set up Saul as king**: God's heart was broken over Saul's disobedience. The man who started out humble and submitted to God eventially went his own way in disobedience.

i. **I greatly regret**: This is the use of *anthropomorphism*, when God explains Himself to man in human terms so man can have *some* understanding of God's heart. God knew from the beginning Saul's heart, ways, and destiny. God already *sought for Himself a man after His own heart* (1 Samuel 13:14). Yet as all this unfolded, God's heart was not emotionless. He didn't sit in heaven with a clipboard, checking off boxes, coldly saying, "All according to plan." Saul's disobedience hurt God, and since we can't grasp all what happens in God's heart, the closest that we can come is for God to express it in the human terms of saying, **"I greatly regret that I have set up Saul as king."**

b. **And it grieved Samuel, and he cried out to the LORD all night**: Samuel had God's heart. It hurt God to reject Saul, and it hurt God's prophet to see him rejected. We are close to God's heart when the things that grieve Him grieve us, and the things that please God please us.

5. (12-13) Saul greets Samuel.

So when Samuel rose early in the morning to meet Saul, it was told Samuel, saying, "Saul went to Carmel, and indeed, he set up a monument for himself; and he has gone on around, passed by, and gone down to Gilgal." Then Samuel

went to Saul, and Saul said to him, "Blessed *are* you of the LORD! I have performed the commandment of the LORD."

a. **Samuel rose early in the morning to meet Saul**: Reluctantly, Samuel (who anointed Saul as king years before) now came to discipline the disobedient king.

b. **He set up a monument for himself**: Saul wasn't grieved over his sin. Saul was quite pleased with himself! There is not the slightest bit of shame or guilt in Saul, even though he directly disobeyed the LORD.

i. In coming chapters, God will raise up another man to replace Saul as king. David, in contrast to Saul, was known as a man after God's own heart (1 Samuel 13:14). Even though David would also disobey God, the difference between him and Saul was great. David felt the guilt and shame one should feel when they sin. Saul didn't feel it. His conscience was dead to shame and his heart was dead to God. Saul's heart was so dead he could directly disobey God and still **set up a monument for himself** on the occasion.

c. **He set up a monument for himself**: This also shows that Saul was not the same humble man who once had a humble opinion of himself (1 Samuel 9:21) and who once hid among the equipment out of shyness (1 Samuel 10:22). The years, the military victories, and prestige of the throne of Israel all revealed the pride in Saul's heart.

i. "But the truth is, he was zealous for his own honour and interest, but lukewarm where God only was concerned." (Poole)

d. **Saul said to him, "Blessed are you of the LORD! I have performed the commandment of the LORD"**: Saul can come to the prophet of God with such boldness, boasting of his obedience because of his pride. Saul is self-deceived. *He probably really believed what he told Samuel.* He probably believed, **"I have performed the commandment of the LORD."** Pride always leads us into self-deception.

i. Maclaren has an insightful comment on Saul's statement, **"I have performed the commandment of the LORD"**: "That is more than true obedience is quick to say. If Saul had done it, he would have been slower to boast of it."

6. (14-16) Saul "explains" his sin to Samuel.

But Samuel said, "What then *is* this bleating of the sheep in my ears, and the lowing of the oxen which I hear?" And Saul said, "They have brought them from the Amalekites; for the people spared the best of the sheep and the oxen, to sacrifice to the LORD your God; and the rest we have utterly destroyed." Then Samuel said to Saul, "Be quiet! And I will tell you what the LORD said to me last night." And he said to him, "Speak on."

a. **What then is this bleating of the sheep in my ears, and the lowing of the oxen which I hear?** The livestock that God clearly commanded to be killed could be heard, seen, and smelled even as Saul said, *"I have performed the commandment of the LORD."*

i. Pride and disobedience make us blind - or deaf - to our sin. What was completely obvious to Samuel was invisible to Saul. We all have blind spots of sin in our lives, and we need to constantly ask God to show them to us. We need to *sincerely* pray the prayer of Psalm 139:23-24: *Search me, O God, and know my heart; try me, and know my anxieties; and see if there is any wicked way in me, and lead me in the way everlasting.*

b. **They have brought them . . . the people spared the best of the sheep and the oxen**: This is the first of a series of excuses from Saul - he blamed the people, not himself. Second, he included himself in the obedience (**the rest we have utterly destroyed**). Third, he justified what he kept because of its fine quality (**the best of the sheep and the oxen**). Fourth, he claimed to do it for a spiritual reason (**to sacrifice to the LORD your God**).

i. In his pride and self-deception, this all made perfect sense to Saul but it meant nothing to God and Samuel. In fact, it was worse than nothing - it showed that Saul was desperately trying to excuse his sin by word games and half-truths.

ii. But even in his excuse, Saul revealed the real problem: he had a poor relationship with God. Notice how he spoke of God to Samuel: **"to sacrifice to the LORD your God."** The LORD was not Saul's God. Saul was Saul's God. The LORD was the God of Samuel, not Saul. In his pride, Saul removed the LORD God from the throne of his heart.

iii. "O sinners, you *do* miscalculate fearfully when you give to God's servants such false explanations of your sins!" (Blaikie)

c. **The rest we have utterly destroyed**: As it turned out, not even this was true. There were still Amalekites left alive. David later had to deal with the Amalekites (1 Samuel 27:8, 30:1, 2 Samuel 8:12). Haman, the evil man who tried to wipe out all the Jewish people in the days of Esther, was a descendant of Agag (Esther 3:1). Most ironic of all, when Saul was killed on the field of battle, an Amalekite claimed to deliver the final thrust of the sword (2 Samuel 1:8-10). When we don't obey God completely, the "left over" portion will surely come back and trouble us, if not kill us.

d. **Then Samuel said to Saul, "Be quiet!"** Samuel has had enough. He will listen to no more from Saul. The excuse was revealed for what it was - just a lame excuse. Now it is time for Saul to be quiet, and to listen to the word of the LORD through Samuel.

i. But even in this, Saul can't shut up. He shows his proud desire to retain some control by replying, **"Speak on"** as if the prophet of God needed Saul's permission. He would speak on, but not because Saul gave him permission. He would speak on because he was a messenger of God.

B. Saul is rejected as king.

1. (17-21) The charge against Saul, and his feeble defense.

So Samuel said, "When you *were* little in your own eyes, *were* you not head of the tribes of Israel? And did not the LORD anoint you king over Israel? Now the LORD sent you on a mission, and said, 'Go, and utterly destroy the sinners, the Amalekites, and fight against them until they are consumed.' Why then did you not obey the voice of the LORD? Why did you swoop down on the spoil, and do evil in the sight of the LORD?" And Saul said to Samuel, "But I have obeyed the voice of the LORD, and gone on the mission on which the LORD sent me, and brought back Agag king of Amalek; I have utterly destroyed the Amalekites. But the people took of the plunder, sheep and oxen, the best of the things which should have been utterly destroyed, to sacrifice to the LORD your God in Gilgal."

a. **Now the LORD sent you on a mission . . . Why did you not obey the voice of the LORD?** This was the *most apparent* of Saul's sins. God gave him a specific command and he directly disobeyed it.

i. Though the disobedience was the most apparent sin, the root of Saul's disobedience was far worse: *pride*. Samuel refers to this when he remembers when things were different with Saul: **When you were little in your own eyes, were you not the head of the tribes of Israel?** It could no longer be said of Saul, "you are **little in your own eyes**." He was *big* in his own eyes and that made God small in his eyes.

b. **But I have obeyed the voice of the LORD**: Saul first insists that he is innocent. But he is so self-deceived he can say, **I have obeyed the voice of the LORD** and then immediately describe how he *did not obey the voice of the LORD* saying that he **brought back Agag king of Amalek**.

i. Saul's claim, "**I have utterly destroyed the Amalekites**" is plain evidence of the power and depth of his self-deception. There was an Amalekite right in front of him whom was not **utterly destroyed**.

c. **But the people took of the plunder**: After insisting he is innocent, Saul then blamed the people for the sin. His statement was a half-truth that was actually a whole lie. It was true that **the people took of the plunder**. But they did so by following Saul's *example* (he spared Agag king of Amalek), and with Saul's *allowance* (because he did nothing to stop or discourage them).

i. Saul was certainly zealous in commanding his army when it suited *him* to be so. In the previous chapter, he commanded a death sentence on anyone who ate anything on the day of battle. He was willing to execute his own son in his zeal to have his command obeyed. Saul was full of fire and zeal when it came to his own will, but not when it came to the will of God.

2. (22-23) Samuel prophesies God's judgment against King Saul.

Then Samuel said: "Has the LORD *as great* delight in burnt offerings and sacrifices, as in obeying the voice of the LORD? Behold, to obey is better than sacrifice, *and* to heed than the fat of rams. For rebellion *is as* the sin of witchcraft, and stubbornness *is as* iniquity and idolatry. Because you have rejected the word of the LORD, He also has rejected you from *being* king."

a. **Has the LORD as great delight in burnt offerings and sacrifices, as in obeying the voice of the LORD? Behold, to obey is better than sacrifice, and to heed than the fat of rams.** Religious observance without obedience is empty before God. The best sacrifice we can bring to God is a repentant heart (Psalm 51:16-17) and our bodies surrendered to His service for obedience (Romans 12:1).

i. One could make a thousand sacrifices unto God, work a thousand hours for God's service, or give millions of dollars to His work. But all these sacrifices mean little if there is not a surrendered heart to God, shown by simple obedience.

ii. In sacrifice we offer the flesh of another creature; in obedience we offer our own will before God. Luther said, "I had rather be obedient, than able to work miracles." (Cited in Trapp)

b. **For rebellion is as the sin of witchcraft, and stubbornness is as iniquity and idolatry**: A rebellious, stubborn heart rejects God just as certainly as someone rejects God by occult practices or idolatry.

i. Saul's problem wasn't just that he neglected some ceremony. That is how Saul thought of obedience to God. In today's world he might say, "What? So God wants me to go to church more? All right, I'll go." But religious observance was not Saul's problem; the problem was that his heart became rebellious and stubborn against God. If religious observance did not help *that* problem, then it was no good.

ii. It would be easy for Saul to point his finger at the Amalekites or the Philistines and say, "Look at those Godless idolaters. They don't worship the true God like I do." But Saul didn't worship the true God either because the real worship of God begins with surrender.

iii. "All conscious disobedience is actually idolatry, because it makes self-will, the human I, into a god." (Keil and Delitszch)

c. **Because you have rejected the word of the LORD, He also has rejected you from being king**: In his empty religious practice, rebellion, and stubbornness against God, Saul rejected God's word. So God rightly rejected him as king over Israel.

i. It would be easy to say, "What, Saul will be rejected as king because he spared a king and a few sheep and oxen? Later kings of Israel would do far worse, and not be rejected as king. Why is God being so tough on Saul?" But God saw Saul's heart, and saw how rebellious and stubborn it was. Saul's condition was like an iceberg: what was visible might be a manageable size, but there was far more under the surface that couldn't be seen. God could see it.

ii. So Saul was **rejected . . . from being king**. Yet it would be almost 25 years before there was another king enthroned in Israel. Saul's rejection was final, but it was not immediate. God used almost 25 years to train up the right replacement for Saul.

3. (24-25) Saul's weak effort towards repentance.

Then Saul said to Samuel, "I have sinned, for I have transgressed the commandment of the LORD and your words, because I feared the people and obeyed their voice. Now therefore, please pardon my sin, and return with me, that I may worship the LORD."

a. **I have sinned, for I have transgressed the commandment of the LORD and your words**: Saul's statement begins like a genuine confession but that changes as he continues and said, "**because I feared the people and obeyed their voice**." Saul refused to own up to his sin and instead blamed the people who "made him" do it.

i. "When he could deny it no longer, at length he maketh a forced and feigned confession; drawn thereto, more by the danger and damage of his sin, than by the offence; mincing and making the best of an ill matter." (Trapp)

ii. To say, "**because I feared the people**" tries to justify one sin with another. "Had he *feared* GOD *more*, he need have *feared the* PEOPLE *less*." (Clarke)

b. **Now therefore, please pardon my sin, and return with me, that I may worship the LORD**: Instead of dealing with the deep issue of his heart of rebellion and stubbornness against God, Saul thought that a word from Samuel could fix everything. But a word or two from Samuel would not change the settled nature of Saul's heart.

i. God knew that Saul's heart was full of rebellion and stubbornness and that it was *settled* in that condition. That is something that no man could know with certainty, looking from the outside. But God knew it and He told Samuel. A simple "**please pardon my sin**" would not do when the heart is settled in rebellion and sin against the LORD.

4. (26-31) God's rejection of Saul as king over Israel is final.

But Samuel said to Saul, "I will not return with you, for you have rejected the word of the LORD, and the LORD has rejected you from being king over Israel." And as Samuel turned around to go away, *Saul* seized the edge of his robe, and it tore. So Samuel said to him, "The LORD has torn the kingdom of Israel from you today, and has given it to a neighbor of yours, *who is* better than you. And also the Strength of Israel will not lie nor relent. For He *is* not a man, that He should relent." Then he said, "I have sinned; *yet* honor me now, please, before the elders of my people and before Israel, and return with me, that I may worship the LORD your God." So Samuel turned back after Saul, and Saul worshipped the LORD.

a. **I will not return with you, for you have rejected the word of the LORD, and the LORD has rejected you from being king over Israel**: Samuel has nothing more to say on this matter, other than what the LORD already said through him (1 Samuel 15:23). There was nothing more to talk about.

i. Why would Samuel say, "**I will not return with you**" when Saul just wanted him to worship with him? Because that worship would no doubt include sacrifice, and offering some of the animals that Saul wickedly spared from the Amalekites.

b. **Saul seized the edge of his robe, and it tore. So Samuel said to him, "The LORD has torn the kingdom of Israel from you today"**: Saul's desperate action provides a vivid object lesson on how the kingdom was torn away from him.

i. As useless as the torn piece of robe was in his hand, so now his leadership of the nation was futile. Now he ruled *against* God, not for Him. Just as the robe tore because Saul grasped it too tightly, so his tight grip on pride and stubbornness meant the kingdom would be taken away from him. In this respect Saul was the opposite of Jesus, of whom it is said He *had always been God by nature, did not cling to His prerogatives as God's Equal, but stripped Himself of all privilege by consenting to be a slave by nature and being born as a mortal man* (Philippians 2:6-7, J.B. Phillips translation). Jesus was willing to let go, but Saul insisted in clinging on. So Saul lost all, while Jesus gained all.

c. **The Strength of Israel will not lie nor relent**: Saul might have thought there was a way out of this. He wondered what he could do to "fix" this. Samuel let him know there was nothing he could do. This was permanent.

i. Samuel uses a title for the LORD found only here in the whole Bible: **The Strength of Israel**. This reminds Saul that the LORD is determined in His purpose and is strong in His will. There will be no change.

ii. The title **Strength of Israel** was also important because at that time Saul probably thought of himself as *the strength of Israel*. But the LORD God was **The Strength of Israel** and Saul needed to hear it.

d. **I have sinned, yet honor me now, please, before the elders of my people and before Israel**: Saul's desperate plea shows the depths of his pride. He is far more concerned with his image than his soul.

i. "Here he plainly discovers his hypocrisy, and the true motive of this and his former confession; he was not solicitous for the favour of God, but for his honour and power with Israel." (Poole)

e. **So Samuel turned back after Saul**: Samuel did not lead an immediate rebellion against Saul because God had not raised up Saul's replacement yet and Saul was better than the anarchy that would come with no king.

f. **So Samuel turned back after Saul, and Saul worshipped the LORD**: Did this do any good? It did no "good" in gaining the kingdom back for Saul. That was a decision God had made and it was final. But it may have done Saul good in moving his proud, stubborn heart closer to God for the sake of saving his soul. At least it had that opportunity, so Samuel allowed Saul to come with him and worship the LORD.

5. (32-33) Samuel carries out God's will.

Then Samuel said, "Bring Agag king of the Amalekites here to me." So Agag came to him cautiously. And Agag said, "Surely the bitterness of death is past." But Samuel said, "As your sword has made women childless, so shall your mother be childless among women." And Samuel hacked Agag in pieces before the LORD in Gilgal.

a. **Then Samuel said, "Bring Agag king of the Amalekites here to me."** The issue was not yet resolved for Samuel - there was still the matter of Saul's incomplete obedience. God's command to *utterly destroy* all of Amalek still stood, even if Saul didn't obey it.

b. **And Agag said, "Surely the bitterness of death is past."** As Agag came to the old prophet he thought, "We will let bygones be bygones. I guess this old prophet will let me go home now." The Living Bible expresses the thought well: *Agag arrived all full of smiles, for he thought "surely the worst is over and I have been spared."*

i. "I who have escaped death from the hands of a warlike prince in the fury of battle, shall certainly never suffer death from an old prophet in time of peace." (Poole)

c. **As your sword has made women childless, so shall your mother be childless among women**: Samuel makes it clear that Agag was not an innocent bystander when it came to the atrocities the Amalekites inflicted on Israel. Agag was the wicked and violent leader of a wicked and violent people. God's judgment against him and the Amalekites was just.

d. **And Samuel hacked Agag in pieces before the LORD in Gilgal**: Samuel was a priest and had officiated at hundreds of animal sacrifices. He knew how it felt when the blade cut into flesh, but he had never killed another person. Now, without hesitation, this old prophet raises a sword - or probably a large knife, as he would use in sacrifices - and brought it down upon this proud, violent king. **Samuel hacked Agag in pieces**.

i. Notably, Samuel did it **before the LORD**. This was not *before Saul*, to show him how weak and proud he was. This was not *before Israel*, to show them how strong and tough Samuel was. This was **before the LORD**, in tough obedience to the LORD God. This scene must have been shockingly violent; the stomachs of those watching must have turned. Yet Samuel did it all **before the LORD**.

ii. "But these are no precedents for private persons to take the sword of justice into their hands; for we must live by the laws of God, and not by extraordinary examples." (Poole)

6. (34-35) The tragic split between Samuel and Saul.

Then Samuel went to Ramah, and Saul went up to his house at Gibeah of Saul. And Samuel went no more to see Saul until the day of his death. Nevertheless Samuel mourned for Saul, and the LORD regretted that He had made Saul king over Israel.

a. **And Samuel went no more to see Saul until the day of his death**: Samuel knew that it wasn't his place to see Saul. It was Saul's place to come to him in humble repentance before the LORD. This probably would not restore the kingdom to Saul but it could restore his heart before God. Sadly, Saul never came to see Samuel. **Ramah** and **Gibeah** were less than ten miles apart, but they never saw each other again.

i. "But we read, chap. xix. 22-24, that *Saul* went to *see Samuel* at Naioth, but this does not affect what is said here. From this time Samuel had no *connection* with Saul; he never more acknowledged him as king; he mourned and prayed for him." (Clarke)

b. **Nevertheless, Samuel mourned for Saul**: Samuel was not a cold, dispassionate messenger of God's word. He hurt for Saul, "For the hardness of his heart, and the hazard of his soul." (Trapp)

1 Samuel 16 - God Chooses David

A. Samuel anoints David as king.

Psalms that may go with this period: 8, 19, 23, and 29.

1. (1-3) God tells Samuel to go and anoint a new king over Israel.

Now the LORD said to Samuel, "How long will you mourn for Saul, seeing I have rejected him from reigning over Israel? Fill your horn with oil, and go; I am sending you to Jesse the Bethlehemite. For I have provided Myself a king among his sons." And Samuel said, "How can I go? If Saul hears *it*, he will kill me." And the LORD said, "Take a heifer with you, and say, 'I have come to sacrifice to the LORD.' Then invite Jesse to the sacrifice, and I will show you what you shall do; you shall anoint for Me the one I name to you."

a. **How long will you mourn for Saul**: There is a time to mourn, but there is also a time to move on. **Fill your horn with oil** must have excited Samuel, because he knew that God wanted him to anoint someone else as king over Israel.

i. God will never allow His work to die with the death or failure of a man. If it is *God's* work, it goes beyond any man. Perhaps Samuel was paralyzed with mourning because of Saul's tragic rebellion, but God was not paralyzed.

b. **I am sending you to Jesse the Bethlehemite**: Israel's next king would be found **among his sons**, the sons of Jesse. Jesse was the grandson of Ruth and Boaz (Ruth 4:17, 22).

c. **How can I go? If Saul hears it, he will kill me**: We can certainly *understand* Samuel's fear. There isn't any doubt that Saul would consider this treason. At the same time, it shows a note of fear in Samuel we are almost surprised to see. Perhaps Samuel's excessive mourning over Saul introduced an element of fear and unbelief in his heart. Samuel didn't have anything to worry about, because God promised **I will show you what you shall do**.

i. Was God telling Samuel to lie? Not at all. "This was strictly *true*; Samuel *did offer a sacrifice*; and it does not appear that he could have done the work which God designed, unless he had offered this sacrifice, and called the elders of the people together, and this collected Jesse's sons. But he did not tell the principle design of his coming; had he done so, it would have produced *evil* and *no good*:." (Clarke)

d. **For I have provided Myself a king among his sons**: Years before this, Israel rejected the LORD as their king and they wanted a human king instead. God gave them a human king after their own desire (Saul) but God was still on the throne, crowning who He pleases as He pleased.

i. The simple fact was that God *did* rule Israel. They could recognize His rule, submit to it, and enjoy the benefits. Or they could resist His reign over Israel and suffer because of it. It does not matter what my attitude towards God is as far as it affects His ultimate victory. The LORD is God and King, and will always triumph. But my attitude matters *a great deal* as it affects my ultimate destiny.

ii. We don't have to fear for the future when we know God has provided for Himself leaders. In some unlikely place God is raising up leaders for His people. He will keep them obscure and hidden until the right time then He will raise them up.

e. **You shall anoint for Me the one I name to you**: The first king of Israel was anointed *for the people*. He was the "king from central casting," the kind of king the *people* wanted. Now the "people's choice" failed and disqualified himself. "Now," the LORD said, "It's time for a king **for Me**." God was going to show Israel *His* king.

2. (4-5) Samuel comes to sacrifice at Bethlehem.

So Samuel did what the LORD said, and went to Bethlehem. And the elders of the town trembled at his coming, and said, "Do you come peaceably?" And he said, "Peaceably; I have come to sacrifice to the LORD. Sanctify yourselves, and come with me to the sacrifice." Then he consecrated Jesse and his sons, and invited them to the sacrifice.

a. **So Samuel did what the LORD said, and went to Bethlehem**: Bethlehem was a small town not very far from Jerusalem. It was the home of Ruth and Boaz, from whom the family of Jesse descended. It was a hilly grain-growing region with many small grain fields carved into the hillsides.

b. **And the elders of the town trembled at his coming, and said, "Do you come peaceably?"** Considering what Samuel had just done with the Amalekite king Agag (1 Samuel 15:33), it is no wonder the elders of Bethlehem were afraid.

c. **Come with me to the sacrifice**: The idea was not that Jesse and his sons were to just watch Samuel sacrifice this heifer. They would watch the sacrifice and then share in a large ceremonial meal, eating the meat that came from the sacrificed animal.

i. When an animal was sacrificed to atone for sin none of it was eaten and it was all burned before the LORD. But when an animal was sacrificed as a peace offering, a fellowship offering, or a consecration offering, then part of the animal was burnt before the LORD, and part of it was eaten in a special ceremonial meal.

3. (6-10) God doesn't choose any of Jesse's older sons.

So it was, when they came, that he looked at Eliab and said, "Surely the Lord's anointed *is* before Him." But the LORD said to Samuel, "Do not look at his appearance or at the height of his stature, because I have refused him. For *the Lord does* not *see* as man sees; for man looks at the outward appearance, but the LORD looks at the heart." So Jesse called Abinadab, and made him pass before Samuel. And he said, "Neither has the LORD chosen this one." Then Jesse made Shammah pass by. And he said, "Neither has the LORD chosen this one." Thus Jesse made seven of his sons pass before Samuel. And Samuel said to Jesse, "The LORD has not chosen these."

a. **Surely the LORD's anointed is before Him**: As Samuel looked at the oldest son **Eliab** he thought, "This man sure looks like a king. This must be the one God will tell me to anoint. That's a good choice, God!" Samuel saw a tall, good looking young man who *looked* like he would be a great king and leader.

b. **Do not look at his appearance or at the height of his stature, because I have refused him**: Samuel made the mistake of judging Eliab based on his **appearance**. This was the same mistake Israel made about their first king. Saul *looked* the part but he didn't have the *heart* a king of God's people should have. It didn't matter how good Eliab *looked* because God said, **"I have refused him."**

c. **For the LORD does not see as man sees; for man looks at the outward appearance, but the LORD looks at the heart**. This was both a *statement of fact*, and an *exhortation to godly thinking*.

i. First, it was a *statement of fact*. **Man looks at the outward appearance, but the LORD looks at the heart.** Even the best of men will look **at the outward appearance**. At the moment, Samuel was guilty of it. We must understand that we can't read the secrets of another's heart and we often do only judge on outward appearance. "The world is full of idolatries, but I question if any idolatry has been more extensively practiced than the idolatry of the outward appearance." (Blaikie)

ii. It was also an *exhortation to godly thinking*. God told Samuel, "Your natural inclination is to only judge on outward appearance. But I can judge the heart that you can't see. So look to Me and don't be so quick to judge a person only on their **outward appearance**." Samuel needed to know his natural inclination to judge only on **outward appearance**, but he didn't have to give into it. He could seek the LORD and seek God's heart and mind when looking at people.

d. **The LORD has not chosen these**: God told Samuel that He had not chosen any of the seven sons of Jesse attending the feast. It wasn't that these sons of Jesse were bad men, but they were not God's choice. God had a man in mind different from Samuel's or Jesse's expectation.

i. Eliab and the seven oldest sons of Jesse were perfect potential kings as far as the flesh is concerned. But God didn't want a king after the flesh. Israel already had a king like that.

4. (11) Samuel asks about an absent son.

And Samuel said to Jesse, "Are all the young men here?" Then he said, "There remains yet the youngest, and there he is, keeping the sheep." And Samuel said to Jesse, "Send and bring him. For we will not sit down till he comes here."

a. **Are all the young men here?** Samuel had a problem. God told him of Jesse, *I have provided Myself a king among his sons* (1 Samuel 16:1). Yet here were the seven sons of Jesse and God did not chose any of them. Since Samuel knew God's word was true he knew there must be another son of Jesse who was not at the sacrificial feast.

b. **There remains the youngest**: This shows the low regard David had among his own family. First, his father didn't even mention him by name. Second, he wasn't even invited to the sacrificial feast. Third, he was only called to come because Samuel insisted on it.

i. "So small was David in his father's esteem that it wasn't considered necessary to include him in the family when the prophet of God called them to sacrifice." (Redpath)

ii. When we consider that David was the youngest of eight sons, we aren't surprised at the low regard he had in his own family. It wasn't because David's character or conduct was unworthy, it was simply because he was the youngest of eight sons.

iii. God often chooses unlikely people to do His work, so that all know the work is God's work, not man's work. He wants to work in a way so that people regard His servants as they regarded Samson: they wondered at the secret of his strength (Judges 16:5).

iv. "You may not be intellectual or well thought of in your family circle; you may be despised by others for your faith in Christ. Perhaps you had only a little share in the love of your parents, as David did. But remember that those who are rejected of men often become beloved of the Lord." (Redpath)

c. **And there he is, keeping the sheep**: David was called for this great anointing when he was out **keeping the sheep**. David simply did his job and was faithful in small things and what his father told him to do.

i. **Keeping the sheep** was a servant's job. The fact that David was out **keeping the sheep** showed that the family of Jesse was not especially wealthy, because if they were wealthy a servant would be **keeping the sheep**. But they were not affluent enough to have servants.

ii. **Keeping the sheep** meant you had time to think. David spent a lot of time looking over the sheep and looking at the glory of God's creation. God built in him a heart to sing about His glory in all creation (Psalm 19:1-4 and Psalm 8 are good examples).

iii. **Keeping the sheep** took a special heart, a special care. It meant you knew how sheep needed the care and help of a good shepherd. You learned that you were a sheep and God was your shepherd. During these years, God built in David the heart that would sing about the LORD as his shepherd (as in Psalm 23).

iv. **Keeping the sheep** meant you had to trust God in the midst of danger. David had lions and bears and wolves to contend with and the sheep had to be protected. "The country round Bethlehem was not a peaceful paradise, and the career of a shepherd was not the easy life of lovesick swains which poets dream." (Blaikie)

v. David's years **keeping the sheep** were not *waiting* time; they were *training* time. David was a great man and a great king over Israel because he *never lost his shepherd's heart.* Psalm 78:70-72 speaks of the connection between David the king and David the shepherd: *He also chose David His servant, and took him from the sheepfolds; from following the ewes that had young He brought him, to shepherd Jacob His people, and Israel His inheritance. So he shepherded them according to the integrity of his heart, and guided them by the skillfulness of his hands.*

5. (12-13) David is chosen and anointed.

So he sent and brought him in. Now he *was* ruddy, with bright eyes, and good-looking. And the LORD said, "Arise, anoint him; for this *is* the one!" Then Samuel took the horn of oil and anointed him in the midst of his brothers; and the Spirit of the LORD came upon David from that day forward. So Samuel arose and went to Ramah.

a. **Now he was ruddy, with bright eyes, and good-looking**: The physical description of David tells us he had a fair complexion (this is probably the meaning of **ruddy**, and a light complexion was considered attractive in that culture). He had **bright eyes**, which speak of vitality and intelligence. David was also **good-looking**.

i. David had a pleasant appearance, but he did not look like Saul, who looked like a leader and a king (1 Samuel 9:2). David looked nice but you didn't look at him and say, "There's a born leader. There is a king." That is what people said when they looked at Saul. When they looked at David they said, "That's a nice looking boy."

ii. We don't know how old David was at this time. The ancient Jewish historian Josephus says that David was ten years old. Others guess he was about fifteen years old. It's safe to say he was in that range.

b. **And the LORD said, "Arise, anoint him; for this is the one!"** By all outward appearances David's seven brothers seemed to be better material for royalty. As unlikely as he was, David was **the one**.

i. David was a shepherd, but there were a lot of shepherds. David was good-looking, but so were a lot of young men. David was young, but there were plenty of young men God could have chosen. God described what made David special in 1 Samuel 13:14: *The LORD has sought for Himself a man after His own heart, and the LORD had commanded him to be commander over His people.* What made David **the one** was that he was *a man after God's own heart.*

ii. God's choice of David shows that we don't have to quit our jobs and enter into full-time ministry to be people after God's own heart. We don't need to be famous or prominent to be people after God's own heart. We don't need to be respected or even liked by others to be people after God's own heart. We don't need status, influence, power, the respect or approval of men, or great responsibilities to be people after God's own heart.

iii. Where did David get this heart? Obviously, from time spent with the LORD. But someone started him on that path. David says nothing of his father, but twice in the Psalms he refers to his mother as a *maidservant* of the LORD (Psalm 86:16 and 116:16). Probably, it was David's godly mother who poured her heart and love and devotion of the LORD into him, and gave him a foundation to build on in his own walk with the LORD. Like Timothy, God used David's mother to pour into him a godly faith (2 Timothy 1:5).

c. **Then Samuel took the horn of oil and anointed him in the midst of his brothers**: From the actions of David, Jesse, and David's brothers, after this we can assume that only God and Samuel knew exactly what happened here.

i. Everyone else probably thought that Samuel just honored David for an unknown reason. Probably no one even dared to think this was a divine royal anointing. But God knew, because He had worked in David's heart for a long time. "The public anointing was the outcome of what had taken place in private between David and God long before." (Redpath)

d. **And the Spirit of the LORD came upon David from that day forward**: The real anointing happened when the Holy Spirit came upon David. The oil on the head was just a sign of this inward reality.

e. **So Samuel arose and went to Ramah**: Samuel did not begin a "Let's Enthrone David" political party and he did not begin to undermine Saul's throne, looking for a way to establish David as king. Samuel took one look at David, and reacted exactly the way God wanted him to: "LORD, I don't know why You chose this kid. But You will have to put him on the throne. I can't do it."

i. God did do it. 1 Samuel 16:13 is the first mention of the name "**David**" in the book of 1 Samuel. He has been referred to prophetically before (as in 1 Samuel 13:14 and 15:28). But this is the first mention of his *name*, which means "Beloved" or "Loved One."

ii. David will become one of the greatest men of the Bible, mentioned more than 1,000 times in the pages of Scripture - more than Abraham, more than Moses, more than any mere man in the New Testament. It's no accident that Jesus wasn't known as the "Son of Abraham" or the "Follower of Moses," but as the *Son of David* (Matthew 9:27 and at least a dozen other places).

iii. "From whatever side we view the life of David, it is remarkable. It may be that Abraham excelled him in faith, and Moses in the power of concentrated fellowship with God, and Elijah in the fiery force of his enthusiasm. But none of these was so many-sided as the richly gifted son of Jesse." (Meyer)

B. Saul's distressing spirit.

1. (14) Saul's **distressing spirit** troubles him.

But the Spirit of the LORD departed from Saul, and a distressing spirit from the LORD troubled him.

a. **The Spirit of the LORD departed from Saul**: In 1 Samuel 16:13, *the Spirit of the LORD came upon David from that day forward.* As the Holy Spirit came upon David, a **distressing spirit** came to Saul and **troubled him**.

b. **A distressing spirit from the LORD troubled him**: If God is all-good, why did He send a **distressing spirit** upon Saul? There are two senses in which God may *send* something. He may send something in the active sense or He may send something in a passive sense. Actively, God never initiates or performs evil; He is *the Father of lights, with whom there is no variation or shadow of turning* (James 1:17). Passively, God may withdraw the hand of His protection and therefore allow evil to come, without being the source of the evil itself.

i. This is indicated by what happened with Saul. First, **the Spirit of the LORD departed from Saul**. This meant Saul lost his spiritual "protection" and covering. So, Satan was more than ready to send a **distressing spirit** to fill the void in Saul.

ii. This is why the continual presence of the Holy Spirit for all Christians is such a comfort. We don't have to fear that God will take the Holy Spirit from us (Romans 8:9-11, 1 Corinthians 6:19-20).

c. **From the LORD**: Perhaps this was to judge Saul's past wickedness and rebellion against the Holy Spirit's guidance. This may be an example of God giving Saul over to his sin.

i. Saul clearly had the Spirit of the LORD upon him at one time (1 Samuel 10:10). As he was proud and rebellious against God, Saul resisted the Holy Spirit. He told the Holy Spirit "No" and "Go away" so many times that God finally gave Saul what he wanted. But Saul never realized the price to pay when **the Spirit of the LORD departed from him**. Saul thought he would be freer to do *his thing* without the **Spirit of the LORD** "bugging" him. He didn't realize he would be in even more bondage to **a distressing spirit** that **troubled him**.

ii. Even in this state Saul could repent. He was not past the place of repentance and restoration. It was up to him to receive God's correction and respond with a tender, repentant heart before the LORD.

d. **A distressing spirit from the LORD troubled him**: Today, Saul would probably be diagnosed as mentally ill. Yet his problem was spiritual in nature, not mental or psychological.

i. There are many people in mental hospitals today that are really suffering from spiritual problems. It is certainly wrong to assume that every case of mental distress is spiritual, because chemical imbalances and physiological problems are also real in this fallen world. Even so, there are certainly some that need liberation from a **distressing spirit** and may never find it in our modern mental health system.

2. (15-17) A solution suggested.

And Saul's servants said to him, "Surely, a distressing spirit from God is troubling you. Let our master now command your servants, *who are* before you, to

seek out a man *who is* a skillful player on the harp; and it shall be that he will play it with his hand when the distressing spirit from God is upon you, and you shall be well." So Saul said to his servants, "Provide me now a man who can play well, and bring *him* to me."

a. **Saul's servants said to him, "Surely a distressing spirit from God is troubling you"**: This was obvious to **Saul's servants**, but it does not seem to be obvious to Saul. Often our spiritual condition is far more apparent to others than it is to our self.

b. **Seek out a man who is a skillful player**: Essentially, Saul's servants advise him to find what we would call a "worship leader." They will **seek out a man** who can, using music, bring the love, peace, and power of God to Saul. King Saul needed to be *led* into worship, so it was important to **seek out a man** to do the job.

i. God created music and gave it the capability to touch people with great power. Music can be used for great good or for great evil, because it is so powerfully communicates to our inner being.

c. **You shall be well**: In the past, Saul received the Spirit of the LORD in the presence of music (1 Samuel 10:10). Perhaps this is an effort to create that experience again.

3. (18) A man is nominated.

Then one of the servants answered and said, "Look, I have seen a son of Jesse the Bethlehemite, *who is* skillful in playing, a mighty man of valor, a man of war, prudent in speech, and a handsome person; and the LORD *is* with him."

a. **Look, I have seen a son of Jesse**: Saul's servants suggested a search; Saul commanded the search, and then one of Saul's servants found this **son of Jesse** name David.

b. **Skillful in playing**: David needed skill to lead Saul in worship and to minister to him in music. The technical quality of his music was important. The heart matters, but so does technical ability.

i. This doesn't mean that a person must be a virtuoso before God can use them. But it does mean that they cannot tolerate a too casual, unconcerned, lazy, "we don't really need to practice" attitude. **Skillful in playing** reflects an *attitude* as much as it reflects *ability*.

c. **A mighty man of valor, a man of war**: David needed the character of a warrior to effectively lead Saul in worship and to minister to him in music. Worship ministry is a constant battleground. There are often conflicts and contentions surrounding worship ministry and if someone isn't equipped and ready for spiritual warfare they will probably be spiritually and emotionally "injured" in worship ministry, and probably "wound" others.

i. So much of what makes a person a good *musician* or a good *artist* goes against true worship ministry. The need for ego satisfaction and the desires for the spotlight, prominence, and attention each work against effective worship.

d. **Prudent in speech**: David needed to speak wisely to effectively lead Saul in worship or to minister to him in music. Good worship ministry needs a lot of diplomacy. Everyone has an opinion on music and a suggestion. Effective worship ministers know when to speak and when to be quiet on the platform, among the team, and in the congregation.

e. **A handsome person**: David was a good-looking young man (1 Samuel 16:12). An effective worship minister doesn't need to be a fashion model, but their appearance is important. They need to present themselves so as to be *invisible.* If they are so dressed up or so dressed down that their appearance calls attention to themselves, it needs to change.

f. **The LORD is with him**: This is the most important attribute. The other measures will grow and develop, but it must be said of any worship minister, **the LORD is with him**. This means that they are called by God, submitting to God, and submitting to whatever leadership the LORD has placed over them.

4. (19-23) David enters Saul's court.

Therefore Saul sent messengers to Jesse, and said, "Send me your son David, who *is* with the sheep." And Jesse took a donkey *loaded with* bread, a skin of wine, and a young goat, and sent *them* by his son David to Saul. So David came to Saul and stood before him. And he loved him greatly, and he became his armorbearer. Then Saul sent to Jesse, saying, "Please let David stand before me, for he has found favor in my sight." And so it was, whenever the spirit from God was upon Saul, that David would take a harp and play *it* with his hand. Then Saul would become refreshed and well, and the distressing spirit would depart from him.

a. **Send me your son David, who is with the sheep**: Since this happened after Samuel anointed David, this means he simply returned to **the sheep** after his anointing. Perhaps David didn't yet understand the significance of what Samuel did. Or if he did, he understood that it was *God's job* to bring him to the throne. In the meantime, David would simply go back to **the sheep**.

b. **Then Saul sent to Jesse, saying, "Please let David stand before me, for he has found favor in my sight"**: David did not have to manipulate his way into the palace or into Saul's favor. He allowed the LORD to open the doors for him. David didn't have to wonder, "Is this of the LORD or is this of me?" because he let the LORD open the doors for him.

i. "Wonder not that David was so suddenly advanced, from a poor contemptible shepherd, to so great a reputation; for these were the effects of that Spirit of the Lord, which he received when he was anointed." (Poole)

c. **And he loved him greatly, and he became his armorbearer**: David was an outstanding young man who was worthy of his name ("Beloved" or "Loved One"). Saul took to him immediately, and gave him the important and trusted position of **armorbearer**, his chief assistant in battle. A soldier's life often depended on the courage and faithfulness of his **armorbearer**, and Saul knew David was worthy of this position.

i. This was an important time in David's life and training for God's destiny for him. For the first time he lived in a royal court and began to learn the customs and manners he needed to know to be a good king later in life.

d. **David would take a harp and play it**: A **harp** is a lyre, the ancient version of the guitar. This isn't one of the big harps you might find in an orchestra.

e. **Then Saul would become refreshed and well**: God used David to minister to Saul. David was happy to be used. What seemed like a great arrangement would not stay great for very long.

i. God was at work in ways no one could see. It seems plain to us from our distant perspective, but at the time perhaps only Samuel knew what was going on. "Unwittingly, Saul was becoming dependent on the one designated to succeed him." (Baldwin)

1 Samuel 17 - David and Goliath

A. Goliath challenges Israel.

1. (1-10) The Philistine Goliath challenges Israel.

Now the Philistines gathered their armies together to battle, and were gathered together at Sochoh, which *belongs* to Judah; they encamped between Sochoh and Azekah, in Ephes Dammim. And Saul and the men of Israel were gathered together, and they encamped in the Valley of Elah, and drew up in battle array against the Philistines. The Philistines stood on a mountain on one side, and Israel stood on a mountain on the other side, with a valley between them. And a champion went out from the camp of the Philistines, named Goliath, from Gath, whose height *was* six cubits and a span. *He had* a bronze helmet on his head, and he *was* armed with a coat of mail, and the weight of the coat *was* five thousand shekels of bronze. And *he had* bronze armor on his legs and a bronze javelin between his shoulders. Now the staff of his spear *was* like a weaver's beam, and his iron spearhead *weighed* six hundred shekels; and a shield-bearer went before him. Then he stood and cried out to the armies of Israel, and said to them, "Why have you come out to line up for battle? *Am* I not a Philistine, and you the servants of Saul? Choose a man for yourselves, and let him come down to me. If he is able to fight with me and kill me, then we will be your servants. But if I prevail against him and kill him, then you shall be our servants and serve us." And the Philistine said, "I defy the armies of Israel this day; give me a man, that we may fight together."

a. **They encamped in the Valley of Elah**: The green rolling hills surrounding the Valley of Elah still stand today and they witnessed one of the most remarkable battles in all the Bible. It began when the Philistines, constant enemies of Israel during this period, assembled their army on a **mountain** and on an opposite **mountain** stood the army of Israel.

b. **And a champion went out from the camp of the Philistines, named Goliath**: He was a large man (**six cubits and a span** can be anywhere from 8'5" to 9'2"), and he had armor and weapons to match his size.

i. Goliath was tall, but his height is not unheard of in history. Poole on Goliath's height: "Besides the giants mentioned in the Scriptures, Herodotus, Diodorus Siculus, and Pliny, and others, make mention of persons seven cubits high, which is near double to an ordinary man's height." Youngblood mentions the documented case of Robert Pershing Wadlow, who was eight feet eleven inches tall at the time of his death on July 15, 1940, at the age of twenty-two.

ii. Goliath was **from Gath** and Joshua 11:22 says that a people known as the Anakim were still there in Joshua's day. That was some 400 years before this, but it shows how there may have continued to be men of unusually large size from the city of Gath.

iii. Different sources give different estimates, but Goliath's armor and weapons together probably weighed somewhere between 150 and 200 pounds. This was a big man, and strong enough to carry and use these huge weapons.

c. **Choose a man for yourselves, and let him come down to me . . . I defy the armies of Israel this day; give me a man, that we may fight together**: Goliath issued a bold challenge to the army of Israel. Adam Clarke says that the word **champion** really comes from the Hebrew word, "a *middle man*, the *man between two*." The idea is that this was a man who stood between the two armies and fought as a representative of his army.

2. (11) The fear of Saul and all Israel.

When Saul and all Israel heard these words of the Philistine, they were dismayed and greatly afraid.

a. **When they heard these words of the Philistine, they were dismayed and greatly afraid**: This was Goliath's *exact intention* in issuing the challenge. The reason why he came out with full battle equipment and paraded in front of the Israelite army was because he *wanted* them to be **dismayed and greatly afraid**. Goliath defeated the Israelites on fear alone.

i. In any contest, it's always useful to *demoralize* your opponent and strike *fear* in their heart. First, it may keep you from ever going to battle with them because they are so afraid. Second, if it does come to battle they will fight with fear and apprehension and so with your words, you've done a lot to win the battle before it even begins. This is a significant strategy of the devil against believers.

b. **When Saul . . . heard these words**: Saul had special reason to be afraid. Goliath was the giant among the Philistines and Saul was head and shoulder taller than other Israelite men (1 Samuel 9:2). Saul was the logical choice to square off against Goliath, and we can expect he knew others expected him to fight Goliath.

c. **Dismayed and greatly afraid**: As battle loomed, this was Saul's state. At one time he was known as a fierce and successful military leader (1 Samuel 14:52). But that was before the Spirit of the LORD departed from Saul (1 Samuel 16:14). As the Spirit left Saul so did his courage.

B. David comes to the camp of Israel.

1. (12-15) David, the youngest of eight brothers, splits his time between the palace and the pasture.

Now David *was* the son of that Ephrathite of Bethlehem Judah, whose name *was* Jesse, and who had eight sons. And the man was old, advanced *in years*, in the days of Saul. The three oldest sons of Jesse had gone to follow Saul to the battle. The names of his three sons who went to the battle *were* Eliab the firstborn, next to him Abinadab, and the third Shammah. David *was* the youngest. And the three oldest followed Saul. But David occasionally went and returned from Saul to feed his father's sheep at Bethlehem.

a. **David occasionally went and returned from Saul to feed his father's sheep**: It seems David was only called to the palace as needed, when Saul was afflicted by the distressing spirit.

b. **David was the youngest**: David is said to be the youngest of eight sons of Jesse. Yet Psalm 89:27 calls David God's *firstborn*, demonstrating that "firstborn" is as much a title and a concept as a description of birth order. Therefore, when Paul calls Jesus *firstborn over all creation* in Colossians 1:15, he isn't trying to say that Jesus is a created being who had a beginning. He is simply pointing to the prominence and preeminence of Jesus.

2. (16-21) David brings gifts from home and comes into Israel's camp.

And the Philistine drew near and presented himself forty days, morning and evening. Then Jesse said to his son David, "Take now for your brothers an ephah of this dried *grain* and these ten loaves, and run to your brothers at the camp. And carry these ten cheeses to the captain of *their* thousand, and see how your brothers fare, and bring back news of them." Now Saul and they and all the men of Israel *were* in the Valley of Elah, fighting with the Philistines. So David rose early in the morning, left the sheep with a keeper, and took *the things* and went as Jesse had commanded him. And he came to the camp as the army was going out to the fight and shouting for the battle. For Israel and the Philistines had drawn up in battle array, army against army.

a. **And the Philistine drew near and presented himself forty days**: Day after day, Goliath taunted and mocked the armies of Israel, exposing them all (and especially Saul) as cowards.

b. **Left the sheep with a keeper**: This little observation shows the shepherd's heart of David. If he left the sheep to run an errand for his father he made sure the sheep were still well cared for.

c. **And he came to the camp as the army was going out to the fight and shouting for the battle**: This must have been the approximate scene for forty days. The armies gathered on each hillside, screaming and shouting at each other across the valley. Goliath made his parade and shouted his insults, and after a while the Israelites slinked away in shame.

3. (22-24) David sees Goliath's challenge and the fear of Israel's soldiers.

And David left his supplies in the hand of the supply keeper, ran to the army, and came and greeted his brothers. Then as he talked with them, there was the champion, the Philistine of Gath, Goliath by name, coming up from the armies of the Philistines; and he spoke according to the same words. So David heard *them*. And all the men of Israel, when they saw the man, fled from him and were dreadfully afraid.

a. **Dreadfully afraid**: *All* of the Israelite army was **dreadfully afraid**. There was not one man among them who would take on Goliath. Every one of them **fled from him** when Goliath came out.

4. (25-27) David *hears* of Saul's reward to the man who beats Goliath, but he *speaks* of God's honor.

So the men of Israel said, "Have you seen this man who has come up? Surely he has come up to defy Israel; and it shall be *that* the man who kills him the king will enrich with great riches, will give him his daughter, and give his father's house exemption *from taxes* in Israel." Then David spoke to the men who stood by him, saying, "What shall be done for the man who kills this Philistine and takes away the reproach from Israel? For who *is* this uncircumcised Philistine, that he should defy the armies of the living God?" And the people answered him in this manner, saying, "So shall it be done for the man who kills him."

a. **The man who kills him, the king will enrich**: The situation had become so desperate that Saul needed to offer a three-part bribe including a cash award, a princess, and a tax exemption - to induce someone, *anyone* to fight and win against Goliath.

b. **Who kills this Philistine and takes away the reproach from Israel . . . who is this uncircumcised Philistine, that he should defy the armies of the living God?** Other soldiers focused on the *danger* of the battle or the *material rewards* to be won. It seems that David alone focused on the reputation of **Israel** and the honor of the **living God**.

i. This truly shows David to be a man after God's own heart. He cares about the things God cares about. He saw the problem in spiritual terms, not in material or fleshly terms.

ii. When the men of Israel said, "**This man**," David said, "**This uncircumcised Philistine**." When the men of Israel said, "**Surely he has come up to defy Israel**," David said, "**That he should defy the**

armies of the living God." When the men of Israel said, "**The man who kills him**," David said, "**The man who kills this Philistine and takes away the reproach from Israel.**" David saw things from the LORD's perspective, but the men of Israel saw things only from man's perspective.

5. (28-30) David is misunderstood and falsely accused by his brother.

Now Eliab his oldest brother heard when he spoke to the men; and Eliab's anger was aroused against David, and he said, "Why did you come down here? And with whom have you left those few sheep in the wilderness? I know your pride and the insolence of your heart, for you have come down to see the battle." And David said, "What have I done now? *Is there* not a cause?" Then he turned from him toward another and said the same thing; and these people answered him as the first ones *did*.

a. **Eliab's anger was aroused against David**: We might have thought that David's visit would please Eliab, especially considering all the things he brought from home. But David's words angered Eliab and there were many reasons why.

i. First, he was angry because he felt David was an insignificant, worthless person who had no right to speak up, especially with such bold words (**Why did you come down here? And with whom have you left those few sheep in the wilderness?**).

ii. Second, he was angry because he *felt* he knew David's motivation (**I know your pride and the insolence of your heart**), but he didn't *really* know David's heart. "Here he taketh upon him that which belongeth to God alone (Jeremiah 17:10), and judgeth David's heart by his own." (Trapp)

iii. Third, he was angry because he thought David tried to provoke someone *else* into fighting Goliath just so he could see a battle (**you have come down to see the battle**). Eliab himself was a tall man of good appearance (1 Samuel 16:7), and he may have felt David was trying to push *him* into battle.

iv. Finally, he was angry because *David was right!* When you are *dismayed and greatly afraid* or *dreadfully afraid*, the last thing in the world you want is someone telling you to be courageous.

b. **What have I done now? Is there not a cause?** David stuck to his position. There is no doubt that what his brother Eliab said *hurt* him, but he would not let it *hinder* him. David kept concerned with God's cause before everything. Before his own personal safety, before his own personal glory, before his only personal honor, he had a passionate concern for God's **cause**.

i. David was more concerned with God's cause (**Is there not a cause?**) than with his own feelings. When David was misunderstood and publicly rebuked by his own brother, probably amid the laughs of the other soldiers, he could have quit. But he showed the strength of the armor of God in his life and replied rightly. He didn't care about his glory or success, but only for the glory and success of the LORD's **cause**. *Goliath was a dead man right then. This is where the battle was won.* If Eliab's hurtful words can get David in the flesh and out of step with the Spirit of the LORD, then David's strength is gone. But when David ruled his spirit and answered softly, he was more in step with the Spirit of the LORD than ever. Goliath was defeated right then.

ii. "Immediately before the encounter with the Philistine he fought a battle which cost him far more thought, prudence, and patience. The word-battle in which he had to engage with his brothers and with king Saul, was a more trying ordeal to him than going forth in the strength of the Lord to smite the uncircumcised boaster. Many a man meets with more trouble from his friends than from his enemies; and when he has learned to overcome the depressing influence of prudent friends, he makes short work of the opposition of avowed adversaries." (Spurgeon)

C. David prepares to fight Goliath.

1. (31-32) David's confident words become known to Saul.

Now when the words which David spoke were heard, they reported *them* to Saul; and he sent for him. Then David said to Saul, "Let no man's heart fail because of him; your servant will go and fight with this Philistine."

a. **They reported him to Saul**: It wasn't as if David's words were all that bold. He never said, "If I went out to fight against that Philistine, I would whip his tail. He's nothing." David didn't talk like that, but at least he stood up to Goliath. David didn't show a lot of backbone but he showed more courage than anyone else in Israel, so it was worth reporting to Saul.

b. **Your servant will go and fight with this Philistine**: Saul waited a long time - at least 40 days - to hear someone say these words. But to hear them now, from the mouth of this boy, almost seemed like a cruel joke. "The good news is that some one finally wants to fight Goliath. The bad news is that he is a little shepherd boy."

i. David's words to Saul almost made the matter worse. "**Let no man's heart fail because of him**" almost sounds like, "All right everyone, calm down, I've got the situation completely under control." It seemed ridiculous coming from this teen-age boy. It seemed like youthful pride and overconfidence, but it wasn't.

c. **Your servant will go and fight with this Philistine**: These are bold words. This is the first time David specifically volunteered to battle Goliath. It is one thing to say, "*Someone* should do something about the enemy." It is entirely another thing to say, "*I* will do something about the enemy."

2. (33-37) David's training as a shepherd prepared him.

And Saul said to David, "You are not able to go against this Philistine to fight with him; for you *are* a youth, and he a man of war from his youth." But David said to Saul, "Your servant used to keep his father's sheep, and when a lion or a bear came and took a lamb out of the flock, I went out after it and struck it, and delivered *the lamb* from its mouth; and when it arose against me, I caught *it* by its beard, and struck and killed it. Your servant has killed both lion and bear; and this uncircumcised Philistine will be like one of them, seeing he has defied the armies of the living God." Moreover David said, "The LORD, who delivered me from the paw of the lion and from the paw of the bear, He will deliver me from the hand of this Philistine." And Saul said to David, "Go, and the LORD be with you!"

a. **You are not able . . . you are but a youth**: Saul thought David was disqualified because of his age, size, and inexperience. This shows that Saul looked at the battle purely in natural, outward terms. The outward "tale of the tape" said there was no way David could win. The "tale of God's tape" said there was no way David could lose.

b. **You are but a youth and he a man of war from his youth**: Saul essentially told David, "He's been a soldier longer than you have been alive. How can you ever defeat him?" Again, this shows that Saul only looked at the outward, not the spiritual dimensions of this battle.

c. **Your servant has killed both lion and bear**: God prepared David for this exact battle when David was a lowly shepherd. A lion attacked the lambs and David fought the lion. A bear came against the sheep and David battled the bear. All along, God prepared David to fight Goliath. How long did David prepare to fight Goliath? All of his life, up to that day.

i. This is generally God's pattern for preparation. He calls us to be faithful right where we are and then uses our faithfulness to accomplish greater things. If David ran scared at the lion or the bear, he would never have been ready to fight Goliath now. But he was faithful then, so he will be faithful now.

d. **Your servant has killed both lion and bear; and this uncircumcised Philistine will be like one of them**: David increases in boldness as the story progresses. First he said someone *should* fight Goliath for a righteous cause (1 Samuel 17:26, 29). Then he said he *would* fight Goliath (1 Samuel 17:32). Now he says he will *kill* Goliath.

e. **The LORD who delivered me from the paw of the lion and from the paw of the bear, He will deliver me from the hand of this Philistine**: As a shepherd facing lions and bears, David had no idea he was being trained to fight a giant. In the midst of our preparation we rarely see how God will use it. Yet now, David can look back and know that the same God who **delivered** him before will also **deliver** him now. David knew that God's help in times past is a prophecy of His help in the future.

3. (38-40) David prepares to fight Goliath.

So Saul clothed David with his armor, and he put a bronze helmet on his head; he also clothed him with a coat of mail. David fastened his sword to his armor and tried to walk, for he had not tested *them*. And David said to Saul, "I cannot walk with these, for I have not tested *them*." So David took them off. Then he took his staff in his hand; and he chose for himself five smooth stones from the brook, and put them in a shepherd's bag, in a pouch which he had, and his sling was in his hand. And he drew near to the Philistine.

a. **So Saul clothed David with his armor**: Saul was still in the natural, in the flesh, in the things that are merely outward. He figured that if this boy were going to beat Goliath, he needed the best **armor** in all Israel - the armor of the king.

b. **He tried to walk . . . David said to Saul, "I cannot walk with these, for I have not tested them."** Saul tried to put his armor on David, but it didn't work. It didn't work because Saul's armor did not *physically fit* David. Everything was too big, and David could not move well with Saul's armor. It also didn't work because Saul's armor did not *spiritually fit* David. Armor, military technology, or human wisdom would not win this battle. The LORD God of Israel would win this battle.

i. Often people try to fight with another person's armor. They see God do something wonderful through someone else and they try to copy it without really making it their own. God's work is never most effectively done in this way.

ii. Sadly, many people would say the same about the armor of God: "**I cannot walk with these, because I have not tested them**." Are you more familiar with the weapons and armor of the flesh or the weapons and armor of the Spirit? "Press some people to their exercise of prayer, or any other piece of the armour of God, and they must say, if they say truly, as here, I cannot do withal, for I have not been accustomed to it." (Trapp)

c. **So David took them off**: David had to *renounce* Saul's armor. He had to vow, "I will not fight with man's armor. I will trust in the LORD and His armor instead." Often we want a safe "middle ground" where we try to wear both kinds of armor. God wants us to trust in Him and Him alone.

d. **A staff in his hand . . . five smooth stones . . . a shepherd's bag, in a pouch which he had, and his sling was in his hand**: David used the same tools he used before as a shepherd to kill the lion and the bear. What God used before, He would use again.

i. A charming - but purely legendary - Rabbinical story says these five particular stones called out to David from **the brook** and said, "*By us you shall overcome the giant!*"

ii. Why did David choose **five** stones? He only needed one to kill Goliath. Perhaps it was because Goliath had four brothers (1 Samuel 21:18-22).

e. **And he drew near the Philistine**: This is where it mattered. David could have said the bold words, renounced Saul's armor, trusted in God's armor, and gathered his shepherd's tools. But if he never went into the battle, what would it matter? Ultimately, David had the faith not just to talk, not just to renounce, not just to prepare, but also to actually **draw near the Philistine**. That's real faith.

D. David defeats Goliath.

1. (41-44) Goliath curses David and his God.

So the Philistine came, and began drawing near to David, and the man who bore the shield went before him. And when the Philistine looked about and saw David, he disdained him; for he was *only* a youth, ruddy and good-looking. So the Philistine said to David, "*Am* I a dog, that you come to me with sticks?" And the Philistine cursed David by his gods. And the Philistine said to David, "Come to me, and I will give your flesh to the birds of the air and the beasts of the field!"

a. **So the Philistine came . . . and the man who bore the shield went before him**: Obviously, because of Goliath's size and experience, it was not a "fair" fight. Adding to that, it was two against one because Goliath had an armor bearer with him.

b. **When the Philistine looked about and saw David, he disdained him**: The idea behind **looked about** is almost that Goliath had to look around to *find* David. David was so small compared to this man that Goliath had a hard time even seeing him. But when he did see him **he disdained him**. There was nothing - *nothing* - in David that struck fear or respect in Goliath's heart. Goliath felt insulted that they sent David (**Am I a dog that you come to me with sticks?**).

i. When Goliath asked, "**Am I a dog?**" it was worse than it sounds. The Hebrew word for **dog** (*kaleb*) is used in passages like Deuteronomy 23:18 for male homosexual prostitutes. Goliath felt that sending David was an insult to his manhood.

c. **And the Philistine cursed David by his gods**: If it hadn't been established before, it is certainly settled now. This *is not a fair fight*. It isn't Goliath and his armor bearer against David. It is Goliath and his armor bearer against David and the LORD God of Israel. The battle is over. Anyone with any spiritual understanding could finish the story from here.

d. **Come to me**: "Bring it on, little boy!" David will be more than happy to oblige Goliath's request.

2. (45-47) David, full of faith, replies to Goliath.

Then David said to the Philistine, "You come to me with a sword, with a spear, and with a javelin. But I come to you in the name of the LORD of hosts, the God of the armies of Israel, whom you have defied. This day the LORD will deliver you into my hand, and I will strike you and take your head from you. And this day I will give the carcasses of the camp of the Philistines to the birds of the air and the wild beasts of the earth, that all the earth may know that there is a God in Israel. Then all this assembly shall know that the LORD does not save with sword and spear; for the battle *is* the Lord's, and He will give you into our hands."

a. **Then David said to the Philistine**: We can imagine Goliath's deep, deep, bass voice reverberating against the tall hills surrounding the Valley of Elah. The sound struck fear into the heart of every Israelite soldier, and probably even some of the Philistine soldiers! Then David answered with his teen-age voice; perhaps even with his voice cracking. The Philistines laughed when they heard David practically screaming in his cracking voice and the Israelites were both horrified and embarrassed.

b. **You come to me with a sword, with a spear, and with a javelin. I come to you in the name of the LORD of hosts, the God of the armies of Israel, whom you have defied**: David makes a contrast between himself and Goliath without giving credit to Goliath himself. "Those are some pretty fancy weapons you've got there, mister. But I've got something far better than your weapons."

i. To say, "**I come to you in the name of the LORD of hosts**" is to say, "I come as a representative of the LORD of hosts, the God who has heavenly armies at His command. I am a sent man, a man on a mission from God."

c. **This day, the LORD will deliver you into my hand**: David is bolder and bolder. It is one thing to tell *Saul* he will kill Goliath (1 Samuel 17:36). It is an entirely different thing to tell *Goliath* he will kill Goliath, and to say the LORD would do it **this day**. Adding **I will strike you down and take your head from you** is a nice, vivid detail.

i. David was careful to say, "**the LORD will deliver you into my hand**."

David was bold, but bold in God not in himself. He knew the battle belonged to the LORD.

d. **That all the earth may know that there is a God in Israel**: This whole incident made David famous. But that was not why he did it. He did it for the fame and the glory of the LORD, not his own name. He wanted **all the earth** to **know that there is a God in Israel**.

e. **Then all this assembly shall know**: At this point, it wasn't enough for **all the earth** to **know that there is a God in Israel**. *Israel needed to know that there was a God in Israel!* Saul and the rest of the soldiers of Israel thought that the LORD only could save with **sword and spear**. They didn't really believe that **the battle is the LORD's** but David will give them proof.

f. **He will give you into our hands**: Again, notice David's humility. It isn't **He will give you into *my* hands**. David knows this was an "**our**" battle, that he fought on behalf of all Israel. If they weren't trusting in the LORD, David would trust for them.

3. (48-49) David kills Goliath.

So it was, when the Philistine arose and came and drew near to meet David, that David hastened and ran toward the army to meet the Philistine. Then David put his hand in his bag and took out a stone; and he slung *it* and struck the Philistine in his forehead, so that the stone sank into his forehead, and he fell on his face to the earth.

a. **When the Philistine arose and came and drew near to meet David, that David hastened and ran toward the army to meet the Philistine**: What a scene! Goliath, enraged at David's boldness, **drew near** to quickly kill David. David didn't run away. He didn't hide. He didn't panic. He didn't drop to his knees and pray. Instead, **David hastened and ran . . . to meet the Philistine**.

i. Many Christians struggle at this very point. Is God supposed to do it or am I supposed to do it? The answer is, "Yes!" God does it and we do it. Trust God, rely on Him, *and then get to work and work as hard as you can - run right at the enemy.* That is how the work of God is done.

ii. "The lazy-bones of our orthodox churches cry, 'God will do his own work'; and then they look out the softest pillow they can find, and put it under their heads, and say, 'The eternal purposes will be carried out: God will be glorified.' That is all very fine talk, but it can be used with the most mischievous design. You can make opium out of it, which will lull you into a deep and dreadful slumber, and prevent your being of any kind of use at all." (Spurgeon)

b. **He slung it and struck the Philistine in his forehead, so that the stone sank into his forehead, and he fell on his face**: David had the calm hand and careful aim of someone who really trusted God. He used the sling - a leather strap with a pouch in the middle - to hurl a stone, killing Goliath.

i. This battle was won out with the sheep. In those lonely hours alone with the lambs, David talked to God and took a lot of target practice with his sling. Now his communion with the LORD and his skill with the sling are both used by God. "In the use of the sling it requires much *practice* to hit the mark; but when once this dexterity is acquired, the sling is nearly as fatal as the musket or bow." (Clarke)

ii. Everyone else thought, "Goliath is so big, I can't beat him." David thought, "Goliath is so big, I can't miss him." "A man of less faith might have been too nervous to take the proper aim." (Balikie)

c. **The stone sank into his forehead, and he fell on his face**: Just as the Philistine god Dagon fell on his face before the LORD (1 Samuel 5:2-5), so now the worshipper of Dagon falls on his face.

4. (50-54) David beheads Goliath and Israel romps over the Philistines.

So David prevailed over the Philistine with a sling and a stone, and struck the Philistine and killed him. But *there was* no sword in the hand of David. Therefore David ran and stood over the Philistine, took his sword and drew it out of its sheath and killed him, and cut off his head with it. And when the Philistines saw that their champion was dead, they fled. Now the men of Israel and Judah arose and shouted, and pursued the Philistines as far as the entrance of the valley and to the gates of Ekron. And the wounded of the Philistines fell along the road to Shaaraim, even as far as Gath and Ekron. Then the children of Israel returned from chasing the Philistines, and they plundered their tents. And David took the head of the Philistine and brought it to Jerusalem, but he put his armor in his tent.

a. **David ran and stood over the Philistine, took his sword and drew it out of its sheath and killed him, and cut off his head with it**: First, David *made certain the enemy was dead.* You can not mess around with sin or your spiritual enemies; you must kill them *dead.* Second, David used Goliath's *own sword* to cut off his head.

i. Later David wrote in Psalm 57:6: *They have prepared a net for my steps; my soul is bowed down; they have dug a pit before me; into the midst of it they themselves have fallen.* God loves to use the devil's weapons against him.

b. **When the Philistines saw that their champion was dead, they fled**: They agreed to surrender to Israel if their champion lost (1 Samuel 17:9). We should never expect the devil to live up to his promises. But the soldiers of Israel pursued and defeated the Philistines. David's example gave them great courage and faith in the LORD.

i. David never read 1 Timothy 4:12, but he lived it: *Let no one despise your youth, but be an example to the believers in word, in conduct, in love, in spirit, in faith, in purity*. David led by example and led Israel to a great victory.

c. **David took the head of the Philistine and brought it to Jerusalem, but he put his armor in his tent**: Since it was many years later that Jerusalem was conquered (2 Samuel 5:6-10), this likely means David *eventually* brought Goliath's head to Jerusalem. But David will use the sword of Goliath later (1 Samuel 21:9). David had some enduring reminders of God's great work.

i. "Presumably David had the head pickled and hung it in his banqueting hall after he had captured Jerusalem." (Ellison)

5. (55-58) Saul meets a victorious David.

When Saul saw David going out against the Philistine, he said to Abner, the commander of the army, "Abner, whose son *is* this youth?" And Abner said, "As your soul lives, O king, I do not know." So the king said, "Inquire whose son this young man *is*." Then, as David returned from the slaughter of the Philistine, Abner took him and brought him before Saul with the head of the Philistine in his hand. And Saul said to him, "Whose son *are* you, young man?" So David answered, "I *am* the son of your servant Jesse the Bethlehemite."

a. **Inquire whose son this young man is**: This doesn't mean that Saul did not recognize David. Perhaps Saul did recognize David, and he simply asked about David's family background (**inquire whose son this young man is**). Saul promised his daughter to the man who killed Goliath, and Saul wanted to know something about his future son-in-law.

i. Or, it may be that Saul indeed did not recognize David. Some think that David played behind a screen or a curtain for Saul so Saul never saw his face. Others think that because of the distressing spirit, Saul was not entirely in his right mind. We also know that David did not spend all his time at the palace, but went home to tend sheep (1 Samuel 17:15). It's possible that David's appearance changed during a time when he was away from Saul, so Saul didn't immediately recognize him. When Saul called David a "**young man**" the word means someone who is full grown, mature, and ready to marry.

b. **David returned from the slaughter of the Philistine**: David won a great victory, but not greater than the victory Jesus won at the cross. David's victory over Goliath is a "picture in advance" of the victory Jesus won for His people.

- Both David and Jesus represented their people. Whatever happened to the representative also happened to God's people

- Both David and Jesus fought the battle on ground that rightfully belonged to God's people, ground they had lost
- Both David and Jesus fought when their enemy was able to dominate the people of God through fear and intimidation alone
- Both David and Jesus were sent to the battleground by their father (1 Samuel 17:17)
- Both David and Jesus were scorned and rejected by their brethren
- Both David and Jesus fought the battle without concern with human strategies or conventional wisdom
- Both David and Jesus won the battle, but saw that their enemies did not then give up willingly
- Both David and Jesus fought a battle where victory was assured even before the battle started

1 Samuel 18 - Conflict Between Saul and David

A. David, Jonathan, and Saul.

1. (1-4) The friendship between David and Jonathan.

Now when he had finished speaking to Saul, the soul of Jonathan was knit to the soul of David, and Jonathan loved him as his own soul. Saul took him that day, and would not let him go home to his father's house anymore. Then Jonathan and David made a covenant, because he loved him as his own soul. And Jonathan took off the robe that *was* on him and gave it to David, with his armor, even to his sword and his bow and his belt.

a. **When he had finished speaking to Saul**: When David finished the "after-killing-Goliath" conversation with Saul, his fame in Israel was assured. He performed a remarkably heroic deed and was initially welcomed by the leadership of Israel.

b. **The soul of Jonathan was knit to the soul of David, and Jonathan loved him as his own soul**: Jonathan, the son of Saul, appeared before in 1 Samuel 14. He is the remarkably brave man of faith who initiated a one-man war against the Philistines.

i. Jonathan was a lot like David. They were approximately the same age, though Jonathan was probably at least five years older. They both were bold, both were men of great trust in God, and both were men of action. Most of all, both had a real relationship with God.

ii. At the same time, Jonathan and David were different. Jonathan was the first-born son of a king (1 Chronicles 9:39) and David was the last-born son of a farmer. This made Jonathan more than a *prince*, he was *the crown prince*. By *everyone's expectation* Jonathan would be the next king of Israel.

c. **The soul of Jonathan was knit to the soul of David**: This happened *after* David **had finished speaking to Saul.** Jonathan heard David give an extended explanation of his heart, his faith in the living God, and Jonathan *knew* that he and David had the same heart. They could not be such close friends until Jonathan knew that about David.

i. The way most people think, Jonathan was the one who had the most to fear from David's success. Yet he loved David, because what they had in common - a real relationship with the LORD God - was bigger than any difference.

d. **Saul took him that day**: David would never again be just a shepherd. David still had a shepherd's heart, but would be *more* than a shepherd.

e. **Then Jonathan and David made a covenant**: Two men, each on track for the same throne - yet they **made a covenant** of friendship that would prove stronger than jealousy, than envy, than ambition.

f. **Jonathan took off the robe that was on him and gave it to David, with his armor, even to his sword and his bow and his belt**: When Jonathan gave David **the robe** and **his armor**, he said by this action, "You will be the next king of Israel. You should be dressed and armed as the crown prince. God's hand is on you and these rightfully belong to you." Because Jonathan was surrendered to God he could see the hand of the LORD upon David. He knew David's destiny and was perfectly willing to set aside his ambition to honor the LORD's choice.

g. **Gave it to David**: For his part, David *received* **the robe** and Jonathan's **armor**. But he did not then say or think, "Good Jonathan. We all see who is boss around here. Now get out of my way because I'm going to replace your father as soon as I can." It would be some *20 years* until David would receive the throne of Israel and replace Saul. If Jonathan was ready to recognize David as God's choice for the next king, David was willing to let *God* put him on the throne, and to do it in *God's* timing. Both of these men were thoroughly submitted to the LORD.

i. David couldn't receive Saul's armor but David received Jonathan's armor, not only because they were more similar in size. More importantly, they shared the same **soul**. They both loved God and lived more for Him and for others more than for themselves. David and Jonathan both knew that if the circumstances were reversed, David would do the exact same thing for Jonathan - because they had the same **soul**.

ii. If the issue of "who will be the next king?" were not settled in the hearts of Jonathan and David, they could never have had this kind of close love and friendship. They loved each other more than the throne of Israel because they loved the LORD more than the throne of Israel.

iii. Some people read a homosexual relationship into the love between David and Jonathan. They suppose that two men cannot love each other without it being something the Bible clearly says is immoral. But the relationship between David and Jonathan shows the Bible doesn't condemn real love between men, only a sexual relationship between men.

2. (5-9) Saul's jealousy of David.

So David went out wherever Saul sent him, *and* behaved wisely. And Saul set him over the men of war, and he was accepted in the sight of all the people and also in the sight of Saul's servants. Now it had happened as they were coming *home*, when David was returning from the slaughter of the Philistine, that the women had come out of all the cities of Israel, singing and dancing, to meet King Saul, with tambourines, with joy, and with musical instruments. So the women sang as they danced, and said: "Saul has slain his thousands, And David his ten thousands." Then Saul was very angry, and the saying displeased him; and he said, "They have ascribed to David ten thousands, and to me they have ascribed *only* thousands. Now *what* more can he have but the kingdom?" So Saul eyed David from that day forward.

a. **David went out wherever Saul sent him, and behaved wisely**: David was fully submitted to Saul and sought to serve him **wisely** in every way. David knew the way to be blessed. It was to work hard to be a blessing to his boss. He would not undercut Saul's position or authority in any way.

i. Where did Saul send David? **Saul set him over the men of war**. This is a remarkable promotion - a man perhaps in his young twenties is now a "general" in the army of Israel.

b. **He was accepted in the sight of all the people and also in the sight of Saul's servants**: David quickly became popular both among **the people** and among the leaders (**Saul's servants**). This was not because David was a yes-man-people-pleaser-sycophant kind of man. David did not *seek* this popularity and did not depend on *any* of those carnal tools to gain it. David became popular because he was a *man after God's own heart* and people could see the *love*, the *wisdom*, and the *peace* of God in him.

i. We might imagine Saul's initial reaction was positive. "Good," he thought. "My new assistant is well received. Everyone thinks I made a brilliant choice in bringing him on staff. This is working out well."

c. **Saul has slain his thousands, and David his ten thousands**: David became unexpectedly popular. When the people of Israel started singing everyone knew David was more popular than Saul.

i. When **women** sing and dance in your honor, you are popular. When it happens in **all the cities of Israel**, you are popular. This song was the number one hit in Israel! David wisely received this popularity because 1 Samuel 18:14 says of this period in David's life, *And David* *behaved wisely in all his ways, and the LORD was with him.* In this environment of praise and popularity, David *behaved wisely in all his ways.*

ii. When you are praised and popular, it isn't *wise* to let it go to your head. David was happy to hear these affirming words, but he didn't let it dominate his thinking or *change* his opinion of himself. He kept the heart and the mind of a shepherd, even in a season of great success.

iii. This wasn't easy. This was a test, one the devil wanted to use to bring David down and one the LORD wanted to use to build David up. David never received this kind of affirmation when he kept the sheep. The sheep never danced and sang a song praising him. Now David faces the challenge of success. Many people who handle adversity well enough fall under the challenge of success.

iv. But because David could be so content and so happy before the LORD in keeping sheep with no praise or popularity, it put his heart in the right place to handle it when he received praise and popularity. Out in the shepherd's field David had his heart set: "I'm doing this for the LORD. I love the LORD, and my reward is from Him." Because his heart was right in the shepherd's field, David *behaved wisely in all his ways* when praise and popularity came.

v. We also see this by David's reaction to the scorn and criticism from his brother Eliab (1 Samuel 17:28-30). When Eliab scorned and criticized David didn't like it, but it didn't crush him. It didn't deter him. Most people are corrupted by praise and popularity to the same degree they are crushed by scorn and criticism. Because of what God built in him out in the shepherd's field, David could live his life more for the LORD than for people. It wasn't that David didn't care about people or what they thought, but he could put the opinion of man in the right perspective because he cared more about the opinion of God.

d. **Then Saul was very angry**: Knowing his character, we are not surprised by Saul's reaction. Saul did not have a right or close relationship with the LORD. All he had to affirm his heart was the praise of man so when David was more praised it really bothered Saul.

i. It is a bad sign in a leader when they resent or feel threatened by the success of a subordinate. It is a certain sign of weakness in the leader.

ii. **Now what more can he have but the kingdom?** This is a typical over-reaction in the proud and insecure. Saul could have thought, "David did well and he has his glory today. I'll keep serving the LORD and have this kind of praise another day." Instead, he over-reacted and said, "**Now what more can he have but the kingdom?**"

iii. However, there is another dynamic at work in Saul: a guilty conscience. He remembered the prophet Samuel told him, "*The LORD has rejected you from being king over Israel.*" Saul knew his sin disqualified him from being king, and he clung to the throne in the energy of his flesh. An honorable man would step down, but if Saul were an honorable man, he wouldn't be in this mess. Instead, Saul constantly worried, "When will God cast me off the throne? Who will He raise up to replace me?" This insecurity, borne of guilt, also made Saul over-react to the praise and popularity given to David.

iv. Yet the crowds *did* praise Saul. They *did* sing, "**Saul has slain his thousands**." For Saul, it wasn't enough to slay thousands as long as someone else was slaying **ten thousands**.

f. **So Saul eyed David from that day forward**: Now Saul's mind is filled with suspicion towards David. He began to hear most everything David said with suspicious ears. He looked at David's actions with suspicious eyes. His thoughts were twisted by suspicion.

i. "He gave way to that devilish vice of envy, which was henceforth as a fire in his bosom, as a worm continually gnawing upon his entrails . . . He looked upon him with an evil eye: prying into all his actions, and making the worst of everything." (Trapp)

B. Saul's first attempt to kill David.

1. (10) The scene in Saul's royal court.

And it happened on the next day that the distressing spirit from God came upon Saul, and he prophesied inside the house. So David played *music* with his hand, as at other times; but *there was* a spear in Saul's hand.

a. **The distressing spirit from God came upon Saul**: This **distressing spirit** was first mentioned in 1 Samuel 16:14. It came upon Saul, permitted by the LORD, when the Spirit of the LORD departed from Saul (1 Samuel 16:14). David was brought into Saul's royal court to play music, so that Saul would be ministered to and soothed when suffering from the **distressing spirit**.

b. **And he prophesied inside the house**: Why would a **distressing spirit** make Saul *prophesy*? Saul wasn't speaking from the LORD at all, and **prophesied** is a bad translation here. The Hebrew grammar here can be used of idle ravings as well as of prophecy from the LORD. Saul simply babbled like a man not in his right mind.

i. "He was *beside himself*; made *prayers*, *supplications*, and incoherent *imprecations*: 'God preserve my life,' 'Destroy my enemies,' or such like prayers, might frequently escape from him in his agitated state." (Clarke)

c. **So David played music with his hand**: The same hands that had killed Goliath and carried the trophy of his severed head now sweetly played music unto the LORD, ministering to a troubled king.

i. David obviously had skillful *hands*, both in war and in music ministry. More remarkable was his *humble heart*. Most men, after the fame that came to David, would consider this kind of service "beneath" them. David was a general in the army, famous in all Israel, and had women dancing and singing his praises. Yet he faithfully performed this job of personally ministering to Saul in music.

d. **But there was a spear in Saul's hand**: David held a harp, and **played music with his hand**. But there was violence **in Saul's hand**.

2. (11) Saul throws a spear at David.

And Saul cast the spear, for he said, "I will pin David to the wall!" But David escaped his presence twice.

a. **And Saul cast the spear**: If a spear is in your hand, you'll probably use it. As Saul held the spear the *distressing spirit* moved upon him, and instead of receiving ministry from David's music the *distressing spirit* prompted Saul to strike out at David.

i. We must say that the *distressing spirit* did not "make" Saul do this. But the spirit *prompted* it. Saul was able to choose, "Will I do this or not?" and he chose to **cast the spear**.

ii. This same music ministry once soothed Saul, and made him *refreshed and well*, giving him relief from the *distressing spirit* (1 Samuel 16:23). Now, it is of no effect at all, and Saul even responds to David's music ministry with a murder attempt. David's music ministry or heart did not change - Saul did, and for the worse. Saul refused to receive from David's ministry and that refusal set the stage for this kind of violence.

b. **For he said, "I will pin David to the wall with it"**: This wasn't an accident. Saul may have wanted it to seem like an accident. Though he wouldn't admit it, his heart was set on killing David. He didn't want to just frighten or wound David. He wanted the spear to deliver a fatal blow, completely through the body.

c. **But David escaped his presence**: Saul threw the spear, and it missed David. Perhaps Saul's aim was bad, affected by his poor mental and emotional state. Perhaps David saw the spear and ducked. Perhaps God simply supernaturally guided the spear to miss. However it happened, the spear missed and was on the floor. And **David escaped his presence**.

i. Of many of us it would be written, "And so-and-so picked the spear up off the floor went over to Saul saying, 'If Goliath couldn't scare me, you sure can't. If Goliath couldn't kill me, you sure can't.' And with one thrust of the spear, so-and-so pinned Saul to the wall."

ii. But David didn't pick up the spear. He didn't throw it back. He simply **escaped his presence**. No one could blame David if he struck back; it could easily be called self-defense. But David had a different heart. It wasn't a matter of what he could get away with, but it was a matter of what God's heart wanted. David was determined to leave the situation in God's hands, and not *take* the throne himself. *God* would have to take care of Saul, because David wouldn't do it.

iii. David said, "LORD, you put Saul on the throne. And I know I'm supposed to the be next king, because You gave me Your promise and Your anointing. But getting Saul out of the way is Your business. I won't touch it, because he is an authority appointed by You. You started his reign, so *You* have to end it."

d. **But David escaped his presence twice**: Perhaps the most remarkable word in this chapter is **twice**. This means that *Saul threw the spear twice*. This means that *Saul missed twice*. This means that *after the first miss, David came back and played again.*

i. This is where many draw the line. "Look, I'll sit with the bulls-eye on my chest once, and I'll dodge the spear. I'll even leave the spear on floor and resist the temptation to throw it back. But one spear whizzing by my head is enough. One miss and I've paid my dues. Once is submission to the LORD. Twice is stupidity."

ii. We might even say that David's submission didn't even *begin* until he sat back down to play for Saul *again* after the first attempt on his life. Now he knew the danger, now he knew Saul's heart, and *now* he had to trust God.

iii. If David struck back after resisting the temptation the first time we can suppose that David still would become king. We can suppose that we still admire David's heart in not throwing the spear back the first time, and we would understand how he struck back the second time. But if David did this, he would have *surrendered his destiny to be the greatest king of Israel.* He still would be a king, but not *the king* the LORD destined him to be.

iv. "In doing this small feat of returning thrown spears, you will prove many things. You are courageous. You stand for the right. You boldly stand against the wrong. You are tough and can't be pushed around. You will not stand for injustice or unfair treatment. You are the defender of the faith, the keeper of the flame, detector of all heresy.

You will not be wronged. All of these attributes then combine to prove that you are also obviously a candidate for kingship. Yes, perhaps you are the Lord's anointed. *After the order of King Saul*." (Gene Edwards, *Tale of Three Kings*)

3. (12-16) David is transferred from the palace to the army.

Now Saul was afraid of David, because the LORD was with him, but had departed from Saul. Therefore Saul removed him from his presence, and made him his captain over a thousand; and he went out and came in before the people. And David behaved wisely in all his ways, and the LORD *was* with him. Therefore, when Saul saw that he behaved very wisely, he was afraid of him. But all Israel and Judah loved David, because he went out and came in before them.

a. **Now Saul was afraid of David, because the LORD was with him**: By all outward appearance, Saul is in control. Saul has the throne. Saul has the army. Saul has the spears. Yet Saul was **afraid of David because the LORD was with him**.

b. **But had departed from Saul**: This made Saul uncomfortable with David, and made it hard for Saul to have David around (**Therefore Saul removed him from his presence**).

c. **Made him his captain**: Saul's desire was not to bless David, but to set him up for harm. Saul's jealousy has made him manipulative, working a hidden, secret agenda on David.

i. "This was under pretence of doing him honour, when it was in effect only to rid himself of the object of his envy." (Clarke)

d. **David behaved wisely in all his ways, and the LORD was with him**: It isn't easy to behave wisely when spears are being thrown at you. It isn't easy to behave wisely when you are put out of the palace. It isn't easy to behave wisely when you have powerful and determined enemies. Even in the midst of all those terrible circumstances, you can behave wisely in all your ways as **the LORD is with** you.

e. **But all Israel and Judah loved David**: David became even more popular because God was with him. David was tempted to use this popularity as a spear against Saul but he refused.

f. **Because he went out and came in**: This is a Hebrew figure of speech meaning, "David conducted successful military operations." God's hand of success was with David even though Saul was against him. Saul might attack and pain David in any number of ways, but God would not allow Saul to have the victory.

i. *David was never a victim.* He *looked* like a victim, because he was attacked. But David **behaved wisely in all his ways**, so he did not give into the victim's state of mind, thinking that *his fate was in the hands of the one attacking him*. David knew his fate was in God's hands, and could have peace in that.

C. Saul sets a trap for David but he escapes and is blessed.

1. (17-19) Saul intends to kill David.

Then Saul said to David, "Here is my older daughter Merab; I will give her to you as a wife. Only be valiant for me, and fight the Lord's battles." For Saul thought, "Let my hand not be against him, but let the hand of the Philistines be against him." So David said to Saul, "Who *am* I, and what *is* my life *or* my father's family in Israel, that I should be son-in-law to the king?" But it happened at the time when Merab, Saul's daughter, should have been given to David, that she was given to Adriel the Meholathite as a wife.

a. **Here is my older daughter Merab**: Saul had promised to *give . . . his daughter* to the man who killed Goliath (1 Samuel 17:25). Now, Saul makes good on the promise, offering his **older daughter Merab** to David.

b. **Let my hand not be against him, but let the hand of the Philistines be against him**: The marriage offer *seemed* like a gesture of kindness and goodness on Saul's part. David was supposed to believe, "Saul has forgiven. He has let bygones be bygones. He threw two spears at me before, but all of that is over now." But Saul didn't think that way at all. In his heart was a different motive.

i. This was a trap because of the dowry that Saul would demand. In that day, a dowry was required whenever a man married. The dowry was paid to the bride's father, and the more important and prestigious the bride and her family, the higher the dowry price. Since David was from a humble family, there was no way he could pay the dowry for the daughter of a king. Saul knew this and will demand that David kill 100 Philistines as a dowry. Saul figured that the job was too big and too dangerous for David, and he would be killed gaining the dowry to marry a king's daughter.

ii. Saul still wanted David dead and gone. But now, instead of throwing spears himself, he used cunning manipulation to have David killed. He thought, "The Philistine spears and swords are just as sharp as mine. I can let them do the work for me." From a fleshly standpoint, this was a pretty smart plan on Saul's part.

iii. It was smart in the flesh, but God would not honor Saul's manipulation. Manipulation uses hidden agendas and concealed motives. It is sneaky and secretive. Manipulation tries to maneuver people and events to accomplish a hidden agenda. It can be smart in the flesh but will never be blessed by God.

c. **Only be valiant for me, and fight the LORD's battles**: Saul works as a clever manipulator. He takes advantage of David's loyalty and patriotism (**only be valiant for me**). He takes advantage of David's courage and heart for the LORD (**fight the LORD's battles**).

d. **So David said to Saul, "Who am I . . . that I should be son-in-law to the king?"** David was not out-maneuvering Saul. David had no idea what was going on in Saul's heart. David simply had a humble heart before the LORD, and God protected him against Saul's manipulation.

i. The question "**Who am I?**" shows David's humble heart. He was nationally famous. All Israel loved him. All Saul's staff loved him. Jonathan the crown prince loved him. All over Israel women sang and danced in his honor. Yet when the hand of Merab is offered to David he didn't think, "Well, this is about time. I'm glad someone noticed."

e. **At the time when Merab, Saul's daughter, should have been given to David, that she was given to Adriel**: When David was initially hesitant to marry Merab, Saul tried another strategy. He suddenly gave her to another man, to try and make David angry or jealous.

i. Saul "treacherously withdrew the offer as the time of nuptials approached - the intention being to arouse his ardent spirit to retaliate, and so become liable to the charge of treason. But all his efforts failed to arouse even a transient impulse for revenge." (Meyer)

2. (20-25) David's agreement to marry Michal.

Now Michal, Saul's daughter, loved David. And they told Saul, and the thing pleased him. So Saul said, "I will give her to him, that she may be a snare to him, and that the hand of the Philistines may be against him." Therefore Saul said to David a second time, "You shall be my son-in-law today." And Saul commanded his servants, "Communicate with David secretly, and say, 'Look, the king has delight in you, and all his servants love you. Now therefore, become the king's son-in-law.'" So Saul's servants spoke those words in the hearing of David. And David said, "Does it seem to you *a* light *thing* to be a king's son-in-law, seeing I *am* a poor and lightly esteemed man?" And the servants of Saul told him, saying, "In this manner David spoke." Then Saul said, "Thus you shall say to David: 'The king does not desire any dowry but one hundred foreskins of the Philistines, to take vengeance on the king's enemies.'" But Saul thought to make David fall by the hand of the Philistines.

a. **Now Michal, Saul's daughter, loved David**: Saul was happy to hear this (**the thing pleased him**). It doesn't surprise us that Michal was attracted to David, because of his character, qualities, and fame. But as is evident later in David's marriage to Michal, she was not really attracted to David's heart for the LORD.

b. **That she might be a snare to him**: This may be meant in two ways. First, obviously Saul wanted David to be snared by the dowry. But it may also be that Saul knew Michal's character and heart, and knew that she would be snare for him as a wife, as turned out to be the case in some regard (2 Samuel 6:16-23).

c. **The king does not desire any dowry but one hundred foreskins of the Philistines**: Now, Saul builds on his clever plan. "David won't marry Michal because he doesn't have a big enough dowry. He's too humble to ask me for terms, so I will suggest them." Even the way he phrases it is clever: "**The king does not desire any dowry**." That makes it sound like Saul doesn't want anything from David. "**But one hundred foreskins of the Philistines**." That makes it sound like Saul isn't asking for much, when he is really asking for something far greater than a lot of money. He asks David to put his life in great jeopardy, because Saul wants him dead.

i. Even the specific request - **one hundred foreskins of the Philistines** - was manipulative. It was designed to goad David on ("Go get those uncircumcised Philistines"). It was designed to be difficult, because the Philistines would obviously have to be dead. And it was designed to make the Philistines completely outraged at David, because from their perspective, not only were their men killed, but also their dead bodies were desecrated. "Here is a fair glove drawn upon a foul hand." (Trapp)

3. (26-27) David fulfills Saul's request for a dowry and marries Michal.

So when his servants told David these words, it pleased David well to become the king's son-in-law. Now the days had not expired; therefore David arose and went, he and his men, and killed two hundred men of the Philistines. And David brought their foreskins, and they gave them in full count to the king, that he might become the king's son-in-law. Then Saul gave him Michal his daughter as a wife.

a. **It pleased David well**: David had such a pure, humble heart that he seemed to be blind to Saul's manipulation and cunning. A simple man can survive amid such treachery when God is with him.

i. David had a humble heart. Many men would say, "Dowry? You want a dowry? You promised to give your daughter to the man who killed Goliath. If you want to see my dowry, look at the ten-foot grave in the Valley of Elah. That's enough of a dowry. I demand my rights!" But David humbly agreed to Saul's demand for a dowry.

b. **Therefore David arose and went, he and his men, and killed two hundred men of the Philistines**: David answered Saul's attempt at manipulation by taking control of the situation and being a humble servant, and by giving *more* than what was required.

c. **And David brought their foreskins, and the gave them in full count to the king**: There are many times we wish we had a visual Bible, or could see Biblical events exactly as they happened. This is one instance where we are happy the Bible is not illustrated.

4. (28-30) David's constantly growing popularity.

Thus Saul saw and knew that the LORD *was* with David, and *that* Michal, Saul's daughter, loved him; and Saul was still more afraid of David. So Saul became David's enemy continually. Then the princes of the Philistines went out *to war*. And so it was, whenever they went out, *that* David behaved more wisely than all the servants of Saul, so that his name became highly esteemed.

a. **Thus Saul saw and knew that the LORD was with David**: Saul did not use this knowledge to stop trying to kill David. He did not find it in his heart to respect David and make a way for the LORD's choice to smoothly come to the throne. Instead, the closer David got to the LORD, the further he got from Saul and **Saul was still more afraid of David**.

b. **Then the princes of the Philistines went out to war**: Saul's cunning plan against David continued. No doubt, **the Philistines went out to war** against David in retaliation for what they felt was a terrible disgrace against the Philistine people. Saul wanted to make David a marked man, and he succeeded.

c. **David behaved more wisely than all the servants of Saul, so that his name became highly esteemed**: Saul's plan has completely backfired. David is not only alive, but also more popular and closer to the LORD than ever. Saul isn't finished, and will use more manipulation, cunning, and outright violence to attack David.

i. David's wise behavior and high esteem were both closely connected to his humble heart. The same is true (in a far greater sense) of the Son of David, Jesus Christ. Philippians 2:9 says of Jesus, *Therefore God also has highly exalted Him and given Him the name which is above every name.* Why was it that the **name** of Jesus **became highly esteemed**? *Let this mind be in you which was also in Christ Jesus, who, being in the form of God, did not consider it robbery to be equal with God, but made Himself of no reputation, taking the form of a bondservant, and coming in the likeness of men. And being found in appearance as a man, He humbled Himself and became obedient to the point of death, even the death of the cross.* (Philippians 2:5-8) This mind, this heart, was in David. This mind, this heart, is in Jesus. God wants this mind, this heart, to be in each of us.

1 Samuel 19 - David Flees from Saul

Psalm relevant to this chapter: Psalm 59.

A. Jonathan defends David before his father Saul.

1. (1a) Saul plots the murder of David, attempting to enlist the help of Jonathan and his servants.

Now Saul spoke to Jonathan his son and to all his servants, that they should kill David.

a. **Jonathan his son**: Saul put Jonathan in a difficult place. Jonathan loved David, and God made a wonderful bond of friendship between them, sealed by a covenant (1 Samuel 18:1-4). Jonathan knew David was destined to be the next king of Israel, even though Jonathan was officially the crown prince. At the same time, his father and king told him to kill David.

b. **And to all his servants**: Saul put his servants in a difficult place. They all loved David (1 Samuel 18:5) yet they are commanded by their king to kill David.

c. **That they should kill David**: Saul put David in a difficult place. Who can he trust? Even if he trusted Jonathan he surely knew there was at least one ambitious man on Saul's staff who would do whatever Saul said, without regard to right or wrong.

2. (1b-3) In loyalty to David, Jonathan warns David.

But Jonathan, Saul's son, delighted greatly in David. So Jonathan told David, saying, "My father Saul seeks to kill you. Therefore please be on your guard until morning, and stay in a secret *place* and hide. "And I will go out and stand beside my father in the field where you *are*, and I will speak with my father about you. Then what I observe, I will tell you."

a. **But Jonathan, Saul's son, delighted much in David**: Without doubt Saul and many on his staff criticized David. They looked for anything they could to bring against him, and if they could find nothing, they made something. Jonathan got an earful of this, but it didn't change his opinion of David. He still **delighted much in David**.

b. **So Jonathan told David**: This made Saul furious, but Jonathan knew he did right. He should not kill David because his father and king told him to do something that was clearly disobedient to God. Jonathan knew the Bible said, *You shall not murder* (Exodus 20:13). The Bible was clear, and Saul was *on record* as saying *that they should kill David* (1 Samuel 19:1).

i. We *are* under authority, and commanded to submit to God's order of authority in many different arenas. There is a Biblical submission from children to their parents, from citizens to their government, from employees to their employers, from Christians to their church leadership, and from wives to their husbands. But in all these relationships, we are never excused from sin because we obeyed an authority that told us to sin. In this case, it would be wrong for Jonathan to obey his father and kill David.

ii. This was a case where Jonathan could say what the apostles said when they were told to stop preaching the gospel: *We ought to obey God rather than men* (Acts 5:29). But Jonathan also had the heart of the apostles in Acts 5; they were beaten severely, and were willing to suffer for what was right before God, rejoicing that they were counted worthy to suffer for His name (Acts 5:40-41). Jonathan was willing to take his lumps for obeying God, and he did not whine about it.

c. **My father Saul seeks to kill you. Therefore please be on your guard until morning, and stay in a secret place and hide**: Jonathan did more than refuse to help Saul. He *helped* David. Jonathan could have said, "Look, I want no part of this. I'm not going to help my father do something I know is wrong. But I won't try to stop it either. I'll just be neutral and let God work it out." But Jonathan didn't take that attitude.

3. (4-5) In loyalty to David, Jonathan speaks to Saul.

Thus Jonathan spoke well of David to Saul his father, and said to him, "Let not the king sin against his servant, against David, because he has not sinned against you, and because his works *have been* very good toward you. For he took his life in his hands and killed the Philistine, and the LORD brought about a great deliverance for all Israel. You saw *it* and rejoiced. Why then will you sin against innocent blood, to kill David without a cause?"

a. **Now Jonathan spoke well of David to Saul his father**: Jonathan did more than secretly help David with information he also **spoke well of David to Saul his father**. Jonathan let Saul know, "Father you have a certain opinion of David. But I don't share that opinion. I love and support David. You should also." That took a lot of courage, and it was the right thing for Jonathan to do.

i. "*Jonathan spake good of David*, which he could not do without hazard to himself. Herein therefore he performed the duty of a true friend, and of a valiant man." (Poole)

b. **Let not the king sin against his servant**: Jonathan was bold enough to tell his father that his anger and jealousy against David was **sin**, and to say, "**he has not sinned against you.**" Saul *felt* that David had sinned against him in some manner and he *felt* righteous in his cause. Jonathan delivered a needed word of correction.

c. **For he took his life in his hands and killed the Philistine, and the Lord brought about a great salvation for all Israel**: Jonathan reminded Saul of these events because Saul colored them with a meaning that justified his jealous desire to murder David.

i. Saul knew that David **killed the Philistine** but he could not believe that David did it for a righteous reason. He thought, "David did it just to become famous and to take my throne. He's a grasping traitor. I'm justified in killing him, because I have to kill him before he kills me."

ii. Jonathan tried to bring Saul back to reality. He reminds his father: "**You saw it and rejoiced.**" "When David first killed Goliath, you **rejoiced** just like everyone. Now Satan has filled your mind with envy and jealousy. Go back to how you thought before."

d. **Why then will you sin against innocent blood, to kill David without a cause?**: In Saul's mind, *there was a cause.* In Saul's mind, David was not *innocent.* But the truth was that David was **innocent**, and there was no **cause** to kill him. Jonathan calls Saul back to reality.

4. (6-7) The reconciliation between Saul and David.

So Saul heeded the voice of Jonathan, and Saul swore, "*As* the Lord lives, he shall not be killed." Then Jonathan called David, and Jonathan told him all these things. So Jonathan brought David to Saul, and he was in his presence as in times past.

a. **So Saul heeded the voice of Jonathan**: This took real humility for Saul. It was easy to say, "I'm the king and I'm right. I don't care what you say." But in this case, Saul **heeded the voice of Jonathan**.

b. **Saul swore, "As the Lord lives, he shall not be killed"**: This shows that the Lord had genuinely touched Saul's heart. God used Jonathan, but it wasn't the work of Jonathan. It was the work of the Lord, and Saul recognized this by declaring this oath.

c. **So Jonathan brought David to Saul and he was in his presence as in times past**: It seems to have all worked. The command to kill David is revoked. Saul and David are together again as in previous days.

5. (8-10) David escapes another attempt on His life.

And there was war again; and David went out and fought with the Philistines, and struck them with a mighty blow, and they fled from him. Now the distressing spirit from the LORD came upon Saul as he sat in his house with his spear in his hand. And David was playing *music* with *his* hand. Then Saul sought to pin David to the wall with the spear, but he slipped away from Saul's presence; and he drove the spear into the wall. So David fled and escaped that night.

a. **And there was war again**: In context this speaks of more war between Israel and the Philistines, but it was also true spiritually. At the end of 1 Samuel 19:7 there was a truce in the spiritual war involving David and Saul. But whenever we are at a time of cease-fire in the spiritual war, we know the battle will begin again before long. It can always be said of our life "**and there was war again**."

b. **David went out and fought with the Philistines, and struck them with a mighty blow, and they fled from him**: Spiritually, these are warning clouds of a coming storm. It was David's success that aroused Saul's jealousy before. When David was successful again, surely Saul would be tempted to jealousy again.

c. **Now the distressing spirit from the LORD came upon Saul**: Evil spirits were more than ready to attack Saul where he was most vulnerable. The attack was on the way.

d. **Saul . . . sat in his house with his spear in his hand**: Saul is in a bad place. He is tempted and spiritually attacked, and now he has put himself in a potentially sinful situation. David was **playing music with his hand**, but Saul knew spears better than praise music.

e. **Then Saul sought to pin David to the wall with the spear**: Saul wavered from his change of heart and broke his oath to not kill David. All of that was thrown away as easily as the spear was thrown. But it didn't "just happen." Saul was unprepared to handle temptation, unprepared to handle spiritual attack, and had the opportunity to sin close at hand. Most of us will trip up under those circumstances.

f. **But he slipped away from Saul's presence; and he drove the spear into the wall**: David was gone, but the spear remained. The thing Saul *didn't* need - the spear - was left. The thing one Saul really *did* need - the person David - was gone. Saul was a loser on both counts.

g. **So David fled and escaped that night**: David never returned to the palace until he was the king of Israel - some 20 years later! From now until the day Saul dies David lives as a fugitive.

B. David flees from Saul.

1. (11-12) David escapes with the help from his wife Michal.

Saul also sent messengers to David's house to watch him and to kill him in the morning. And Michal, David's wife, told him, saying, "If you do not save your life tonight, tomorrow you will be killed." So Michal let David down through a window. And he went and fled and escaped.

a. **Saul also sent messengers to David's house to watch him and to kill him**: Previously, Saul *swore, "As the LORD lives, he shall not be killed."* (1 Samuel 19:6). Now for the second time Saul goes back on that oath.

b. **Michal, David's wife, told him**: She saved the day. Michal was Saul's daughter, so this was a conflict of loyalties for Michal. Should she act in her father's interests or in her husband's interests? Here, she made the right choice and supported her husband David.

i. Michal acts according to the principle of Genesis 2:24: *Therefore a man shall leave his father and mother and be joined to his wife, and they shall become one flesh.* Though the Genesis passage speaks specifically of the husband it expresses a principle that applies to both partners in a marriage: that the former family loyalties and obligations take a back seat to the loyalty and obligation to the new family.

c. **Told him**: Michal helped by *warning* David. She perhaps saw the "hit men" coming before he did, and she also knew the character of her father better than David did. Michal was probably less surprised than David was to find "hit men" from Saul against him.

i. David did well to receive this warning from his wife. Sometimes men are so hard headed and so hard hearted that they never hear how God might warn them through their wives. If David would have ignored this warning because he didn't like the source, he might have ended up dead.

d. **Michal let David down through a window**: As David decided on a course of action, she was there to support and help him put it into practice. Michal's help was successful, because David **fled and escaped**.

i. During this night, when men watched his house and David escaped he composed a song unto the LORD found in Psalm 59. The introduction of that Psalm says, *when Saul sent men, and they watched the house in order to kill him.* In a time of danger David could *sing* unto the LORD.

2. (13-17) Michal deceives the men who came to kill David.

And Michal took an image and laid *it* in the bed, put a cover of goats' *hair* for his head, and covered *it* with clothes. So when Saul sent messengers to take David, she said, "He *is* sick." Then Saul sent the messengers *back* to see David, saying, "Bring him up to me in the bed, that I may kill him." And when the

messengers had come in, there was the image in the bed, with a cover of goats' *hair* for his head. Then Saul said to Michal, "Why have you deceived me like this, and sent my enemy away, so that he has escaped?" And Michal answered Saul, "He said to me, 'Let me go! Why should I kill you?'"

a. **Michal took an image**: The **image** was a *teraphim*, a figurine used as a household idol or as a fertility and good luck charm. In ancient Israel *teraphim* were intended as helps in worshipping the true God. They didn't think of the *teraphim* as other gods, but as representing the God of Israel.

i. Clearly God's people had no business having or using an **image** like this. We can't imagine that this **image**, this *household idol*, belonged to David; so it shows that Michal didn't have the kind of relationship with God she should have. This weak relationship with God will reveal itself in Michal as the story of David's life unfolds (2 Samuel 6:16-23). "When we read of these images we are not surprised by the defects of character which we see in Michal." (Balikie)

b. **Bring him up to me in the bed, that I may kill him**: This means Saul was not taken in by his daughter's deception. This also shows something of the depth of Saul's hatred for David, because he wanted to deliver the death-blow himself (**bring him up to me . . . that I may kill him**).

c. **My enemy**: These are the saddest words in this passage. Saul, when describing David, calls him **my enemy**. David was really Saul's friend and David did more to help Saul than just about anyone else. David was only the **enemy** of Saul because Saul *wanted* to see him that way.

C. David, pursued by Saul, flees to Naioth.

1. (18) David visits Samuel at Ramah.

So David fled and escaped, and went to Samuel at Ramah, and told him all that Saul had done to him. And he and Samuel went and stayed in Naioth.

a. **Went to Samuel at Ramah and told him all that Saul had done to him**: David did the right thing when in a difficult and confusing situation. He spent some time with a godly man. We can imagine David pouring out his heart to the prophet: "Samuel, you anointed me king and look what happened! I guess it isn't time yet, but why is it so hard? Does God want me dead? Why is the LORD allowing this?"

b. **Stayed in Naioth**: The word **Naioth** comes from the Hebrew word for *residence*. This spoke of Samuel's home (which may have had "**Naioth**" title itself), or it may have been some landmark or specific place in Ramah. Whenever **Naioth** is mentioned it is associated with Ramah.

2. (19-21) Saul sends messengers to capture David, but they are touched by the Holy Spirit and prophesy in the presence of Samuel and other prophets.

Now it was told Saul, saying, "Take note, David *is* at Naioth in Ramah!" Then Saul sent messengers to take David. And when they saw the group of prophets prophesying, and Samuel standing *as* leader over them, the Spirit of God came upon the messengers of Saul, and they also prophesied. And when Saul was told, he sent other messengers, and they prophesied likewise. Then Saul sent messengers again the third time, and they prophesied also.

a. **Saul sent messengers to take David**: Saul is wicked, but persistent. We never admire the devil's work but we can admire the devil's work ethic.

b. **When they saw the group of prophets prophesying, and Samuel standing as leader over them**: When the messengers of Saul came to capture David, they came in the middle of a worship meeting. Samuel and his "students" (**the group of prophets**) were waiting on the LORD, worshipping Him, speaking to the LORD and hearing from Him.

i. When it says that they were all **prophesying** it isn't that they were all predicting the future. The Hebrew word simply has the idea of speaking under the inspiration of the Holy Spirit. They probably all gave spontaneous and inspired praise to God.

c. **The Spirit of God came upon the messengers of Saul, and they also prophesied**: They were caught up in the atmosphere of worship and devotion to God, and the **Spirit of God came upon** them.

i. This was an unusual work of the Holy Spirit - to come upon men who did not seek after God, who did not long to be filled with the Spirit. God did this to protect David, and this was His way of "disarming" those who came to capture David.

ii. This was also the Holy Spirit's warning to these men and to Saul. It is as if the Spirit said, "I don't want David captured. I am sending these men home empty handed. Instead of seeking to kill David, you should seek to be filled with the **Spirit of God**."

d. **He sent other messengers**: Saul didn't get the message. So, **he sent other messengers**, but the same thing happened - **they prophesied likewise**. Saul still didn't get the message, so he **sent messengers again the third time, and they prophesied also**. Three sets of messengers came back and God said the same thing each time through each of them.

3. (22-24) Saul pursues David himself, but he also prophesies in the presence of Samuel and the prophets.

Then he also went to Ramah, and came to the great well that *is* at Sechu. So he asked, and said, "Where *are* Samuel and David?" And *someone* said, "Indeed *they are* at Naioth in Ramah." So he went there to Naioth in Ramah. Then the Spirit of God was upon him also, and he went on and prophesied until he came

to Naioth in Ramah. And he also stripped off his clothes and prophesied before Samuel in like manner, and lay down naked all that day and all that night. Therefore they say, "*Is* Saul also among the prophets?"

a. **Then he also went to Ramah**: Three times, the Holy Spirit said to Saul, "Leave David alone. My Spirit is stronger than you are. You will never win this battle against Me and against David." But Saul didn't listen. Instead, to an even greater degree, Saul took matters into his own hands: **he also went to Ramah**.

b. **Then the Spirit of God was upon him also**: As before, the Holy Spirit worked to prevent David's capture. It also told Saul, "Hands off My servant David. I am in charge here."

i. There may have been an additional message to Saul in this: "Saul, you are prophesying now, speaking beautiful words of praise and wonder to Me. This is how I could work in you all the time if you were humble and willing."

c. **He also stripped off his clothes and prophesied**: The Spirit prompted Saul to do this as an expression of deep humility. Saul would not humble himself before God, and so God *will* find a way to humble him.

i. It is unlikely - though possible - that Saul stripped himself bare. The Hebrew word for **naked** can indicate just stripping down to the undergarments. Saul probably took off all the royal robes that said "prestige" and "royalty," and laid himself out before the LORD in his plain linen undergarments. It was a way for the LORD to say, "You really aren't a king any more, Saul. I've stripped you of your royal glory."

ii. A person can be *affected* by the power of God (resulting in amazing experiences), but not *surrendered* to the power of God, which results in a changed life.

d. **Is Saul also among the prophets?** This phrase was first mentioned in 1 Samuel 10:10-12, and it expressed astonishment that someone became a religious enthusiast. Saul was an unspiritual man who became very spiritual at the moment the Spirit of the LORD came upon him.

1 Samuel 20 - Jonathan's Final Attempt to Reconcile His Father and David

A. David, coming from Naioth, meets Jonathan.

1. (1-4) David asks Jonathan about Saul's intentions towards him; Jonathan promises his help to David.

Then David fled from Naioth in Ramah, and went and said to Jonathan, "What have I done? What *is* my iniquity, and what *is* my sin before your father, that he seeks my life?" So Jonathan said to him, "By no means! You shall not die! Indeed, my father will do nothing either great or small without first telling me. And why should my father hide this thing from me? It *is* not *so*!" Then David took an oath again, and said, "Your father certainly knows that I have found favor in your eyes, and he has said, 'Do not let Jonathan know this, lest he be grieved.' But truly, *as* the LORD lives and *as* your soul lives, *there is* but a step between me and death." So Jonathan said to David, "Whatever you yourself desire, I will do *it* for you."

a. **Then David fled from Naioth**: The Spirit of God protected David in Naioth in a powerful way. He could have simply stayed there for however long it took Saul to give up or die. Yet David left for a good reason: He wanted to know if Saul's heart had changed, and if there was still a chance to reconcile with Saul.

b. **What have I done?** Here David checked his relationship with Jonathan. He wanted to know what *Saul* thought but it was more important for David to know what *Jonathan* thought. In asking, "**What have I done?**" David wanted to know if Jonathan has come to a place of agreement with his father Saul.

c. **So Jonathan said to him, "By no means!"** This assured David that Jonathan was still his loyal friend, and that Jonathan hadn't bought into Saul's lies about David. Jonathan also assured David of his protection by warning David of Saul's intentions.

i. **Why should my father hide this thing from me? It is not so!** Apparently, David wondered why Jonathan didn't tell him about the attempted arrest at Naioth. Jonathan expressed astonishment that his father did not tell him, but assures David of his heart towards him.

d. **There is but a step between me and death**: This reveals David's *discouragement.* He knew that Saul attempted to kill him many times, and it seemed Saul would not quit until David was gone. David felt that his death was inevitable and that he walked on a slippery plank over a great canyon.

e. **Whatever you yourself desire, I will do it for you**: Jonathan continued to reassure David, bringing encouragement and an offer of help to a discouraged man. Conceivably, he could have said, "Where is your faith, brother? Why aren't you just trusting God?" Instead Jonathan knew David's heart was pointed in the right direction, and he offered *to help.*

2. (5-11) David proposes to test Saul's attitude.

And David said to Jonathan, "Indeed tomorrow *is* the New Moon, and I should not fail to sit with the king to eat. But let me go, that I may hide in the field until the third *day* at evening. If your father misses me at all, then say, 'David earnestly asked *permission* of me that he might run over to Bethlehem, his city, for *there is* a yearly sacrifice there for all the family.' If he says thus: '*It is* well,' your servant will be safe. But if he is very angry, *then* be sure that evil is determined by him. Therefore you shall deal kindly with your servant, for you have brought your servant into a covenant of the LORD with you. Nevertheless, if there is iniquity in me, kill me yourself, for why should you bring me to your father?" But Jonathan said, "Far be it from you! For if I knew certainly that evil was determined by my father to come upon you, then would I not tell you?" Then David said to Jonathan, "Who will tell me, or what *if* your father answers you roughly?" And Jonathan said to David, "Come, and let us go out into the field." So both of them went out into the field.

a. **If your father misses me**: David asked Jonathan to observe Saul's reaction to David's absence at an important feast held monthly for the high officials of state. David wondered if Saul would take the opportunity to reconcile or take the opportunity to kill him.

i. **The New Moon, and I should not fail to sit with the king to eat**: Special sacrifices were commanded for the new moon (Numbers 28:11-15).

b. **If there is iniquity in me**: Again, David seems somewhat shaken by the fact that Jonathan did not tell him about the attempted arrest at Naioth. David is asking Jonathan, "Am I in the wrong here? Are you still behind me?" Essentially, David says "If you really are working for your father and agree with him that I deserve to die, then just kill me now."

i. We have to see all of this from David's perspective. He remembered that Jonathan's support for him was challenged by the fact that *his father* was against David. He also remembered that Jonathan's support for him was challenged by the fact that Jonathan *is next in line for the throne* and therefore might set himself against David.

ii. Jonathan's response is the same as in 1 Samuel 20:2. He *didn't know* that Saul set out to get David at Naioth, though previously his father told him everything.

c. **Far be it from you!** With this encouragement Jonathan told David to no longer doubt his loyalty. Jonathan senses that David is in a vulnerable place and he wants to give him encouragement in the midst of it.

d. **Who will tell me?** David now poses a practical problem. If Saul has determined evil against David and Jonathan intends to warn him, how will he do it? How will Jonathan get the message to David?

B. Jonathan's agreement.

1. (12-13) Jonathan will discover the state of his father's heart towards David.

Then Jonathan said to David: "The LORD God of Israel *is witness*! When I have sounded out my father sometime tomorrow, *or* the third *day*, and indeed *there is* good toward David, and I do not send to you and tell you, may the LORD do so and much more to Jonathan. But if it pleases my father *to do* you evil, then I will report it to you and send you away, that you may go in safety. And the LORD be with you as He has been with my father.

a. **When I have sounded out my father**: Jonathan will find out his father's heart and will **report it to** David, to say if it is good or bad towards David.

b. **And send you away, that you may go in safety**: Jonathan knows that if his father Saul intends evil against David it means that David must go **away**. He will not be welcome again in the palace and he would not be safe again at home. By giving David early warning of this Jonathan will help David **go in safety**.

c. **And the LORD will be with you as He has been with my father**: Jonathan wants to give David more than a warning; he gives him *encouragement* also. "David, even if you must leave the palace and your home behind and flee as a fugitive, **the LORD will be with you**. You can be sure of it."

i. Jonathan shows his spiritual maturity when he says, "**as He has been with my father**," because one might think that the LORD was really *against* Saul instead of *for* him. Jonathan knew that God was really *for* Saul because God offered Saul opportunities for repentance.

2. (14-17) In response, Jonathan asks David to commit himself in a covenant.

"And you shall not only show me the kindness of the Lord while I still live, that I may not die; but you shall not cut off your kindness from my house forever, no, not when the Lord has cut off every one of the enemies of David from the face of the earth." So Jonathan made *a covenant* with the house of David, *saying*, "Let the Lord require *it* at the hand of David's enemies." Now Jonathan again caused David to vow, because he loved him; for he loved him as he loved his own soul.

a. **You shall not cut off your kindness from my house forever**: Jonathan was aware of the political dynamic between the family of David and the family of Jonathan. In those days when one royal house replaced another it was common for the new royal house to kill all the potential rulers from the old royal house. Jonathan knew that one day David and his descendants would rule over Israel and he wanted a promise that David and his descendants will not kill or mistreat the descendants of Jonathan.

b. **So Jonathan made a covenant with the house of David**: Jonathan and David agreed to care for one another. Jonathan agreed to care for David in the face of Saul's threat and David agreed to care for Jonathan and his family in the future. David fulfilled this promise to Jonathan (2 Samuel 9:1-8 and 21:7).

3. (18-23) Jonathan proposes a signal to inform David of Saul's reaction.

Then Jonathan said to David, "Tomorrow *is* the New Moon; and you will be missed, because your seat will be empty. And *when* you have stayed three days, go down quickly and come to the place where you hid on the day of the deed; and remain by the stone Ezel. Then I will shoot three arrows to the side, as though I shot at a target; and there I will send a lad, *saying*, 'Go, find the arrows.' If I expressly say to him, 'Look, the arrows *are* on this side of you; get them and come'; then, as the Lord lives, *there is* safety for you and no harm. But if I say thus to the young man, 'Look, the arrows *are* beyond you'; go your way, for the Lord has sent you away. And as for the matter which you and I have spoken of, indeed the Lord *be* between you and me forever."

a. **I will shoot three arrows**: After Jonathan learned his father's heart and intention towards David, he would communicate to David through a signal. Jonathan would take target practice and where he shot the arrows would tell David the answer.

b. **Three arrows**: These would bring one of two messages. Either Saul's heart has changed towards David and **there is safety for you**, or Saul was still determined to kill David and **the Lord has sent you away**.

i. This was a crucial time in David's life. Either he would be welcomed back to the palace and his home or he would be a fugitive until Saul gave up the hunt for David. A lot was riding on the message brought through a few arrows.

C. Saul's settled hatred towards David.

1. (24-34) Saul is enraged when he learns of David's absence.

Then David hid in the field. And when the New Moon had come, the king sat down to eat the feast. Now the king sat on his seat, as at other times, on a seat by the wall. And Jonathan arose, and Abner sat by Saul's side, but David's place was empty. Nevertheless Saul did not say anything that day, for he thought, "Something has happened to him; he *is* unclean, surely he *is* unclean." And it happened the next day, the second *day* of the month, that David's place was empty. And Saul said to Jonathan his son, "Why has the son of Jesse not come to eat, either yesterday or today?" So Jonathan answered Saul, "David earnestly asked *permission* of me *to go* to Bethlehem. And he said, 'Please let me go, for our family has a sacrifice in the city, and my brother has commanded me *to be there*. And now, if I have found favor in your eyes, please let me get away and see my brothers.' Therefore he has not come to the king's table." Then Saul's anger was aroused against Jonathan, and he said to him, "You son of a perverse, rebellious *woman*! Do I not know that you have chosen the son of Jesse to your own shame and to the shame of your mother's nakedness? For as long as the son of Jesse lives on the earth, you shall not be established, nor your kingdom. Now therefore, send and bring him to me, for he shall surely die." And Jonathan answered Saul his father, and said to him, "Why should he be killed? What has he done?" Then Saul cast a spear at him to kill him, by which Jonathan knew that it was determined by his father to kill David. So Jonathan arose from the table in fierce anger, and ate no food the second day of the month, for he was grieved for David, because his father had treated him shamefully.

a. **But David's place was empty**: David was expected to be at this special feast of the **New Moon**, and so he his absence was clearly noticed. At first this did not trouble Saul greatly, because **he thought, "Something has happened to him; he is unclean, surely he is unclean."** Ceremonial uncleanliness might cause a person to miss a feast such as this but the ceremonial uncleanliness only lasted a day (Leviticus 22:3-7). So when **it happened the next day . . . that David's place was empty**, Saul demanded an explanation.

i. Meyer on **the son of Jesse**: "Speaking of him derisively as 'the son of Jesse,' thus accentuating his lowly birth, and ignoring the relationship that bound him to the royal family."

b. **Jonathan answered Saul, "David earnestly asked permission of me to go to Bethlehem"**: Jonathan covered for David, trying to give Saul a plausible (and truthful) explanation for David's absence.

i. "It seems probably that he went first to Bethlehem, as he bade Jonathan to tell his father, ver. 6, and thence returned to the field, when the occasion required; else we must charge him with a downright lie, which ought not to be imagined (without any apparent cause) concerning so good a man." (Poole)

c. **Saul's anger was aroused . . . "You son of a perverse, rebellious woman!"** Jonathan knew from this response that Saul's heart was settled on evil against David. If Saul's heart was different towards David he might have been disappointed but not furious.

d. **He shall surely die**: Certainly this was Saul's intention, despite his previous oath (*As the LORD lives, he shall not be killed*, 1 Samuel 19:6). Despite Saul's intentions, David would not die at the hands of Saul or any other enemy. Man proposes, but God disposes.

e. **Why should he be killed? What has he done?** Jonathan responded by defending not only David, but *right* in this cause. His support of David wasn't a *blind* support; it was based on what was *right* before the LORD. Jonathan's support of David enraged Saul and **Saul cast a spear at him to kill him**. This shows how deep Saul's hatred of David was - he would kill his own son for siding with David.

i. "Jonathan made one vain attempt to reason with the furious monarch; he might as well have tried to arrest the swelling of Jordan in the time of flood." (Meyer)

2. (35-40) Jonathan reports to David through the signal of the arrows.

And so it was, in the morning, that Jonathan went out into the field at the time appointed with David, and a little lad *was* with him. Then he said to his lad, "Now run, find the arrows which I shoot." As the lad ran, he shot an arrow beyond him. When the lad had come to the place where the arrow was which Jonathan had shot, Jonathan cried out after the lad and said, "*Is* not the arrow beyond you?" And Jonathan cried out after the lad, "Make haste, hurry, do not delay!" So Jonathan's lad gathered up the arrows and came back to his master. But the lad did not know anything. Only Jonathan and David knew of the matter. Then Jonathan gave his weapons to his lad, and said to him, "Go, carry *them* to the city."

a. **Is not the arrow beyond you?** It took courage for Jonathan to communicate with David, even secretly - because he knew that if his father became aware of it, he would focus his murderous rage against Jonathan *again*. Jonathan had a noble commitment to David as a friend.

i. "But there is something still nobler - when one dares in any company to avow his loyalty to the Lord Jesus. Like David, he is now in obscurity and disrepute; his name is not popular; his gospel is misrepresented; his followers are subjected to rebuke and scorn. These are days when to stand up for anything more than mere conventional religion must cost something; and for this reason let us never flinch." (Meyer)

b. **Jonathan and David knew of the matter**: A small thing - the signal of a single arrow - told David his whole life was changed. He would no longer be welcome at the palace. He would no longer be welcome among the army of Israel. He could no longer go home. David was now a fugitive on the run from an angry, jealous king determined to destroy him.

i. Sometimes our life turns on a small thing. One night of carelessness may change a girl's life forever. One night with the wrong crowd may give a boy an arrest record. It often does not seem fair that so much in life should turn on small moments, but a lifetime is made of nothing but many small moments.

3. (41-42) The tearful farewell of David and Jonathan.

As soon as the lad had gone, David arose from *a* place toward the south, fell on his face to the ground, and bowed down three times. And they kissed one another; and they wept together, but David more so. Then Jonathan said to David, "Go in peace, since we have both sworn in the name of the Lord, saying, 'May the Lord be between you and me, and between your descendants and my descendants, forever.'" So he arose and departed, and Jonathan went into the city.

a. **They wept together**: David and Jonathan loved each other and had a strong bond of friendship. Jonathan and David probably envisioned working *together*, as partners, as friends, both before and after the time David became king. But now all that was gone because David couldn't stay and Jonathan couldn't go, so they **wept together**.

b. **But David more so**: If Jonathan had reason to weep, David had **more so**. The pain of being apart was bad enough, but it was worse for David because he was cut off from everything and destined to live the life of a fugitive for many years.

i. "Behind you is the sunny morning, before you a lowering sky; behind you the blessed enjoyment of friendship, wife, home, royal favor, and popular adulation, before you an outcast's life." (Meyer)

c. **Go in peace, since we have both sworn in the name of the Lord**: Jonathan knew he might never see David again. In fact, David and Jonathan will only meet once more, shortly before Jonathan's death. Yet as David now left for a life of hiding and danger, Jonathan could send David away **in peace** because they both agreed to honor each other not only in life, but also to honor each other's families beyond their own lifetimes.

d. **So he arose and departed**: David will not return to "normal life" until Saul is dead and David is king. This was a pretty bleak road for David to walk, but it was *God's* road for him.

i. Was David in God's will? How can anyone set out on such a bleak road and be in the will of God? Because God often has His people spend at least some time on a bleak road, and He appoints some of His favorites to spend a lot of time on that road - think of Job, Joseph, Paul, and even Jesus.

ii. This bleak road was important in David's life because if God would put David in a place where people must depend on him, God would teach David to depend upon God alone. Not himself, not Saul, not Jonathan, not anyone except God

iii. This bleak road was important in David's life because if David would be safe now and promoted to king later, David must learn to let God be his defense and his promoter.

iv. This bleak road was important in David's life because if David was to be set in such a great position of authority, David must learn to submit to God's authority, even if it were through a man like Saul.

v. "Let God empty you out that He may save you from becoming spiritually stale, and lead you ever onward. He is always calling us to pass beyond the thing we know into the unknown. A throne is God's purpose for you; a cross is God's path for you; faith is God's plan for you." (Redpath)

1 Samuel 21 - David at Nob and at Gath

A. David meets Ahimelech the priest at Nob.

1. (1-2) David, fleeing from Saul, comes to the city of Nob.

Now David came to Nob, to Ahimelech the priest. And Ahimelech was afraid when he met David, and said to him, "Why *are* you alone, and no one is with you?" So David said to Ahimelech the priest, "The king has ordered me on some business, and said to me, 'Do not let anyone know anything about the business on which I send you, or what I have commanded you.' And I have directed *my* young men to such and such a place."

a. **To Ahimelech the priest**: In his uncertain circumstances David went to the right place - the house of the LORD.

b. **Ahimelech was afraid when he met David**: It seemed unusual to Ahimelech that a prominent man like David wandered around the villages of Judea by himself. It made Ahimelech think something was wrong so he asked David, "**Why are you alone, and no one is with you?**"

i. It seems that Ahimelech knew nothing of the conflict between David and Saul. It seemed strange and dangerous to him that David traveled alone. Plus, we can imagine that David looked tired, weary, disheveled, and probably looked like he had been crying a lot.

c. **The king has ordered me on some business**: This was a plain lie. David came to the house of the LORD but he lied to protect himself. David elaborated on his lie when he put false words in the mouth of Saul to establish an environment of secrecy (**Do not let anyone know anything about the business on which I send you**), and when he refered to "**my young men**"(David was all alone).

i. In many ways, we can understand why David lied and even sympathize with him. Many of us would have done the same or worse in the same situation. At the same time, David would come to horribly regret this lie (as he says in 1 Samuel 22:22).

ii. "Some go about to excuse David's lying here: but that cannot be. The consequences of it were very sad . . . and afterward made his soul melt for very heaviness." (Trapp)

2. (3-6) David asks for and receives holy bread.

"Now therefore, what have you on hand? Give *me* five *loaves of* bread in my hand, or whatever can be found." And the priest answered David and said, "*There is* no common bread on hand; but there is holy bread, if the young men have at least kept themselves from women." Then David answered the priest, and said to him, "Truly, women *have been* kept from us about three days since I came out. And the vessels of the young men are holy, and *the bread is* in effect common, even though it was sanctified in the vessel this day." So the priest gave him holy *bread*; for there was no bread there but the showbread which had been taken from before the LORD, in order to put hot bread *in its place* on the day when it was taken away.

a. **Give me five loaves of bread**: When David came to the tabernacle in Nob he was hungry and knew he needed food both now and later.

b. **There is no common bread on hand; but there is holy bread**: The tabernacle of the LORD had a table that held twelve loaves of bread, symbolizing God's continual fellowship with Israel.

i. The importance and meaning of the bread is found in its name. Literally, *showbread* means "bread of faces." It is bread associated with, and to be eaten before, *the face of God*. F.B. Meyer calls the *showbread* "presence-bread." To eat the showbread was to eat God's bread in God's house as a friend and a guest of the LORD, enjoying His hospitality. In that culture eating together formed a bond of friendship that was permanent and sacred.

ii. The showbread was always to be *fresh*. Ahimelech would give David the old showbread, **which had been taken from before the LORD, in order to put hot bread in its place**. God wants our fellowship with Him, our time before His face, to be *fresh*.

c. **If the young men have at least kept themselves from women**: The showbread was not to be treated casually. In fact, it was to be eaten by the priests: *And it shall be for Aaron and his sons, and they shall eat it in a holy place* (Leviticus 24:9). While this passage in Leviticus does not specifically say that *only* priests can eat the showbread, it establishes the principle that it must be regarded as holy and can't be distributed casually. So Ahimelech asked David for a basic level of ceremonial cleanness before he gave him the showbread.

d. **Truly, women have been kept from us**: David acted as if he traveled with a group. What he said was true of himself, but there were no others traveling with him.

e. **So the priest gave him holy bread; for there was no bread there but the showbread**: In giving David the bread, Ahimelech broke with priestly custom but not with God's Word. He rightly understood that human need was more important that Levitical observance.

i. When Jesus' disciples were criticized for breaking religious custom by eating against traditions, Jesus used what Ahimelech did to explain the matter (Matthew 12:1-8). Jesus approved of what Ahimelech did, and Jesus honored him by standing on Ahimelech's same ground.

ii. The point with Ahimelech and Jesus is powerful: human traditions are never more important than God's word itself. If God had said, "*Only* the priests can eat this bread," it would have been different. But God never said that. To put the *only* in there seemed logical, but it was adding to God's Word. We must never elevate our *extension* or *application* of God's Word to the same level as God's word itself.

3. (7-9) David receives a sword, and is spotted by one of Saul's royal officials.

Now a certain man of the servants of Saul *was* there that day, detained before the Lord. And his name *was* Doeg, an Edomite, the chief of the herdsmen who *belonged* to Saul. And David said to Ahimelech, "Is there not here on hand a spear or a sword? For I have brought neither my sword nor my weapons with me, because the king's business required haste." So the priest said, "The sword of Goliath the Philistine, whom you killed in the Valley of Elah, there it is, wrapped in a cloth behind the ephod. If you will take that, take *it*. For *there is* no other except that one here." And David said, "*There is* none like it; give it to me."

a. **Doeg the Edomite**: We meet a character we will meet again. Doeg was **chief of the herdsmen who belonged to Saul**, and he was not an Israelite but an **Edomite**.

i. **Chief of the herdsmen**: The word translated **chief** means *mighty*, but can also be used to mean *violent* or *obstinate*. Doeg will show himself to be a violent and obstinate man.

ii. **Detained before the Lord**: By what we see of Doeg and his character, it is hard to think that he did real spiritual business before the Lord at the tabernacle. He was probably fulfilling some ceremonial requirement related to his employment for the king of Israel.

b. **Is there not here on hand a spear or a sword?** We can understand why David wanted a weapon and why he asked. But it is also sad that David continued his lie about being on **the king's business**. David is desperately trying to avoid **the king's business** because right now, the king's business is to kill David.

i. Considering what **the king's business** was, David told the truth when he said, "**The king's business required haste.**" That was true, but not in the way David meant it.

ii. "It is painful to the last degree to see one whose faith towered to such a lofty height in the encounter with Goliath, coming down from that noble elevation, to find him resorting for self-protection to the lies and artifices of an impostor." (Balikie)

c. **The sword of Goliath**: David was happy to have a good weapon (**There is none like it**). As David held this sword, he should have remembered how he came to win it. He didn't do it with lies and half-truths. He did it with a bold trust in God, a trust that believed God and trusted *Him* to sort out the consequences.

i. David can have the sword of Goliath in his arsenal but he would be better equipped if he had the faith that killed Goliath. Is David now trusting in Philistine swords more than the shepherd tools? There was nothing wrong with Goliath's sword - the LORD used it before (1 Samuel 17:51), but only in the context of radical *faith*.

ii. "David lost confidence in God and in fulfillment of God's purpose for his life which had been revealed to him. He went to God's house for comfort and help and guidance, but he was detected as being wrong in his soul. Instead of acknowledging the truth to the only one who could help him and confessing that he had been telling a lie, he ran for his life again." (Redpath)

d. **There is none like it; give it to me**: Knowing that something is *precious* and *wonderful* makes us want it. Being in a time of *trial* or *stress* makes us want the wonderful thing all the more. If this was true of Goliath's sword, it is even truer of the sword of the Spirit, God's Word. We should always say of God's Word, "**give it to me**."

i. "There are some who are bent on taking away the Word of God. Well, if *they* discard it, 'Give it to *me*.' There are some who want to put it up on the self, as a thing that has seen its best days. *They* suppose the old sword is rusty, and worn out, but *we* can say, 'There is none like that; give is me!' " (Spurgeon)

B. David at Gath.

1. (10) David flees to Gath.

Then David arose and fled that day from before Saul, and went to Achish the king of Gath.

a. **David arose and fled that day**: David's attempt to protect himself with clever lies instead of trusting God to protect him didn't bring lasting results. He had to flee.

b. **Went to Achish the king of Gath**: David was now among the Philistines. He must be discouraged or deceived to think he could find peaceful refuge among these enemies of Israel - especially as he carried Goliath's sword into Goliath's hometown.

i. It didn't make sense for the man who carried Goliath's sword to go to Goliath's hometown (1 Samuel 17:4). It didn't make sense for the man who was sustained by the sacred bread of God to find refuge among the pagans. It didn't make sense for the man after God's own heart to change his address to Gath.

2. (11-12) David's predicament in Gath.

And the servants of Achish said to him, "*Is* this not David the king of the land? Did they not sing of him to one another in dances, saying: 'Saul has slain his thousands, And David his ten thousands'?" Now David took these words to heart, and was very much afraid of Achish the king of Gath.

a. **Is this not David the king of the land?** The Philistines of Gath recognized David as **the king of the land** of Israel. These ungodly men understood David's destiny better than King Saul.

b. **Did they not sing of him to one another in dances**: The song and dance about David that swept the nation of Israel (1 Samuel 18:6-7) was also popular among the Philistines. If he didn't know it before, now David found that there was real price for fame.

c. **David took these words to heart, and was very much afraid**: David knew he was discovered and understood that King Achish would not let the man who killed Goliath go.

i. David's words in Psalm 56 help us understand what happened here. The title of that Psalm identifies as the song he wrote *when the Philistines captured him in Gath.* Apparently, although 1 Samuel 21 doesn't detail it, the Philistines *captured* David when he came to Gath. David thought he could find anonymity or sympathy among the ungodly Philistines in Gath, but he was wrong. Psalm 56 describes David's journey from fear to praising as a prisoner in Gath.

ii. Psalm 56 shows that the slide that started on the road from Jonathan and continued on into Gath is now stopped. David is on higher ground again. This was the difference between David and Saul. Both of them slipped but Saul kept sliding, while David turned back to the LORD.

3. (13-15) To escape, David pretends madness.

So he changed his behavior before them, feigned madness in their hands, scratched on the doors of the gate, and let his saliva fall down on his beard. Then Achish said to his servants, "Look, you see the man is insane. Why have

you brought him to me? Have I need of madmen, that you have brought this *fellow* to play the madman in my presence? Shall this *fellow* come into my house?"

a. **Pretended madness in their hands**: David acted in a strange manner, scratching on the doors of the gate and letting **saliva fall down on his beard**. It was as if David foamed at the mouth.

i. Basically, David humiliated himself before the Philistines and acted like a madman. The **saliva** on the **beard** was especially convincing, because men in that culture would consider this something only a man out of his right mind would allow. "An indignity to the beard was considered an intolerable insult and would not have been permitted by a normal person." (Jamieson, Fausset, and Brown)

b. **This man is insane. Why have you brought him to me?** David's plan worked. Achish decided that this wasn't David after all, or if it was he was such a pathetic specimen that he may as well let him go.

i. Was David walking in the Spirit or in the flesh when he pretended madness? Some commentators believe that David was in the flesh and trusting in himself. But the change of Psalm 56 happened before David's escape, and it made sense that the LORD would guide David into a path of escape that would *humble* him. When David tried to protect himself with lies and tried to find refuge among the ungodly, he really was acting *crazy*. When David repented, asked for mercy, and trusted again in the LORD, it was as if the LORD said, "You've been acting like a madman. Keep the act going and I'll get you out of this."

c. Psalm 34 is David's declaration of joy when he escaped from Gath with his life. The title of Psalm 34 reads, *A Psalm of David when he pretended madness before Abimelech, who drove him away, and he departed.*

i. Psalm 34 begins beautifully: *I will bless the LORD at all times; His praise shall continually be in my mouth. My soul shall make its boast in the LORD; the humble shall hear of it and be glad. Oh, magnify the LORD with me, and let us exalt His name together. I sought the LORD, and He heard me, and delivered me from all my fears* (Psalm 34:1-4). David was amazed with gratitude to the LORD.

ii. David is especially joyful because the LORD got him out of a mess that David himself made. God's amazing goodness is shown when He delivers us when we don't really deserve it.

1 Samuel 22 - David at the Adullam Cave, Saul Murders the Priests

A. David at Adullam cave.

1. (1a) David's distress at Adullam.

David therefore departed from there and escaped to the cave of Adullam.

a. **David therefore departed from there**: David had been through a lot. He had the high of immediate fame, a recent marriage, dangers from the Philistines, repeated attempts on his life, and a heartbreaking farewell from everyday life to live as a fugitive for who knows how long. Then David had a brief but intense period of backsliding, a dramatic turn to the LORD and deliverance from a life-threatening situation.

b. **Escaped to the cave of Adullam**: This was David's place of refuge. He couldn't go to his house, he couldn't go to the palace, he couldn't go to Samuel, he couldn't go to Jonathan, he couldn't go to the house of the LORD, and he couldn't go to the ungodly. But he could go to a humble **cave** and find refuge.

i. The name **Adullam** means *refuge*, but the cave wasn't to be David's refuge. God wanted to be David's refuge in this discouraging time.

ii. Most archaeologists believe that the Cave of Adullam was not too far from the place where David defeated Goliath, in the hills of Judah. David couldn't help but consider how far he had come from a great victory to running around like a criminal, hiding in a cave.

c. The title of Psalm 142 reads: *A Contemplation of David. A prayer when he was in the cave.* So, Psalm 142 described David's discouraged heart: *I cry out to the LORD with my voice; with my voice to the LORD I make my supplication. I pour out my complaint before Him; I declare before Him my trouble. When my spirit was overwhelmed within me, then You knew my path. In the way in which I walk they have secretly set a snare for me. Look on my right hand and see, for there is no one who acknowledges me; refuge has failed me; no one cares for my soul.* (Psalm 142:1-4)

d. The title of Psalm 57 reads *A Michtam of David when he fled from Saul into the cave*. Psalm 57 describes David as the LORD strengthened him in the cave and prepared him for what was next.

i. Psalm 57 shows David with a humble heart: *Be merciful to me, O God, be merciful to me!* (Psalm 57:1)

ii. Psalm 57 shows David with a prayerful heart: *I will cry out to God Most High, to God who performs all things for me.* (Psalm 57:2)

iii. Psalm 57 shows David with a realistic heart: *My soul is among lions . . . they have prepared a net for my steps.* (Psalm 57:4, 6)

iv. Psalm 57 shows a heart of trusting praise to the LORD: *I will praise You, O LORD, among the peoples; I will sing to You among the nations . . . Be exalted, O God, above the heavens; let Your glory be above all the earth.* (Psalm 57:9, 5, 11)

v. The LORD brought David into this place while He was still in the **Adullam cave**. We often think we have to get out of the cave until we can have the heart David had in Psalm 57. But we can have it now, no matter what our circumstances.

2. (1b-2) Others come to David at the Adullam cave.

And when his brothers and all his father's house heard *it*, they went down there to him. And everyone *who was* in distress, everyone who *was* in debt, and everyone *who was* discontented gathered to him. So he became captain over them. And there were about four hundred men with him.

a. **So when his brothers and all his father's house heard it, they went down there to him**: First, David's *family* came to him. This is a precious gift from God because previously all David had was trouble and persecution from his father and his brothers (1 Samuel 16:11 and 1 Samuel 17:28). Now they join him at the Adullam cave.

b. **And everyone who was in distress, everyone who was in debt, and everyone who was discontented gathered to him**: God called an unlikely and unique group to David in the Adullam cave. These were not the men David would choose for himself but they were the ones God called to him.

i. These men were **in distress**. Their own lives weren't easy or together. They had problems of their own, yet God called them to David at the Adullam cave.

ii. These men were **in debt**. They hadn't seen a lot of success in the past, and were stung from their past failures. They had problems of their own, yet God called them to David at the Adullam cave.

iii. These men were **discontented**. The Hebrew word for **discontented** means *bitter of soul.* They knew the bitterness of life, and they were not satisfied with their lives or with King Saul. They wanted something different, and something better, and God called them to David at the Adullam cave.

iv. These men all came to David when he was down and out, hunted and despised. Once David came to the throne, there were a lot of people who wanted to be around him. The glory of these 400 is that they came to David in the cave.

v. "These are the kind of men who came to David: distressed, bankrupt, dissatisfied. These are the kind of people who come to Christ, and they are the only people who come to Him, for they have recognized their distress, their debt, and bankruptcy, and are conscious that they are utterly discontented. The sheer pressures of these frustrations drives them to the refuge of the blood of Christ that was shed for them." (Redpath)

c. **So he became captain over them**: This was not a mob. This was a team that needed a leader, and David **became captain over them**. God doesn't work through mobs. He works through called men and women, but He also calls others to stand with and support those men and women.

i. **Four hundred men**, and desperate men at that. This was a solid beginning to a rebel army if David wanted it. An unprincipled leader might make these 400 men into a gang of rebels or cutthroats, but David did not allow this to become a rebel army against King Saul.

ii. These men *came* to David in distress, in debt, and discontented, but they didn't *stay* that way. David made them into the kind of men described in 1 Chronicles 12:8: *Mighty men of valor, men trained for battle, who could handle the shield and spear, whose faces were like the faces of lions, and were as swift as gazelles on the mountains.*

d. **And there were about four hundred men with him**: David was the one anointed by God to be the next king over Israel, and he became Israel's greatest earthly king. But just as much as God called David, God called these four hundred to come beside David.

i. Each principle is important. The principle that *God leads through a called and anointed man* is important. When an ark had to be built, God didn't call 400 men. When Israel needed deliverance from Egypt, God didn't call a committee. Over and over again in the Scriptures, God's work is led by a called and anointed man.

ii. At the same time, the principle that *God rarely calls that man to work alone* is important. David *needed* these 400 men, even if he never thought so before. They are just as called and anointed as David is, but they are called and anointed to follow and support David and he is called and anointed to lead them.

iii. David had his followers, and so does the Son of David, Jesus Christ. "Do you see the truth of which this Old Testament story is so graphic a picture? Just as in David's day, there is a King in exile who is gathering around Him a company of people who are in distress, in debt, and discontented. He is training and preparing them for the day when He shall come to reign." (Redpath)

3. (3-4) David cares for his parents.

Then David went from there to Mizpah of Moab; and he said to the king of Moab, "Please let my father and mother come here with you, till I know what God will do for me." So he brought them before the king of Moab, and they dwelt with him all the time that David was in the stronghold.

a. **He said to the king of Moab, "Please let my father and mother come here with you."** David took his parents to Moab because his great-grandmother Ruth was a Moabite (Ruth 4:18-22, 1:4). He wanted his parents to be safe in whatever battles he may face in the future.

b. **Till I know what God will do for me**: David doesn't know the whole story. He knew he was called and anointed to be the next king of Israel but he had no idea how God would get him there. David had to trust and obey when he didn't **know what God** would do.

4. (5) David hears from the prophet Gad.

Now the prophet Gad said to David, "Do not stay in the stronghold; depart, and go to the land of Judah." So David departed and went into the forest of Hereth.

a. **Now the prophet Gad said to David**: David enjoyed support and aid from the prophets. Saul's dealing with the prophets (such as Samuel) was almost always negative because Saul resisted the word of God. David received God's word.

b. **Go to the land of Judah**: Gad counseled David to leave his own **stronghold** and to go back to the very stronghold of Saul. This probably wasn't what David really wanted to hear but he obeyed anyway. David had to learn to trust God *in the midst* of danger, not on the other side of danger.

i. "Hereby also God would exercise David's faith, and wisdom, and courage; and so prepare him for the kingdom, and uphold and increase his reputation among the people." (Poole)

B. Saul murders the priests.

1. (6-8) Feeling sorry for himself, Saul accuses his aides of treason.

When Saul heard that David and the men who *were* with him had been discovered; now Saul was staying in Gibeah under a tamarisk tree in Ramah, with his spear in his hand, and all his servants standing about him; then Saul said to his servants who stood about him, "Hear now, you Benjamites! Will the son of Jesse give every one of you fields and vineyards, *and* make you all captains of thousands and captains of hundreds? All of you have conspired against me, and *there is* no one who reveals to me that my son has made a covenant with the son of Jesse; and *there is* not one of you who is sorry for me or reveals to me that my son has stirred up my servant against me, to lie in wait, as *it is* this day."

a. **David and the men who were with him had been discovered**: When it was just David hiding out from Saul, he could remain hidden for a long time. But you can't hide 400 men. When David came back into Judah, Saul's network of informants quickly discovered them.

b. **With a spear in his hand, and all his servants standing about him**: When Saul had a spear in his hand, it usually meant he was going to try to hurt someone.

c. **Will the son of Jesse give everyone of you fields and vineyards**: Saul appealed to the truly worst in these men, asking them if a man from Judah will favor the tribe of Benjamin with riches and promotions.

i. Also, notice how Saul referred to David: "**the son of Jesse**." He didn't say, "The Man Who Killed Goliath," or "The Man Who Killed 200 Philistines," or "The Man Anointed by God." Saul knew that David came from a family of simple farmers, so he called him by the humblest name he could think of - **the son of Jesse**.

d. **All of you have conspired against me . . . there is not one of you who is sorry for me**: In his fleshly, self-focused world, everything revolved around Saul. He became paranoid and whiny, and he led through guilt and accusation.

e. **My son has stirred up my servant against me**: Jonathan never did any such thing but Saul could not accept the truth that David and Jonathan were in the right and he was in the wrong. So Saul constructed elaborate conspiracies against him.

2. (9-10) Doeg reports on Ahimelech and David to King Saul.

Then answered Doeg the Edomite, who was set over the servants of Saul, and said, "I saw the son of Jesse going to Nob, to Ahimelech the son of Ahitub. And he inquired of the LORD for him, gave him provisions, and gave him the sword of Goliath the Philistine."

a. **Doeg the Edomite**: This man was last seen in 1 Samuel 21:7 in Nob, at the tabernacle at the same time David came there.

b. **He inquired of the LORD for him, gave him provisions, and gave him the sword of Goliath**: Doeg implicated the priest Ahimelech as David's accomplice. "Look at all the help Ahimelech gave David. Surely, they are working together against you Saul, and Ahimelech probably knows exactly where David is and where he is going."

i. Doeg was more than an ambitious man looking to promote himself. He also knew how to divert Saul's anger and suspicion from his own staff to the priests.

3. (11-15) Saul accuses Ahimelech of conspiracy with David.

So the king sent to call Ahimelech the priest, the son of Ahitub, and all his father's house, the priests who *were* in Nob. And they all came to the king. And Saul said, "Hear now, son of Ahitub!" And he answered, "Here I am, my lord." Then Saul said to him, "Why have you conspired against me, you and the son of Jesse, in that you have given him bread and a sword, and have inquired of God for him, that he should rise against me, to lie in wait, as it is this day?" So Ahimelech answered the king and said, "And who among all your servants *is as* faithful as David, who is the king's son-in-law, who goes at your bidding, and is honorable in your house? Did I then begin to inquire of God for him? Far be it from me! Let not the king impute anything to his servant, *or* to any in the house of my father. For your servant knew nothing of all this, little or much."

a. **Here I am, my lord**: Ahimelech answered Saul with the honesty of a man with a clear conscience. He simply and honestly said, "**Let not the king impute anything to his servant**."

i. Saul continued in his reckless paranoia. He accused Ahimelech and David of conspiracy against him (**you conspired against me, you and the son of Jesse**). He also thought that David was out to kill him (**that he should rise against me, to lie in wait**). Saul thought of *himself* as the victim, that David and Ahimelech were *out to get him.*

b. **For your servant knew nothing of all this, little or much**: Ahimelech told the exact truth. When David came to Ahimelech, the priest questioned him carefully (*Why are you alone, and no one is with you*, 1 Samuel 21:1). Instead of telling Ahimelech the truth, David lied to him. This put Ahimelech in a very vulnerable position.

i. Ahimelech was so unaware of the hatred Saul has for David that he praised David before the jealous king: "**And who among all your servants is as faithful as David**." This is because David told Ahimelech that he was on Saul's bidding when he was really running for his life (1 Samuel 21:2).

4. (16-19) Saul commands the execution of the priests and their families, and Doeg the Edomite carries it out.

And the king said, "You shall surely die, Ahimelech, you and all your father's house!" Then the king said to the guards who stood about him, "Turn and kill the priests of the LORD, because their hand also *is* with David, and because they knew when he fled and did not tell it to me." But the servants of the king would not lift their hands to strike the priests of the LORD. And the king said to Doeg, "You turn and kill the priests!" So Doeg the Edomite turned and struck the priests, and killed on that day eighty-five men who wore a linen ephod. Also Nob, the city of the priests, he struck with the edge of the sword, both men and women, children and nursing infants, oxen and donkeys and sheep; with the edge of the sword.

a. **"You shall surely die, Ahimelech, you and your father's house!"** Any man in the place of sin and rebellion Saul was in can't stand to see an innocent, guileless man like Ahimelech disagree with him. So he commanded him to be *murdered.*

i. Saul was reluctant to kill the enemies of the LORD when he was commanded to (1 Samuel 15:9). But he wasn't reluctant to murder the priests of the LORD in cold blood. Saul is clearly going off the deep end. "His anger was bent against the Lord himself, for taking away his kingdom, and giving it to another: and because he could not come at the Lord, therefore he wreaketh his rage upon his priests." (Trapp)

ii. "This is one of the worst acts in the life of Saul; his malice was implacable, and his wrath was cruel, and there is no motive of justice or policy by which such a barbarous act can be justified." (Clarke) "A bloody sentence, harshly pronounced and as rashly executed, without any pause or deliberation, without any remorse or regret. This was the worst act that ever Saul did." (Trapp)

b. **The servants of the king would not lift their hands to strike the priests**: To their credit, Saul's servants feared God more than Saul and they refused to murder the priests.

c. **So Doeg the Edomite turned and struck the priests**: Doeg, who was not a Jew but an Edomite, didn't hesitate to murder the priests and their families. Doeg was *detained before the LORD* at the tabernacle (1 Samuel 21:7) but it didn't change his heart at all.

5. (20-23) David protects Abiathar, the only survivor of Ahimelech's family.

Now one of the sons of Ahimelech the son of Ahitub, named Abiathar, escaped and fled after David. And Abiathar told David that Saul had killed the Lord's priests. So David said to Abiathar, "I knew that day, when Doeg the Edomite *was* there, that he would surely tell Saul. I have caused *the death* of all the persons of your father's house. Stay with me; do not fear. For he who seeks my life seeks your life, but with me you *shall be* safe."

a. **I knew that day, when Doeg the Edomite was there, that he would surely tell Saul**: David showed how he felt about this in Psalm 52, which says in its title *A Contemplation of David when Doeg the Edomite went and told Saul, and said to him, "David has gone to the house of Ahimelech."*

i. In Psalm 52, David showed his outrage against Doeg: *Why do you boast in evil, O mighty man? Your tongue devises destruction, like a sharp razor, working deceitfully. You love evil more than good, lying rather than speaking righteousness. You love all devouring words, you deceitful tongue.* (Psalm 52:1a, 2-4)

ii. In Psalm 52, David showed his confidence in God's judgments: *God shall likewise destroy you forever; He shall take you away, and pluck you out of your dwelling place, and uproot you from the land of the living.* (Psalm 52:5)

iii. In Psalm 52, David showed his focus on the LORD: *But I am like a green olive tree in the house of God; I trust in the mercy of God forever and ever. I will praise You forever, because You have done it; and in the presence of Your saints I will wait on Your name, for it is good.* (Psalm 52:8-9)

b. **I have caused the death of all the persons of your father's house**: David meant this in two ways. In the greater way, it was David's mere presence with Ahimelech that made him guilty before Saul and there really wasn't anything David or anyone could do about that. In the lesser way, David's lying to Ahimelech made the priest vulnerable before Saul.

i. David's lies did not directly kill Ahimelech and the other priests. But at the very least, he kept Ahimelech from dying with greater honor. If Ahimelech knew of the conflict between David and Saul he could have chosen to stand with David and die with greater honor.

ii. We know from both 1 Samuel and the Psalms that David turned his heart back to the LORD and asked forgiveness after his lies to Ahimelech. David was restored, but there was still bad fruit to come of the lies, and now David sees and tastes that bad fruit.

c. **With me you shall be safe**: David could not do anything about the priests who were already murdered. He confessed his guilt in the matter, and sought forgiveness from the LORD. Now, all he can do is minister to the need in front of him - Abiathar, the surviving priest.

1 Samuel 23 - David Saves Keliah; David Escapes from Saul

A. David saves Keliah from the Philistines.

1. (1-4) God directs David to fight against the Philistines and deliver the city of Keliah.

Then they told David, saying, "Look, the Philistines are fighting against Keilah, and they are robbing the threshing floors." Therefore David inquired of the LORD, saying, "Shall I go and attack these Philistines?" And the LORD said to David, "Go and attack the Philistines, and save Keilah." But David's men said to him, "Look, we are afraid here in Judah. How much more then if we go to Keilah against the armies of the Philistines?" Then David inquired of the LORD once again. And the LORD answered him and said, "Arise, go down to Keilah. For I will deliver the Philistines into your hand."

a. **The Philistines are fighting against Keliah, and they are robbing the threshing floors**: They brought this plea for help to David and not to King Saul because Saul was not fulfilling his role as king over Israel. It was *Saul's* job to protect Keliah and it was *Saul's* job to fight the Philistines but Saul wasn't doing his job and the LORD called David to do it.

i. God loved His people too much to let them suffer with an unfaithful king. If Saul wasn't up to the task, God would raise up a man who was, and David was the one. God directed David to act like a king even if he was not the king yet.

b. **Therefore David inquired of the LORD**: This showed David's wisdom and godliness. Some might have immediately said, "This isn't my responsibility, let Saul deal with it." Others might have immediately said, "Let's go! I can fix this problem!" Either course was foolish, but David was wise because he **inquired of the LORD**.

c. **Go, and attack the Philistines, and save Keliah**: By all outward appearance, this was a crazy thing to do. First, David had 400 men with thin resumes and bad credit reports (1 Samuel 22:2) - not exactly a regular army. Second, David had enough trouble with Saul and he didn't need to add trouble from the Philistines - one enemy is usually enough. Third, this would bring David wide open out before King Saul. This was a dangerous course of action.

i. David did this for two reasons. He had the command of God, and the need of the people. David was willing to endanger himself to obey the command of God and to meet the need of the people.

d. **But David's men said to him, "Look, we are afraid here in Judah."** David's men counseled him to *not go to Keliah.* We can understand their counsel; but we should not agree with it. It was good that David *became captain over them* (1 Samuel 22:2) and that this wasn't a democracy.

e. **David inquired of the LORD once again**: Wisely, David took the words from his men into great account. He wrestled with their advice and saw that in many ways it made a lot of sense. At the same time he knew this was an issue that had to be decided before the LORD.

f. **Arise, go down to Keiliah, for I will deliver the Philistines into your hand**: God likes to confirm His word, especially when He directs us to do something hard or unusual. This time the LORD not only confirmed His previous command but He also gave *a promise* with the confirmation: "**I will deliver the Philistines into your hand.**"

2. (5) David rescues the people of Keliah.

And David and his men went to Keilah and fought with the Philistines, struck them with a mighty blow, and took away their livestock. So David saved the inhabitants of Keilah.

a. **So David and his men went to Keliah and fought**: David did what God told him to do. It isn't enough to ask or know God's will. We must have a commitment to *obey* God's will, even when it is difficult.

b. **Struck them with a mighty blow . . . David saved the inhabitants of Keliah**: God blessed the obedience of David. God perfectly kept His promise to David (1 Samuel 23:4-5).

3. (6-8) Saul comes against David at Keliah.

Now it happened, when Abiathar the son of Ahimelech fled to David at Keilah, *that* he went down *with* an ephod in his hand. And Saul was told that David had gone to Keilah. So Saul said, "God has delivered him into my hand, for he has shut himself in by entering a town that has gates and bars." Then Saul called all the people together for war, to go down to Keilah to besiege David and his men.

a. **So Saul said, "God has delivered him into my hand."** Saul thought that **God** had blessed him and given him victory over David. It was true that God lead David to Keliah and it was true that this exposed David to Saul's attack. But it was *not true* that the LORD had **delivered him into my hand**, as Saul said.

b. **The Saul called all the people together for war**: This was not a war against the Philistines, against the Edomites, against the Amelekites, or against the Moabites. This was against David. Saul made the common mistake of assuming that someone is an enemy of the LORD just because they are *our* enemy.

i. Saul *wouldn't* go to Keliah to save the people against the Philistines, but he *would* go there to try and save himself against David. Saul was totally motivated by self-interest.

4. (9-13) David escapes from Keliah.

When David knew that Saul plotted evil against him, he said to Abiathar the priest, "Bring the ephod here." Then David said, "O LORD God of Israel, Your servant has certainly heard that Saul seeks to come to Keilah to destroy the city for my sake. Will the men of Keilah deliver me into his hand? Will Saul come down, as Your servant has heard? O LORD God of Israel, I pray, tell Your servant." And the LORD said, "He will come down." Then David said, "Will the men of Keilah deliver me and my men into the hand of Saul?" And the LORD said, "They will deliver *you*." So David and his men, about six hundred, arose and departed from Keilah and went wherever they could go. Then it was told Saul that David had escaped from Keilah; so he halted the expedition.

a. **Bring the ephod here**: David was in a bad place, and he was in a bad place because the LORD led him there. Some might be angry with the LORD but David did the right thing - he inquired of the LORD again.

i. "Here is a second inquiry. God loveth to be often sought unto by his praying people (Luke 18:1), and the therefore answereth them by degrees, that he may frequently hear from them." (Trapp)

b. **He will come down . . . They will deliver you**: This is another example of David seeking God through the priest using the *Urim and Thummim.* Notice how the questions are presented in a "Yes or No" format, because that is how the *Urim and Thummim* were used.

i. This was a true word of the LORD. Obviously, the word of the Lord to David was true *depending on David's actions.* If David stayed in Keliah the word would have surely come to pass.

c. **So David and his men . . . arose and departed from Keliah**: David could have stood and fought and there was something in him that probably wanted to. But David knew that it was not of the LORD and that a lot of innocent people would get hurt in the battle. So David, who was a great warrior, humbled himself and escaped. David was not the kind of man to sneak away from a battle but he didn't let his pride get the best of him in this matter.

d. **Saul . . . halted the expedition**: David's humble heart saved the city of Keliah. In this, he shows the same heart as the greater Son of David, Jesus, who through His humble action spared us against not only Satan, but against the righteous judgment of God.

B. David narrowly escapes Saul in the Judean wilderness.

1. (14-15) David takes refuge in Wilderness of Ziph.

And David stayed in strongholds in the wilderness, and remained in the mountains in the Wilderness of Ziph. Saul sought him every day, but God did not deliver him into his hand. So David saw that Saul had come out to seek his life. And David *was* in the Wilderness of Ziph in a forest.

a. **The Wilderness of Ziph**: Ziph was a town below the southern tip of the Dead Sea, with a dramatically varied landscape. It was not a comfortable or easy place to be. God guided and protected David, but it wasn't comfortable or easy. This was an essential time for God's work in David's life. He became a man after God's heart in the shepherd's field but he became a king in the wilderness.

b. **Saul sought him every day**: Saul was a determined enemy, unrelenting in his pursuit of David. Saul was so obsessed with killing David that he didn't give attention to the work God called him to do.

c. **But God did not deliver him into his hand**: Saul can be as determined as he pleases but he does not dictate these events - God does. Man can intend, attempt, and work all kinds of evil **but God** is still in charge.

2. (16-18) Jonathan and David meet each other for the last time.

Then Jonathan, Saul's son, arose and went to David in the woods and strengthened his hand in God. And he said to him, "Do not fear, for the hand of Saul my father shall not find you. You shall be king over Israel, and I shall be next to you. Even my father Saul knows that." So the two of them made a covenant before the LORD. And David stayed in the woods, and Jonathan went to his own house.

a. **Strengthened his hand in God**: This is what Jonathan did for David. Jonathan could not rescue David but he **strengthened his hand in God**. Jonathan couldn't give David all the answers but he **strengthened his hand in God**. Jonathan couldn't stay with David but he **strengthened his hand in God**. This was a precious gift.

b. **Do not fear**: In encouraging David, Jonathan gave him reasons to **not fear**. David could reject fear because God would ultimately protect him (**Saul my father shall not find you**). David could reject fear because

God's promise would come to pass (**You shall be king over Israel**). David could reject fear because he had loyal friends like Jonathan (**I shall be next to you**).

i. Because of their great friendship, David and Jonathan looked forward to the day when David would be king and Jonathan would support and help him. But it would never come to pass because Jonathan would die before David became king. Jonathan's encouragement was a mix of divine promises and an expression of hope and desire.

c. **Even my father knows that**: Saul knew that David would be the next king, that the LORD had ordained it. Yet he fought against the will of God with everything he had.

d. **The two of them made a covenant before the LORD**: David and Jonathan already made a covenant (1 Samuel 18:3, 20:16) but now they confirm it again. Renewing or reconfirming a covenant does not make the previous covenant less precious; it makes it more precious and valid.

i. This was the last time David and Jonathan saw each other on earth and their relationship was still confirmed in **covenant**.

3. (19-23) The Ziphites betray David.

Then the Ziphites came up to Saul at Gibeah, saying, "Is David not hiding with us in strongholds in the woods, in the hill of Hachilah, which *is* on the south of Jeshimon? Now therefore, O king, come down according to all the desire of your soul to come down; and our part *shall be* to deliver him into the king's hand." And Saul said, "Blessed *are* you of the LORD, for you have compassion on me. Please go and find out for sure, and see the place where his hideout is, *and* who has seen him there. For I am told he is very crafty. See therefore, and take knowledge of all the lurking places where he hides; and come back to me with certainty, and I will go with you. And it shall be, if he is in the land, that I will search for him throughout all the clans of Judah."

a. **Our part shall be to deliver him into the king's hand**: For every faithful Jonathan there is also a **Ziphite** willing to betray. Many a godly man or woman has known both friends and betrayers, just as Jesus did.

b. **Blessed are you of the LORD**: Saul was so spiritually warped that he said to the betrayers of an innocent man, "**Blessed are you of the LORD.**"

c. **I am told that he is very crafty**: It wasn't David's craftiness that kept him from Saul's clutches; it was the goodness and faithfulness of the LORD. Saul didn't want to believe that, so he thought and said David's protection was due to being **very crafty**.

d. At this time, David expressed his feelings to the LORD in song, and that song is Psalm 54. The title to that Psalm reads, *A Contemplation of David when the Ziphites went and said to Saul, "Is David not hiding with us?"*

i. In Psalm 54, David called out to the LORD for help: *Save me, O God, by Your name, and vindicate me by Your strength* (Psalm 54:1).

ii. In Psalm 54, David understood his enemies: *For strangers have risen up against me, and oppressors have sought after my life; they have not set God before them* (Psalm 54:3).

iii. In Psalm 54, David expressed his confidence in the LORD: *Behold, God is my helper; the LORD is with those who uphold my life* (Psalm 54:4).

iv. In Psalm 54, David let go of the bitterness and fear and praised the LORD instead: *I will freely sacrifice to You; I will praise Your name, O LORD, for it is good* (Psalm 54:6).

v. "He is now looking at God. First he was looking at his enemies and these supposed friends of his, but now he sees them through God. If you begin with God, your enemies grow small. If you begin with the enemy, you may never reach God." (Redpath)

4. (24-29) David's dramatic, narrow escape.

So they arose and went to Ziph before Saul. But David and his men *were* in the Wilderness of Maon, in the plain on the south of Jeshimon. When Saul and his men went to seek *him*, they told David. Therefore he went down to the rock, and stayed in the Wilderness of Maon. And when Saul heard *that*, he pursued David in the Wilderness of Maon. Then Saul went on one side of the mountain, and David and his men on the other side of the mountain. So David made haste to get away from Saul, for Saul and his men were encircling David and his men to take them. But a messenger came to Saul, saying, "Hasten and come, for the Philistines have invaded the land!" Therefore Saul returned from pursuing David, and went against the Philistines; so they called that place the Rock of Escape. Then David went up from there and dwelt in strongholds at En Gedi.

a. **Saul went on one side of the mountain, and David and his men on the other side of the mountain**: If only Saul knew David was so close! They were on the same **mountain** (what we would think of as a large hill), separated by the ridge. Saul did his best to trap David, and it looked like he would.

b. **But a messenger came to Saul**: Out of the blue - actually, out of heaven - **a messenger came to Saul**, and drew him away from David to fight the Philistines. The hand of God was so evident that David and his men made a memorial of the spot: **they called that place the Rock of Escape**.

1 Samuel 24 - David Spares Saul's Life

A. David doesn't kill Saul when he has the opportunity.

1. (1-2) Saul seeks David in the Wilderness of En Gedi.

Now it happened, when Saul had returned from following the Philistines, that it was told him, saying, "Take note! David *is* in the Wilderness of En Gedi." Then Saul took three thousand chosen men from all Israel, and went to seek David and his men on the Rocks of the Wild Goats.

a. **When Saul had returned from following the Philistines**: In the previous chapter, God miraculously delivered David by drawing Saul away to fight the Philistines at the moment Saul was ready to capture David. But when Saul was done with the Philistines, he went back to pursuing David.

i. We often wish that our next victory would be a *permanent* victory. We wish that the spiritual enemies who pursue us like Saul pursued David would simply give up, and we wouldn't have to bother with them any more. But even when we have victory and they are sent away, they come back, and will keep coming back until we go to glory with the LORD. That is the only *permanent* victory we will find.

b. **The Wilderness of En Gedi**: The **En Gedi** canyon runs westward from the Dead Sea. One can still see the good sized creek flowing down the canyon, making **En Gedi**, with its waterfalls and vegetation seem more like a tropical paradise than the middle of the desert.

i. One can also see the numerous *caves* dotting the hills. This was a great place for David and his men to hide out. In the middle of barren desert, scouts could easily detect approaching troops. There was plenty of water and wildlife and many caves and defensive positions.

2. (3) Saul unkowingly comes to a cave where David and his men are hiding.

So he came to the sheepfolds by the road, where there *was* a cave; and Saul went in to attend to his needs. (David and his men were staying in the recesses of the cave.)

a. **The sheepfolds**: This indicates that this was a large cave, big enough to shelter a flock of sheep. All or most of David's 600 men could hide in the recesses of the cave.

b. **Saul went in to attend to his needs**: Since the Bible is a real book, dealing with real people living real lives, we aren't surprised to see it describe Saul's attention to his personal needs. But something as basic and common as this was timed and arranged by God, without Saul having any knowledge of God's timing or arrangement of things.

i. The fact that Saul **went in to attend to his needs** also meant that he went into the cave *alone*. His soldiers and bodyguards were out of the cave waiting for him.

c. **David and his men were staying in the recesses of the cave**: What are the chances? Saul must attend to his personal needs at the very moment he passes by the very cave where David hides. This was no coincidence but arranged by God to test David, to train David, and display David's godly heart.

3. (4-7) David restrains himself and his men from killing Saul.

Then the men of David said to him, "This is the day of which the LORD said to you, 'Behold, I will deliver your enemy into your hand, that you may do to him as it seems good to you.' " And David arose and secretly cut off a corner of Saul's *robe*. Now it happened afterward that David's heart troubled him because he had cut Saul's robe. And he said to his men, "The LORD forbid that I should do this thing to my master, the Lord's anointed, to stretch out my hand against him, seeing he *is* the anointed of the LORD." So David restrained his servants with *these* words, and did not allow them to rise against Saul. And Saul got up from the cave and went on *his* way.

a. **The men of David said to him**: David's men were excited at the opportunity and believed it was a gift from God. They knew it was no coincidence that Saul came alone into that cave at that moment. They thought this was an opportunity from God to kill Saul.

i. Apparently, on some previous occasion God promised David, "**Behold, I will deliver your enemy into your hand, that you may do to him as it seems good to you.**" They believed that this was the fulfillment of the promise and that David needed to seize the promise by faith and by the sword.

b. **David arose and secretly cut off a corner of Saul's robe**: We can imagine David listening to this counsel from his men and with his sword creeping quickly towards Saul, covered by the darkness of the cave. David's men are excited; their lives as fugitives are about to end, and they will soon be installed as friends and associates of the new King of Israel. But as

David came close to Saul and put forth his sword he didn't bring it crashing down on Saul's neck or thrust it through his back. Instead he **secretly cut off a corner of Saul's robe**.

i. Some wonder how David could have done this without being detected. Saul may have laid his robe down in one part of the cave, and attended to his needs in another part, so David did not have to get right next to Saul to cut off a corner of his robe. Or, it may also be that there was enough noise and commotion from the thousands of men outside of the cave along with their horses that David was simply undetectable.

ii. David decided to spare Saul because he knew that God's promise said, "You will inherit the throne of Israel." He knew that Saul was in the way of that promise. But he also knew it was disobedient of him to kill Saul, because God put Saul in a position of authority and it was *God's* job to take care of Saul not David's. David wanted the promise to be fulfilled but he *refused to try and fulfill God's promise through his own disobedience.*

iii. Sometimes when we have a promise from God we think we are justified in sinning to pursue that promise. This is *always wrong*. God will fulfill His promises, but He will do it *His way*, and do it *righteously*. Instead, we need to be like Abraham, who obeyed God even when it seemed to be at the expense of God's promise, willing to sacrifice the son of promise (Genesis 22). Even more, we need to be like Jesus, who didn't take Satan's offer to "win back the world" at the expense of obedience (Luke 4:5-8).

iv. In all this, we see that David knew not only how to wait *on* the LORD, but he also knew how to wait *for* the LORD. "We wait *on* the Lord by prayer and supplication, looking for the indication of his will; we wait *for* the Lord by patience and submission, looking for the interposition of his hand." (Meyer) David was determined that when he sat on the throne of Israel it wouldn't be because *he* got Saul out of the way but because *God* got Saul out of the way. He wanted God's fingerprints on that work, not his own, and he wanted the clean conscience that comes from knowing it was God's work.

v. We also see that David's heart didn't store up bitterness and anger towards Saul. Even as Saul made David's life completely miserable, David kept taking it to the LORD, and he received the cleansing from the hurt and the bitterness and the anger that the LORD can give. If David stored up bitterness and anger towards Saul he probably wouldn't have been able to resist the temptation to kill him at what seemed to be a "risk free" opportunity.

c. **David's heart troubled him**: This is a remarkably tender conscience in David. Many would only be troubled that they did not take the opportunity to kill Saul. David only cut off the corner of Saul's robe, yet his **heart troubled him**. Why? Because the robe was a symbol of Saul's royal authority, and David felt bad - rightly so, according to the heart of God - that he had done *anything* against Saul's God appointed authority.

i. David expresses this when he said, **"The LORD forbid that I should do this thing to my master, the LORD's anointed . . . seeing he is the anointed of the LORD."** David knew better than anyone that Saul was a troubled and corrupt leader, yet it was in God's power to take him away and David wouldn't do what was only the LORD's to do.

ii. "It was a trifling matter, and yet it seemed dishonouring to God's anointed king; and as such it hurt David to have done it. We sometimes in conversation and criticism cut off a piece of a man's character, or influence for good, or standing in the esteem of others. Ought not our heart to smite us for such thoughtless conduct? Ought we not to make confession and reparation?" (Meyer)

d. **So David restrained his servants with these words**: David not only kept himself from taking vengeance upon Saul, he also **restrained his servants**. Many men in the same situation, would say, "Well, I won't kill Saul now, but if one of my servants does, what can I do?" and therefore leave the door wide open for Saul to be killed. But David wouldn't do that, and he **restrained his servants**.

i. **With these words**: These were the words of a humble, tender conscience before God. They were the words of a man who was convicted at merely cutting off a corner of Saul's robe. When David's servants saw his godliness and how he wanted to please God in *everything*, their hearts were **restrained** from doing any evil against Saul.

B. David appeals to Saul.

1. (8) David reveals his presence to Saul.

David also arose afterward, went out of the cave, and called out to Saul, saying, "My lord the king!" And when Saul looked behind him, David stooped with his face to the earth, and bowed down.

a. **David . . . went out of the cave**: David took a big chance here, because he could simply remain in hiding, secure in the fact that Saul had not found him. But he surrendered himself to Saul because he saw the opportunity to show Saul his heart towards him and reconcile.

b. **My lord the king . . . David stooped with his face to the earth and bowed twice**: This was great submission to Saul. We might think that David had the right to come to Saul as an *equal*. "Well Saul, we've both been anointed to be king. You've got the throne right now, but I'll have it some day and you know it. So from one anointed man to another, look at how I just spared your life." That wasn't David's attitude at all. Instead he said: "Saul, you are the boss and I know it. I respect your place as my leader and as my king."

i. When **David stooped with his face to the earth and bowed twice** he also showed great trust in God, because he made himself completely vulnerable to Saul. Saul could have killed him very easily at that moment, but David trusted that if he did what was right before God then God would protect him and fulfill the promise.

2. (9-15) David's speech to Saul.

And David said to Saul: "Why do you listen to the words of men who say, 'Indeed David seeks your harm'? Look, this day your eyes have seen that the LORD delivered you today into my hand in the cave, and *someone* urged *me* to kill you. But *my eye* spared you, and I said, 'I will not stretch out my hand against my lord, for he *is* the Lord's anointed.' Moreover, my father, see! Yes, see the corner of your robe in my hand! For in that I cut off the corner of your robe, and did not kill you, know and see that *there is* neither evil nor rebellion in my hand, and I have not sinned against you. Yet you hunt my life to take it. Let the LORD judge between you and me, and let the LORD avenge me on you. But my hand shall not be against you. As the proverb of the ancients says, 'Wickedness proceeds from the wicked.' But my hand shall not be against you. After whom has the king of Israel come out? Whom do you pursue? A dead dog? A flea? Therefore let the LORD be judge, and judge between you and me, and see and plead my case, and deliver me out of your hand."

a. **Why do you listen to the words of men**: David showed great kindness and tact to Saul. David knew very well that Saul's fear of David came from Saul himself and not from anyone else. But David put the blame on nameless others so that it was easier for Saul to say, "*They* were wrong" instead of "*I* was wrong." Even in confrontation, David covers Saul's sin.

i. "He prudently and modestly translates the fault from Saul to his followers and evil counselors." (Poole)

ii. Some might have said, "David, lay it on the line! Tell it like it is!" and David will, to some extent. But even as he does he will show mercy and kindness to Saul. David will fulfill Proverbs 10:12: *Love covers all sins*, and 1 Peter 4:8: *Love will cover a multitude of sins.*

b. **I will not stretch out my hand against my lord, for he is the LORD's anointed**: This principle of not striking out against God's anointed leaders is good and important but sometimes has been misused.

i. The phrase *touch not the Lord's anointed* is in vogue among some Christians and among many leaders. Often to them it means: "You should never speak against a pastor or a leader. He is above your criticism or rebuke, so just keep quiet." Sometimes it is used even to prevent a Biblical evaluation of teaching. But when David recognized that Saul was **the Lord's anointed** and refused to harm him, what David would not do is *kill* Saul. He did humbly confront Saul with his sin, hoping Saul would change his heart. But it is entirely wrong for people to use the idea of *touch not the Lord's anointed* to insulate a leader from all evaluation or accountability.

c. **See the corner of your robe in my hand**: This was proof that David had full opportunity to kill Saul but did not take that opportunity. As David showed Saul the **corner of** his **robe**, Saul must have heard the Spirit of God speaking loudly in his heart.

i. Through this cut robe, God sent a message to Saul. The robe was a picture of Saul's royal authority, and through this God said, "I am cutting away your royal authority."

ii. In 1 Samuel 15:27-28 the prophet Samuel rebuked Saul for his hard-hearted disobedience to God. In his distress, Saul tried to keep Samuel from leaving, and grabbed his robe, and a portion of the prophet's robe tore away. When Saul was left holding the torn piece of Samuel's robe, Samuel said to him: *The Lord has torn the kingdom of Israel from you today, and has given it to a neighbor of yours, who is better than you.* Now, when David confronts Saul with the torn robe, Saul *must* be reminded of this incident, and God's message to him was loud and clear.

d. **Let the Lord judge between you and me**: David didn't need to do anything more to defend himself before Saul; he referred the matter to the Lord. David would let God plead his case and be his judge. David didn't just say, "**My hand shall not be against you**," he *proved* it by not killing Saul when he had the opportunity.

i. The Living Bible gives a good sense of 1 Samuel 24:12: *Perhaps the Lord will kill you for what you are trying to do to me, but I will never harm you.* In fact, David *protected* Saul by restraining his men.

ii. It was inevitable that Saul would be judged, and that he would lose the throne. But it was absolutely God's business to accomplish that and it was the business of no one else. Jesus established the same principle in Matthew 18:7 when He said, *offenses must come, but woe to that man by whom the offense comes*! God's judgment is *God's* business. We put ourselves in a bad place when we make ourselves instruments of God's judgment.

e. **Wickedness proceeds from the wicked**: David used this proverb to make a point. "Saul, if I was really as wicked as your advisors say I am, if I really was out to kill you, I would have done that wicked act in the cave. Because no wickedness proceeded from me when I had the opportunity, it shows my heart is not wicked towards you."

f. **Therefore let the LORD be judge . . . and see and plead my case, and deliver me out of your hand**: David told Saul, "I'm still trusting God, that He will deliver me out of your hand." Instead of finding a way out of his trial in the flesh, David did the harder thing - he trusted in God to deliver him instead of trusting in himself.

C. Saul's reaction to David.

1. (16-19) Saul honors David's mercy towards him.

So it was, when David had finished speaking these words to Saul, that Saul said, "*Is* this your voice, my son David?" And Saul lifted up his voice and wept. Then he said to David: "You *are* more righteous than I; for you have rewarded me with good, whereas I have rewarded you with evil. And you have shown this day how you have dealt well with me; for when the LORD delivered me into your hand, you did not kill me. For if a man finds his enemy, will he let him get away safely? Therefore may the LORD reward you with good for what you have done to me this day."

a. **Is this your voice, my son David?** Saul responded so emotionally because Saul lived on the delusion that David was out to get him, and David's refusal to kill Saul when he had the chance proved beyond doubt that this was false. David's *obedience to God* and his *love to Saul* made all the difference in softening Saul's heart.

b. **You are more righteous than I . . . you have dealt well with me . . . you did not kill me . . . the LORD reward you with good for what you have done to me this day**: This was a dramatic change of heart in Saul. Every change David could have hoped for in Saul has happened, and Saul really seemed sincere about it (**Saul lifted up his voice and wept**). David heaped coals of kindness upon Saul's head and it melted Saul's heart.

2. (20-22) Saul looks to the future.

"And now I know indeed that you shall surely be king, and that the kingdom of Israel shall be established in your hand. Therefore swear now to me by the LORD that you will not cut off my descendants after me, and that you will not destroy my name from my father's house." So David swore to Saul. And Saul went home, but David and his men went up to the stronghold.

a. **I know indeed that you shall surely be king**: Saul knew it all along (1 Samuel 23:17) but now he *really* knows it.

b. **Therefore swear to me know by the Lord that you will not cut off my descendants after me**: Saul simply wanted the same kind of promise from David that he made to Jonathan in 1 Samuel 20:13-16. In that day, when one royal house replaced another it was common for the new royal house to kill all the potential rulers from the old royal house. Saul knew that one day, David and his descendants would rule over Israel, and he wants David to promise that David and his descendants will not kill or mistreat the descendants of Saul.

i. "How then could David destroy so many of Saul's sons, 2 Samuel 21:8-9? David could bind himself by his oaths, but he could not bind God, to whose good pleasure all promises, vows, and oaths must in all reason be submitted; and that was done by God's command, and God was well pleased with it, 2 Samuel 21:14." (Poole)

c. **And Saul went home, but David and his men went up to the stronghold**: David didn't go back home with Saul and be restored to his home and his place at the palace because David knew that as much as Saul meant it at the moment, the struggle would be to *remain* in the place of victory.

i. Many times, a person repents and claims to recognize their sinful ways just like Saul did. But the validity of repentance and a changed heart isn't demonstrated by the emotion or sincerity of a moment. It is demonstrated by the ongoing direction of one's life and David had every right to say, "I'm going to stay in the stronghold until I see the direction of Saul's life."

ii. "What a miserable picture Saul is! What is the use of saying, 'I have played the fool,' if he goes on playing the fool? What use are his tears and confession before David if he doesn't act upon his remorse?" (Redpath)

iii. In fact, it is *worse* to have this kind of emotional response if it *doesn't* result in true repentance. "If a man is emotionally upset, as Saul was, and awakens to his condition, but only weeps about it and still doesn't obey God, his second state is a thousand times worse than the first. Emotion that does not lead to action only leads deeper into sin and rebellion." (Redpath)

1 Samuel 25 - David, Nabal, and Abigail

A. David's anger at Nabal.

1. (1) Samuel, the great prophet and judge over Israel, dies.

Then Samuel died; and the Israelites gathered together and lamented for him, and buried him at his home in Ramah. And David arose and went down to the Wilderness of Paran.

a. **Then Samuel died**: This great man dedicated unto the LORD and serving Him from his youngest days, now dies. As godly as he was, it did not save him from an earthly death because he was still a descendant of Adam. But God's work in Israel did not end when Samuel died. God's work never is dependent on only one man.

i. If it is written "**then Samuel died**," it is also written "**and David arose**." God's work may begin with a man but it never ends with one man. God continues and sustains His work as He pleases.

b. **The Israelites gathered together and lamented for him**: Samuel seemed to be unappreciated by Israel during his life (1 Samuel 8:1-7) but at least he was honored in his death.

i. Samuel's heritage lived on in a remarkable way. 1 Chronicles 9:22 suggests he organized the Levites in the service of the sanctuary which was completed by David and Solomon. 1 Chronicles 26:27-28 says Samuel began collecting treasures for building the temple in Solomon's day. 2 Chronicles 35:18 reports that Samuel remembered the Passover, and kept Israel in remembrance of God's great deliverance. Psalm 99:6 and Jeremiah 15:1 commemorate Samuel as a man of great intercession. Hebrews 11:33 puts Samuel in God's "Hall of Faith."

2. (2-3) A man named Nabal, his wife and his character.

Now *there was* a man in Maon whose business *was* in Carmel, and the man *was* very rich. He had three thousand sheep and a thousand goats. And he was shearing his sheep in Carmel. The name of the man *was* Nabal, and the name of his

wife Abigail. And *she was* a woman of good understanding and beautiful appearance; but the man *was* harsh and evil in *his* doings. And he *was of the house of* Caleb.

a. **And the man was very rich**: The first thing we learn about this man is where he lived (**Maon**, with his business in **Carmel**), and that he was a **very rich** man (**three thousand sheep and a thousand goats**).

i. There are four kinds of riches. There are riches in what you *have*, riches in what you *do*, riches in what you *know*, and riches in what you *are* - riches of *character*. Nabal was a **very rich** man, but only rich in what he had. He had the lowest kind of riches.

b. **And he was shearing his sheep in Carmel**: This was the "harvest time" for a sheep rancher. Because it was like "harvest time" sheep shearing was a time of lavish hospitality towards others.

i. "Sheep-shearing was traditionally celebrated by feasting, with enough and to spare." (Baldwin)

c. **The name of the man was Nabal**: This is another indication of his character, because the name **Nabal** means *fool*. In ancient Israel names were often connected with a person's character. We don't know if Nabal was given this name or he earned it but he certainly lived up to it.

i. The fact that **he was of the house of Caleb** may also be a bad description of Nabal, because **Caleb** means *dog*, and to be **of the house of** *a dog* was no compliment. "As the word *caleb* signifies *a dog*, the *Septuagint* have understood it as implying a man of a *canine disposition*, and translate it thus . . . *he was a doggish man*. It is understood in the same way by the *Syriac* and *Arabic*." (Clarke)

d. **Abigail . . . a woman of good understanding and beautiful appearance**: Nabal's wife was both **beautiful** and wise, in contrast to Nabal himself. The Bible gives Abigail great praise when it says she was of **beautiful appearance**, because the only other women who have this Hebrew phrase applied to them are Rachel (Genesis 29:17) and Esther (Esther 2:7).

i. How did a woman like this ever get matched up with a man like Nabal? We can understand it in that day of arranged marriages. But there are many Abigails today who are in that place not because the marriage was arranged but because they chose it. "It is remarkable how many Abigails get married to Nabals. God-fearing women, tender and gentle in the sensibilities, high-minded and noble in their ideals, become tied in an indissoluble union with men for whom they can have no true affinity, even if they have not an unconquerable repugnance." (Meyer)

ii. "May I say to you lovingly, but firmly, if such a circumstance has befallen you, that is no reason for you to invoke the law of the country to get out of the entanglement. Perhaps God knew that you needed the fiery trial to humble you and make you a testimony to your partner. The Bible says you must stay as you are. Maybe there will come to you one day, as there came to Abigail, a new opportunity; but until then, it is for you to prove the grace and power of the Lord in your heart to strengthen you and keep you pure." (Redpath)

3. (4-9) David asks for compensation for his valuable service to Nabal.

When David heard in the wilderness that Nabal was shearing his sheep, David sent ten young men; and David said to the young men, "Go up to Carmel, go to Nabal, and greet him in my name. And thus you shall say to him who lives *in prosperity*: 'Peace *be* to you, peace to your house, and peace to all that you have! Now I have heard that you have shearers. Your shepherds were with us, and we did not hurt them, nor was there anything missing from them all the while they were in Carmel. Ask your young men, and they will tell you. Therefore let *my* young men find favor in your eyes, for we come on a feast day. Please give whatever comes to your hand to your servants and to your son David.'" So when David's young men came, they spoke to Nabal according to all these words in the name of David, and waited.

a. **Please give whatever comes to your hand to your servants and your son David**: David made this request because he performed a valuable service for Nabal, protecting his flocks when Philistine raids were common. To our modern ears it might sound like David ran some kind of "protection racket," but that wasn't the case at all. He performed a worthy, valuable service for Nabal and expected to be compensated.

b. **Nabal was shearing his sheep**: This means David waited until the right time to ask for compensation for his services. David protected Nabal's shepherds and flocks a long time, but did not expect to be compensated until Nabal himself made his money at the "harvest" of sheep shearing.

c. **David sent ten young men**: This shows that David made the request politely. He did it through messengers so Nabal would not be intimidated. He sent the messengers with a greeting full of warmth and kindness (**Peace be to you**), so Nabal would not give out of fear or intimidation.

d. **Your shepherds were with us . . . nor was there anything missing . . . ask your young men, and they will tell you**: This shows that David made the request properly, carefully and patiently giving Nabal an "itemized receipt" for services rendered.

e. **For we come on a feast day**: David politely reminded Nabal of the traditions of generosity surrounding harvest and sheep shearing time.

f. **Please give whatever comes to your hand**: David did not demand any specific payment from Nabal, or set a price - he simply left it up to Nabal's generosity. Then David's messengers simply waited for the reply.

4. (10-12) Nabal's reply to David's request.

Then Nabal answered David's servants, and said, "Who *is* David, and who *is* the son of Jesse? There are many servants nowadays who break away each one from his master. Shall I then take my bread and my water and my meat that I have killed for my shearers, and give *it* to men when I do not know where they *are* from?" So David's young men turned on their heels and went back; and they came and told him all these words.

a. **Who is David, and who is the son of Jesse?** It can't be that Nabal did not know who David was, because David was famous throughout all Israel (1 Samuel 18:5-7). Nabal said this as a direct insult to David - knowing who he was, but refusing to recognize him. In our modern way of speaking, Nabal said, "Who does he think he is?"

b. **There are many servants nowadays who break away each one from his master**: Nabal deepened his insult, saying that David is simply a rebellious servant. This was completely false because David had continually (though not perfectly) conducted himself wisely when attacked by Saul.

c. **Shall I then take my bread . . . my water . . . my meat . . . my shearers, and give it**: Nabal showed what an ungenerous man he was. He looked at everything as *his*, instead of the *LORD's*. True and Biblical generosity doesn't think, "This is mine and I will share it with you." It thinks, "All that I have belongs to the LORD so you can have some of it also."

5. (13) David reacts to Nabal's insulting response.

Then David said to his men, "Every man gird on his sword." So every man girded on his sword, and David also girded on his sword. And about four hundred men went with David, and two hundred stayed with the supplies.

a. **Then David said to his men, "Every man gird on his sword."** David received Nabal's response exactly the way Nabal intended it to be received: with great insult. But Nabal is not dealing with a weak, no-account man; David was a great soldier and warrior. In our modern way of speaking, David would have said to his men, "Lock and load!" In a western movie, he would have said, "Mount up, boys!" David was ready to fight.

i. This is not a high moment for David. He doesn't respond the way the LORD would have him respond to an insult, or even to an attack. God would have us bear insults with love and kindness, returning their evil with our good. This is high ground to walk on, but it is commanded by Jesus: *Whoever slaps you on your right cheek, turn the other to him also.* (Matthew 5:38-39)

ii. David didn't show Nabal the same kindness and longsuffering that he showed to Saul. In just the previous chapter, David spared Saul's life when Saul not only insulted David but also actually attacked him and tried to kill him. David was able to be kind and longsuffering to Saul, but it seems to have been harder to do it towards someone he perceived as his equal or lower than himself. Often, this is true measure of our character - not how we treat our superiors, but how we treat our equals or those "beneath" us in some way or another.

b. **About four hundred men went with David**: David is not coming to Nabal just to make a statement, but to wipe him out. That is why he arms himself and his men and why he left some men behind to watch the stuff and serve as reinforcements.

B. Abigail intercedes between David and Nabal.

1. (14-17) Abigail hears of how Nabal responded to David.

Now one of the young men told Abigail, Nabal's wife, saying, "Look, David sent messengers from the wilderness to greet our master; and he reviled them. But the men *were* very good to us, and we were not hurt, nor did we miss anything as long as we accompanied them, when we were in the fields. They were a wall to us both by night and day, all the time we were with them keeping the sheep. Now therefore, know and consider what you will do, for harm is determined against our master and against all his household. For *he is* such a scoundrel that *one* cannot speak to him."

a. **He reviled them**: One of the servants who witnessed Nabal's response to David's men tells Nabal's wife Abigail that Nabal **reviled** David's men and by extension, David. To **revile** means, "to treat with contemptuous language."

b. **The men were very good to us**: Nabal's servants told Abigail of the valuable service David's men performed. Abigail then knew that David and his men *deserved* compensation.

c. **Know and consider what you will do, for harm is determined**: Nabal's servants read the handwriting on the wall. They knew that David would not take such an insult (theft, actually) lying down. For their own sake and for the sake of the household they asked Abigail to do something (**consider what you will do**).

d. **He is such a scoundrel that one cannot speak to him**: This explains why they did not appeal directly to Nabal. The Book of Proverbs had not been written yet, but they still knew the truth of Proverbs 17:12: *Let a man meet a bear robbed of her cubs, rather than a fool in his folly.* Therefore, they made this life-or-death appeal to Abigail.

2. (18-20) Abigail prepares a present for David and his men.

Then Abigail made haste and took two hundred *loaves* of bread, two skins of wine, five sheep already dressed, five seahs of roasted *grain*, one hundred clusters of raisins, and two hundred cakes of figs, and loaded *them* on donkeys. And she said to her servants, "Go on before me; see, I am coming after you." But she did not tell her husband Nabal. So it was, *as* she rode on the donkey, that she went down under cover of the hill; and there were David and his men, coming down toward her, and she met them.

a. **Abigail made haste**: Since she was *a woman of good understanding* (1 Samuel 25:3), she knew that time was of the essence and something had to be done quickly.

b. **Two hundred loaves of bread . . . two skins of wine . . . five sheep already dressed . . . one hundred clusters of raisins**: Abigail did what Nabal *should* have done, but what he *didn't* do.

i. The fact that Abigail was able to gather so much food so quickly shows how wealthy Nabal was. If this much food was on hand, it makes Nabal's ungenerous reply to David all the worse.

3. (21-22) David vows to massacre Nabal and his entire household.

Now David had said, "Surely in vain I have protected all that this *fellow* has in the wilderness, so that nothing was missed of all that *belongs* to him. And he has repaid me evil for good. May God do so, and more also, to the enemies of David, if I leave one male of all who *belong* to him by morning light."

a. **And he has repaid me evil for good**: David was accurate, but not right in his heart. He ha the facts straight, but not his heart.

b. **If I leave one male of all who belong to him by morning light**: This made David's intention clear - he planned to massacre Nabal and all the males of his household. This was the expected reaction (Nabal's own servants expected it according to 1 Samuel 25:17) but God called David to go further than what the world expected.

4. (23-31) Abigail's appeal to David.

Now when Abigail saw David, she hastened to dismount from the donkey, fell on her face before David, and bowed down to the ground. So she fell at his feet and said: "On me, my lord, *on* me *let* this iniquity *be*! And please let your maidservant speak in your ears, and hear the words of your maidservant. Please, let not my lord regard this scoundrel Nabal. For as his name *is*, so *is* he: Nabal *is* his name, and folly *is* with him. But I, your maidservant, did not see the young men of my lord whom you sent. Now therefore, my lord, *as* the LORD lives and *as* your soul lives, since the LORD has held you back from coming to bloodshed and from avenging yourself with your own hand, now then, let your enemies and

those who seek harm for my lord be as Nabal. And now this present which your maidservant has brought to my lord, let it be given to the young men who follow my lord. Please forgive the trespass of your maidservant. For the LORD will certainly make for my lord an enduring house, because my lord fights the battles of the LORD, and evil is not found in you throughout your days. Yet a man has risen to pursue you and seek your life, but the life of my lord shall be bound in the bundle of the living with the LORD your God; and the lives of your enemies He shall sling out, *as from* the pocket of a sling. And it shall come to pass, when the LORD has done for my lord according to all the good that He has spoken concerning you, and has appointed you ruler over Israel, that this will be no grief to you, nor offense of heart to my lord, either that you have shed blood without cause, or that my lord has avenged himself. But when the LORD has dealt well with my lord, then remember your maidservant."

a. **When Abigail saw David**: Because of the hilly terrain (*she went down under cover of the hill*, 1 Samuel 25:20), Abigail could remain hidden from David right up until they met face to face. It also seems that **Abigail saw David** first, and when David first saw her, she was humbled before him, at the head of a great train of gifts and provisions.

i. In his angry, agitated state, something unexpected made David and his whole company come to an immediate stop: a great procession of gifts, and at the head of that procession, a beautiful woman bowing down before David. This had to make a startling impression on David.

b. **She hastened to dismount from the donkey, fell on her face before David, and bowed down to the ground**: Abigail made her appeal in utmost humility. She didn't come to David as a superior (as the beautiful, rich, and privileged often do) or even as an equal; she came to David as his humble servant.

c. In this appeal, Abigail did many things very right.

i. When she first heard of the crisis, she immediately went into action (*Then Abigail made haste*, 1 Samuel 25:18). She knew this was an urgent situation, so she acted with urgency.

ii. With her first words to David Abigail immediately took the blame on herself (**On me, my lord, on me let this iniquity be!**). Abigail didn't do this because she really believed she was guilty. She took the blame because she knew that David would punish her differently than he might punish her husband Nabal.

iii. Abigail asked permission to speak instead of taking command of the conversation (**Please let your maidservant speak in your ears**).

iv. Abigail smoothly suggested the positive outcome to David in her appeal (**the LORD has held you back from coming to bloodshed**

and from avenging yourself with your own hand). She stated it in a way that almost guided David towards her suggested outcome.

v. Abigail brought David a present (**now this present**), but was wise enough to say that it was for **the young men who follow** David, not for David himself. To say that it was for David would suggest that he was in this just for the money, and that David's insulted dignity could be bought off with money.

vi. Abigail plainly, straightforwardly, asked for forgiveness (**Please forgive the trespass of your maidservant**).

vii. Despite David's present anger and agitation - which is clearly sin - Abigail spoke of David's character in high terms, regarding his present unmentioned state as an aberration (**my lord fights the battles of the Lord, and evil is not found in you throughout your days**).

viii. Abigail reminded David of the Lord's promise for his life (**the Lord will certainly make for my lord an enduring house**). She guided David to look beyond the immediate aggravating circumstances to the bigger promise of God.

ix. Abigail asked David not to do something he would later regret, when God's promise was ultimately fulfilled (**that this will be no grief to you . . . that you have shed blood without cause**). This is perhaps the single best thing that Abigail said; she wisely asked David to consider the outcome of his present course and how bad it would be. She asked him to let the Lord settle the matter instead of taking vengeance into his own hands.

d. Abigail also did some things wrong in her appeal to David.

i. She did all this without her husbands counsel or approval (*But she did not tell her husband Nabal*, 1 Samuel 25:19).

ii. She openly and severely criticized her husband to David (**this scoundrel Nabal . . . Nabal is his name, and folly is with him**). No wife should speak this way of her husband and no husband should speak this way of his wife.

iii. She almost suggested to David that he kill the guilty Nabal (**let your enemies and those who seek harm for my lord be as Nabal**), but that he spare the rest of the household because they were innocent (**shed blood without cause**).

iv. She made herself available for David's future consideration, perhaps in an inappropriate way (**When the Lord has dealt well with my lord, then remember your maidservant**).

v. Abigail was not outstandingly submissive or respectful to her husband Nabal. Though there is no explanation in the Bible perhaps it was justified because this was a legitimate life-or-death situation. If Abigail didn't do what she did, then Nabal and scores of innocent men would die. But the point of the passage is how submissive and respectful Abigail is towards David, not Nabal.

e. **The life of my lord shall be bound in the bundle of the living with the LORD your God; and the lives of your enemies He shall sling out, as from the pocket of a sling**: This perhaps is the strongest point of Abigail's appeal and she used a wonderful turn of speech. She said, "David, you are like a bundle that the LORD holds closely and securely to Himself. Your enemies are like rocks that the LORD will sling away." This invites David to *act* like a man who is close to the LORD.

i. David took his 400 men to do what God could do as easily as throwing a stone out of sling. This had to remind David of a time when he really did trust God for the victory - when he cast a stone out of a sling and killed Goliath. Through her wise words, Abigail focused David's attention from Nabal back unto the LORD.

ii. Abigail's appeal to David was so glorious because it *lifted him up* instead of *beating him down*. David was clearly in the wrong, and Abigail wanted to guide him into the right. But she didn't do it by being negative, by emphasizing to David how wrong and angry and stupid he was - though in fact he was. Instead, Abigail emphasized David's glorious calling and destiny, and the general integrity of his life, and simply asked him to consider if what his present course of action was consistent with that destiny and integrity.

iii. Abigail is a marvelous model of "sweetly speaking submission." Many Christian wives have the idea of "silent submission." They say, "I know my husband is wrong, but I won't tell him. Submission means I should shut up." That is wrong, and they should look to Abigail as an example. Other Christian wives have the idea of "sharply speaking submission." They say, "I know my husband is wrong, and God has appointed me to tell him. And boy, will I!" That is wrong, and they should look to Abigail as an example. Abigail gives the right example - submission that speaks, but speaks sweetly instead of sharply.

iv. Abigail's submission to Nabal was not outstanding but her submission to David was. And David's submission to the LORD was equally outstanding; by giving up the fight, he had to trust God to take care of Nabal.

5. (32-35) David thanks God for Abigail's appeal, and receives her advice.

Then David said to Abigail: "Blessed *is* the LORD God of Israel, who sent you this day to meet me! And blessed *is* your advice and blessed *are* you, because you have kept me this day from coming to bloodshed and from avenging myself with my own hand. For indeed, *as* the LORD God of Israel lives, who has kept me back from hurting you, unless you had hastened and come to meet me, surely by morning light no males would have been left to Nabal!" So David received from her hand what she had brought him, and said to her, "Go up in peace to your house. See, I have heeded your voice and respected your person."

a. **Blessed be the LORD God of Israel**: David was on a sinful course and Abigail, through her bold, quick, and wise appeal, stopped him from sin. He knew God spoke to him through Abigail (**who sent you this day**).

i. David is being taught a good lesson - our hurt feelings never justify disobedience. When others sin against us, we may *feel* justified in sinning against them, but we are never justified by our hurt feelings.

b. **You have kept me this day from coming to bloodshed and from avenging myself with my own hand**: David can also thank God because Abigail successfully reminded him of his destiny - to reign over Israel in righteousness and integrity. If David had slaughtered Nabal and his household it would forever be a black mark against David among Israelites. They would forever wonder if they could really trust him. It might also seal his doom before Saul, because for the first time David would have given Saul a legitimate *reason* to hunt him down as a criminal.

c. **Blessed is your advice, and blessed are you**: David was man enough and wise enough to take counsel from a woman. He knew that the issue wasn't Abigail's gender but that God used her at that time and place. David did well both to receive her advice and to praise her for her boldness in bringing it.

d. **So David received from her hand**: It is important to remember that Abigail did not come to David empty-handed. One reason her appeal was effective was because she *paid David what was owed to him.* When David received it from Abigail he acknowledged that Nabal had paid the bill and there was nothing outstanding.

i. Here David knew the blessing of being *kept from sin.* It surely is a blessing to be forgiven our sins; but it is an even greater blessing to be kept from sin.

C. Nabal dies and David marries Abigail.

1. (36-38) God strikes Nabal dead.

Now Abigail went to Nabal, and there he was, holding a feast in his house, like the feast of a king. And Nabal's heart *was* merry within him, for he *was* very

drunk; therefore she told him nothing, little or much, until morning light. So it was, in the morning, when the wine had gone from Nabal, and his wife had told him these things, that his heart died within him, and he became *like* a stone. Then it came about, *after* about ten days, that the LORD struck Nabal, and he died.

a. **There he was, holding a feast in his house**: Nabal lived up to his name; he was a fool. His life was in imminent danger - his wife knew it, all his servants knew it, but he didn't know it. He eats and gets drunk as if all were fine, and didn't have a care in the world.

i. In this regard, Nabal is a picture of the sinner who goes on rejecting God without regard to God's coming judgment. David certainly would have killed Nabal and it is certain that God will judge the sinner who continues to reject Him.

b. **Like the feast of a king**: All Nabal had to do was invite David to this tremendous feast and Nabal's life would have been spared. Nabal's own greed and foolishness was his undoing.

c. **His heart died within him, and he became like stone . . . the LORD struck Nabal, and he died**: Abigail's wise action saved Nabal from David and saved David from himself. But it could not save Nabal from God's judgment. Nabal was never out of God's reach and when it was the right time, God took care of him.

i. In 1 Samuel 25:33, David was grateful that Abigail's appeal had kept him *from avenging myself with my own hand.* This proves that David did not need to avenge himself with his own hand; God was more than able to do it.

ii. Jesus may have had Nabal in mind when He taught the Parable of the Rich Fool (Luke 12:15-21). That parable describes a man who dies with everything - and nothing.

iii. "All which time he lay like a block in his bed, without repentance or confidence in God; but condemned of his own conscience, he went to his place without noise. Let this be a warning to drunkards." (Trapp)

2. (39-44) David marries Abigail.

So when David heard that Nabal was dead, he said, "Blessed *be* the LORD, who has pleaded the cause of my reproach from the hand of Nabal, and has kept His servant from evil! For the LORD has returned the wickedness of Nabal on his own head." And David sent and proposed to Abigail, to take her as his wife. When the servants of David had come to Abigail at Carmel, they spoke to her saying, "David sent us to you, to ask you to become his wife." Then she arose, bowed her face to the earth, and said, "Here is your maidservant, a servant to

wash the feet of the servants of my lord." So Abigail rose in haste and rode on a donkey, attended by five of her maidens; and she followed the messengers of David, and became his wife. David also took Ahinoam of Jezreel, and so both of them were his wives. But Saul had given Michal his daughter, David's wife, to Palti the son of Laish, who *was* from Gallim.

a. **For the LORD has returned the wickedness of Nabal on his own head**: David knew the death of Nabal was God's judgment, which the LORD showed when David decided to let the LORD avenge him instead of avenging himself.

b. **David sent and proposed to Abigail**: In 1 Samuel 25:31, Abigail asked David, *then remember your maidservant.* Here, David certainly remembered her and he took her as his wife.

i. Was this inappropriate? Wasn't David already married to Saul's daughter Michal? (1 Samuel 18:27) The writer of 1 Samuel explains that at this time, David was not married to Michal, because Saul had taken her away and given her to another man to spite David (David will get Michal back in 2 Samuel 3:13-16). So, Abigail is not really David's second wife; she is his "second first wife."

c. **David also took Ahinoam of Jezreel, and so both of them were his wives**: Though Abigail was David's "second marriage," with **Ahinoam** David took a second wife and will add many more wives.

i. Was this inappropriate? It wasn't directly sin, because God hadn't commanded against it. But it did go against God's ideal, His plan for oneness in a marriage relationship. David was a man of great passions and as a part of that he had many wives. But because David never really followed God's plan and purpose for marriage, his family life was never blessed and peaceful. Family trouble brought David some of the greatest trials of his life.

d. **Here is your maidservant, a servant, to wash the feet of the servants of my lord**: Abigail did not allow her success with David or the death of Nabal make her arrogant or bossy. She greeted the servants of David with the greatest humility.

1 Samuel 26 - David Spares Saul's Life Again

A. David's second opportunity to kill Saul.

1. (1-4) The Ziphites betray David again.

Now the Ziphites came to Saul at Gibeah, saying, "Is David not hiding in the hill of Hachilah, opposite Jeshimon?" Then Saul arose and went down to the Wilderness of Ziph, having three thousand chosen men of Israel with him, to seek David in the Wilderness of Ziph. And Saul encamped in the hill of Hachilah, which *is* opposite Jeshimon, by the road. But David stayed in the wilderness, and he saw that Saul came after him into the wilderness. David therefore sent out spies, and understood that Saul had indeed come.

a. **Now the Ziphites came to Saul**: The people of the city of Ziph - had betrayed David's whereabouts to Saul before (1 Samuel 23:19-23). Now they try to gain King Saul's favor again, by helping Saul find David again.

b. **Having three thousand chosen men of Israel with him, to seek David**: This means Saul went back on his previous repentance shown in 1 Samuel 24:16-21. At that time David had opportunity to kill Saul, but did not take it. When David boldly demonstrated this to Saul, the king was greatly moved emotionally and publicly repented for his murderous intentions toward David. Saul's repentance was deep, sincere, and emotional - but it didn't last very long.

i. **Three thousand chosen men** reminds us that Saul had a great numerical advantage. 3,000 against 600 is a significant advantage.

c. **David therefore sent out spies**: As a wise and capable commander David constantly monitored the movements of Saul. David knew where Saul was but Saul did not know where David was.

2. (5-8) David's second opportunity to kill Saul.

So David arose and came to the place where Saul had encamped. And David saw the place where Saul lay, and Abner the son of Ner, the commander of his army. Now Saul lay within the camp, with the people encamped all around him.

Then David answered, and said to Ahimelech the Hittite and to Abishai the son of Zeruiah, brother of Joab, saying, "Who will go down with me to Saul in the camp?" And Abishai said, "I will go down with you." So David and Abishai came to the people by night; and there Saul lay sleeping within the camp, with his spear stuck in the ground by his head. And Abner and the people lay all around him. Then Abishai said to David, "God has delivered your enemy into your hand this day. Now therefore, please, let me strike him at once with the spear, right to the earth; and I will not *have to strike* him a second time!"

a. **Now Saul lay within the camp**: The King James Version says that *Saul lay within the trench*. That translation is accurate from the Hebrew but gives the wrong idea. The idea is that the perimeter of Israeli army camp was marked by the tracks of their wagons, and it was within the perimeter of the camp that Saul slept. **Saul lay within the camp** is a good translation of the idea.

b. **So David arose and came to the place where Saul had encamped**: The last time David and Saul met David was simply hiding from Saul and Saul happened upon the place where David hid. This time David actively sought Saul out.

i. **So David arose** means that David himself went. He could send any of his 600 men to do this job, and from a military sense it made more sense to send someone else. Why should David go on such a dangerous mission? The fact that David did this shows his boldness and courage; the outcome of it all shows God was leading him in it.

c. **David saw the place where Saul lay, and Abner the son of Ner, the commander of his army**: As the entire army slept Saul slept near **the commander of his army**. Then David, with a trusted assistant (**Abishai the son of Zeruiah**), secretly crept down to where Saul and Abner slept. With Saul's **spear stuck in the ground by his head** and all asleep, Saul was completely vulnerable.

d. **Then Abishai said to David, "God has delivered your enemy into your hand this day"**: As with the last time David could have killed Saul (1 Samuel 24:4), David's associates pointed out that this circumstance was not an accident but designed by God - and the design was for David to take righteous vengeance upon Saul.

i. Abishai made it easy for David: **Please let me strike at once with the spear**. David would not raise his hand against Saul but Abishai would do it, and not feel bad about it in the slightest way. David could say to himself and everyone else, "*I* did not kill Saul."

ii. Abishai also weaves into the matter an element of poetic justice: **the spear** used to kill Saul would be the king's own spear, stuck in the ground by his head. The spear that was thrown at David in attempted murder before (1 Samuel 18:10-11 and 19:9-10) would now be used as the instrument of the LORD's righteous judgment. It all might have seemed to be perfectly given from the hand of God.

3. (9-12) David's response to the opportunity to kill Saul.

And David said to Abishai, "Do not destroy him; for who can stretch out his hand against the Lord's anointed, and be guiltless?" David said furthermore, "*As* the LORD lives, the LORD shall strike him, or his day shall come to die, or he shall go out to battle and perish. The LORD forbid that I should stretch out my hand against the Lord's anointed. But please, take now the spear and the jug of water that *are* by his head, and let us go." So David took the spear and the jug of water *by* Saul's head, and they got away; and no man saw *it* or knew *it* or awoke. For they *were* all asleep, because a deep sleep from the LORD had fallen on them.

a. **Do not destroy him; for who can stretch out his hand against the LORD's anointed, and be guiltless**: It wasn't that David thought Saul was right. David knew more than anyone that Saul was deeply in sin. But David knew that even a sinning Saul was still the **anointed** king over Israel (1 Samuel 10:1). That would only change when God changed it; David would not **stretch out his hand against the LORD's anointed**.

i. We might think that David had more righteous reason than ever to kill Saul. Now, Saul went back on a previous promise to leave David alone. In David's position many would say, "I showed love and let him off once before. I'm full of love, but I'm not stupid. Saul had his chance and he blew it."

b. **The LORD shall strike him, or his day shall come to die, or he shall go out to battle and perish**: David knew that it wasn't "hard" for God to kill Saul. The LORD was more than able to kill Saul at any time. Every breath Saul took was a gift from God. God could allow a wicked man to kill Saul at any time. When it came to striking down an anointed king of Israel, God did not need the services of a godly, righteous man like David.

i. *"Vengeance is Mine, I will repay," says the Lord* (Romans 12:17-21). If vengeance belongs to God, it does not belong to us, so we are to love our enemies and never repay evil with evil.

c. **David took the spear and the jug of water by Saul's head**: David would not kill Saul, but he did take the spear and the jug of water as evidence that he had the opportunity to kill Saul. Probably, David noticed that **a deep sleep from the LORD had fallen on them** all, and knew there was a reason for it.

B. David confronts Saul again with the evidence of his mercy.

1. (13-16) David chides Abner, Saul's bodyguard.

Now David went over to the other side, and stood on the top of a hill afar off, a great distance *being* between them. And David called out to the people and to Abner the son of Ner, saying, "Do you not answer, Abner?" Then Abner answered and said, "Who *are* you, calling out to the king?" So David said to Abner, "*Are* you not a man? And who *is* like you in Israel? Why then have you not guarded your lord the king? For one of the people came in to destroy your lord the king. This thing that you have done *is* not good. *As* the LORD lives, you deserve to die, because you have not guarded your master, the Lord's anointed. And now see where the king's spear *is*, and the jug of water that *was* by his head."

a. **Are you not a man? And who is like you in Israel? Why then have you not guarded your lord the king?** In this vivid scene, David implied that *he* cared more for Saul's life than Abner did.

b. **See where the king's spear is, and the jug of water that was by his head**: This dramatic evidence - like the evidence of the corner of Saul's robe in 1 Samuel 24:11 - was undeniable proof that David had the opportunity to kill Saul, but did not do it.

2. (17-20) David calls out to Saul.

Then Saul knew David's voice, and said, "*Is* that your voice, my son David?" And David said, "*It is* my voice, my lord, O king." And he said, "Why does my lord thus pursue his servant? For what have I done, or what evil *is* in my hand? Now therefore, please, let my lord the king hear the words of his servant: If the LORD has stirred you up against me, let Him accept an offering. But if *it is* the children of men, *may* they *be* cursed before the LORD, for they have driven me out this day from sharing in the inheritance of the LORD, saying, 'Go, serve other gods.' So now, do not let my blood fall to the earth before the face of the LORD. For the king of Israel has come out to seek a flea, as when one hunts a partridge in the mountains."

a. **My lord, O king . . . my lord . . . please let my lord . . . his servant**: This phrasing shows that David spoke to Saul with genuine humility. Since David was so right and Saul was so wrong, it was easy for David to project a superior attitude towards Saul, but he didn't.

b. **What have I done, or what evil is in my hand?** David first asked Saul to consider the facts and to clearly think about what David did.

c. **If the LORD has stirred you up against me . . . if it is the children of men**: David made it easier for Saul to repent. David knew very well that the LORD or other men had not stirred up Saul but that it came from Saul's own bitterness, carnality, and jealousy. But he offered these suggestions to Saul to give him an easier way to repent. He could admit that his actions against David were wrong without admitting that they originated with himself.

d. **They have driven me out this day from abiding in the inheritance of the LORD, saying, "Go, serve other gods."** David revealed his own heart's struggle under the pressure from Saul's relentless persecution. What hurt David the most was that he couldn't go to the house of God and openly be with the people of God, living his life after the LORD as he longed to. The pressure of all this tempted David to consider leaving Israel altogether and to go among those who worshipped other gods.

e. **Now therefore, do not let my blood fall to the earth before the face of the LORD**: David concluded his appeal to Saul with a simple request. "Saul, please don't kill me!"

i. "There is a vast deal of dignity in this speech of David, arising from a consciousness of his own innocence. He neither begs his life from Saul, nor offers one argument to prevail upon him to desist [stop] from his felonious attempts, but refers the whole matter to God, as the judge and vindicator of oppressed innocence." (Clarke)

f. **As when one hunts a partridge in the mountains**: "It is worthy of remark that the Arabs, observing that partridges, being put up several times, soon become so weary as not to be able to fly; they in this manner hunt them upon the mountains, till at last they can knock them down with their clubs. It was in this manner that Saul hunted David, coming hastily upon him, and putting him up from time to time, in hopes that he should at length, by frequent repetitions of it, be able to destroy him." (Clarke)

3. (21) Saul apologizes to David.

Then Saul said, "I have sinned. Return, my son David. For I will harm you no more, because my life was precious in your eyes this day. Indeed I have played the fool and erred exceedingly."

a. **I have sinned**: The last time Saul was in this situation he was overcome with emotion. His feelings seemed right but his life was not changed (1 Samuel 24:16-21). This time there is something cold and mechanical about Saul's words. The words seem right but the feelings aren't there.

b. **For I will harm you no more . . . Indeed I have played the fool and erred exceedingly**: It *seems* - both from the "feel" of the verse and Saul's subsequent actions - that Saul isn't repentant but only ; bitterly realizes that David got the better of him again. His words in 1 Samuel 26:25 express this also: *You shall both do great things and also still prevail.*

i. "The Apostle makes a great distinction, and rightly, between the sorrow of the world and the sorrow of a godly repentance which needeth not to be repented of. Certainly Saul's confession of sin belonged to the former; while the cry of the latter comes out in Psalm 51, extorted from David by the crimes after the years." (Meyer)

c. Morgan on **I have played the fool**: "In these words we have a perfect autobiography. In them the complete life-story of this man is told."

4. (22-25) David explains to Saul why he did not kill him.

And David answered and said, "Here is the king's spear. Let one of the young men come over and get it. May the Lord repay every man *for* his righteousness and his faithfulness; for the Lord delivered you into *my* hand today, but I would not stretch out my hand against the Lord's anointed. And indeed, as your life was valued much this day in my eyes, so let my life be valued much in the eyes of the Lord, and let Him deliver me out of all tribulation." Then Saul said to David, "*May* you *be* blessed, my son David! You shall both do great things and also still prevail." So David went on his way, and Saul returned to his place.

a. **May the Lord repay every man for his righteousness and his faithfulness**: David trusted in God who blesses the righteous and the faithful. David knew the truth of Hebrews 6:10 before it was written: *For God is not unjust to forget your work and labor of love which you have shown toward His name.*

i. David understood the principle Jesus spoke of in Matthew 7:2: *With the same measure you use, it will be measured back to you.* David wanted the "extra big scoop" of God's mercy for himself, so David gave Saul the "extra big scoop" of mercy. That generous measure of mercy will be a great blessing to David later in his life.

b. **So let my life be valued much in the eyes of the Lord**: David wanted to fulfill his call to be the next king of Israel. But he wanted *both* the throne and the blessing of God. He refused to take the throne through murder or rebellion. He would wait until it came to him God's way. In this, David trusted that God would protect him when he did eventually come to reign over Israel.

i. David held on to this principle, and when he became king, he recognized that his righteousness was rewarded (Psalm 18:20-27).

c. **David went on his way**: Saul invited David to *return* (1 Samuel 26:21) but David did not take the invitation. He waited to see if the repentant words Saul spoke showed a genuine repentance in his life. But as David went **on his way** he was faced with the temptation he spoke of in 1 Samuel 26:19 - tempted to flee Israel all together and live among the ungodly.

i. "Knowing Saul's unstable and deceitful heart, he would not trust to any of his professions or promises, but kept out of his reach." (Poole)

ii. "Since now there is nothing more to be said, David and Saul part, never to see each other again." (Youngblood)

1 Samuel 27 - David Flees to the Philistines

A. David joins with the Philistine leader Achish.

1. (1) David's discouraged decision.

And David said in his heart, "Now I shall perish someday by the hand of Saul. *There is* nothing better for me than that I should speedily escape to the land of the Philistines; and Saul will despair of me, to seek me anymore in any part of Israel. So I shall escape out of his hand."

a. **David said in his heart**: The sad story of 1 Samuel 27 begins with something **David said in his heart**. He may have never said it out loud; he may have never said it to anyone else; he may have never said it to God. But **David said** it **in his heart**. What we say in our heart has a tremendous power to shape our thinking, our actions, even our whole destiny.

b. **Now I shall perish someday by the hand of Saul**: This is what David said in his heart. That was a word of discouragement coming from a heart tired of trusting God for His continued deliverance. In his discouragement David forgot God's past deliverance.

i. "I remember on one occasion, to my shame, being sad and doubtful of heart, and a kind friend took out a paper and read to me a short extract from a discourse upon faith. I very soon detected the author of the extract; my friend was reading to me from one of my own sermons. Without saying a word he just left it to my own conscience, for he had convicted me of committing the very fault against which I had so earnestly declaimed." (Spurgeon)

c. **There is nothing better for me than that I should speedily escape to the land of the Philistines**: David decided to leave Israel and live among the idol worshipping Philistines. David was so discouraged that he thought there was **nothing better** for him in Israel and among God's people.

d. **Saul will despair of me, to seek me anymore in any part of Israel. So I shall escape out of his hand**. Before David trusted in the LORD to protect him from the hand of Saul. Now, David gave up trusting in the LORD and instead left the land of promise, left the people of God, and found "protection" among the Philistines.

i. **Saul will despair**: Saul will not despair if David leaves the land of promise. Saul will not despair if David forsakes the people of God and joins the ungodly. It is David who is in **despair**, not Saul.

ii. Saul could never drive David to the Philistines. If Saul told David, "You must leave the people of God and go live among the Philistines," David would never bow to it. But *discouragement* and *despair* are more powerful enemies than Saul. *Discouragement* and *despair* will drive David to do something that Saul could never make him do.

2. (2-4) David goes over to Achish, leader of Gath.

Then David arose and went over with the six hundred men who *were* with him to Achish the son of Maoch, king of Gath. So David dwelt with Achish at Gath, he and his men, each man with his household, *and* David with his two wives, Ahinoam the Jezreelitess, and Abigail the Carmelitess, Nabal's widow. And it was told Saul that David had fled to Gath; so he sought him no more.

a. **David arose and went over with the six hundred men**: David's discouraged and despairing heart didn't only affect himself; he led **six hundred men** out of the land of promise to live with the ungodly. Before David sunk into his pit of discouragement and despair, he would have never dreamed of doing this.

i. 1 Samuel 27:3 makes it even worse: **Each man with his household**. David's defection to the Philistines touched even more than the **six hundred men**, it touched all their families. It directly touched David's household also, because **Ahinoam** and **Abigail** were with him.

b. **So David dwelt with Achish at Gath**: Previously (recorded in 1 Samuel 21:10-15), David briefly went over to Achish of the Philistines, believing there might be a place of refuge for him. God allowed that experience to quickly turn sour, and David pretended to be a madman so he could escape. In his discouragement and despair David will go down a road of sin he has been down before.

i. Achish received David this time when he would not in 1 Samuel 21:10-15 for two reasons. First, it is clear now when it wasn't clear before that David and Achish share the same enemy, Saul. Second, David now brings with him 600 fighting men, whom Achish can use as mercenaries.

c. **It was told Saul that David had fled to Gath; so he sought him no more**: David accomplished his immediate goal, because Saul stopped pursuing him. But now David is in a place of compromise that will leave him worse off than before. He is actually submitting to a Philistine master.

i. We have no record of any Psalms that David wrote during this time. This was not a high point in his spiritual life. He didn't write sweet Psalms unto the LORD.

ii. "The sweet singer was mute. He probably acquired a few new strains of music, or even mastered some fresh instruments, while sojourning at Gath, a memory of which is perpetuated in the term *Gittith*, a term which frequently occurs in the inscriptions of the psalms composed afterward. But who would barter a song for a melody, a psalm for a guitar? It was a poor exchange." (Meyer)

B. David becomes a bandit.

1. (5-7) David receives the city of Ziklag.

Then David said to Achish, "If I have now found favor in your eyes, let them give me a place in some town in the country, that I may dwell there. For why should your servant dwell in the royal city with you?" So Achish gave him Ziklag that day. Therefore Ziklag has belonged to the kings of Judah to this day. Now the time that David dwelt in the country of the Philistines was one full year and four months.

a. **David said to Achish, "If I have now found favor in your eyes."** Before, David never cared about finding favor in the eyes of a Philistine ruler. This is a great change in David.

b. **Why should your servant dwell in the royal city with you?** It smarts to hear David say to a Philistine ruler, "**your servant**." David wanted his own city because "he needed freedom to operate his own independent policy without being observed too closely." (Baldwin)

c. **Let them give me a place . . . that I may dwell there**: In David's mind, this isn't just a visit to the Philistines. He may say to himself that he will someday return to Israel, but he isn't planning on a short stay among the ungodly. He wants to **dwell there** and he did for **one full year and four months**.

i. Now David, his 600 men and their families lived in a completely new situation. They lived in a fortified city, a formal place of defense. But apart from God, they aren't safer in the city.

2. (8-9) David's new occupation: a roving bandit.

And David and his men went up and raided the Geshurites, the Girzites, and the Amalekites. For those nations were the inhabitants of the land from of old,

as you go to Shur, even as far as the land of Egypt. Whenever David attacked the land, he left neither man nor woman alive, but took away the sheep, the oxen, the donkeys, the camels, and the apparel, and returned and came to Achish.

a. **David and his men went up and raided**: The Hebrew word **raided** comes from the verb *to strip*, with the idea of stripping the dead for loot. David attacked these villages or encampments, killed some of the men, stripped them for treasure or armor, and robbed the people of the village or encampment. This was no way of life for a man after God's own heart.

b. **The Geshurites, the Girzites, and the Amalekites**: David hasn't *totally* turned against God and His people. For now, he only attacks the enemies of Israel. This probably gave David some comfort but it is a small consolation to know that you aren't as bad as you possibly could be.

c. **He left neither man nor woman alive, but took away**: Even though he attacked the enemies of Israel, David was nothing more than an armed robber and murderer. He killed all the people of the village or encampment, took the spoil, and did it without the approval or guidance of God. He now fought wars for profit instead of for God's honor.

3. (10-12) David lies to Achish.

Then Achish would say, "Where have you made a raid today?" And David would say, "Against the southern *area* of Judah, or against the southern *area* of the Jerahmeelites, or against the southern *area* of the Kenites." David would save neither man nor woman alive, to bring *news* to Gath, saying, "Lest they should inform on us, saying, 'Thus David did.' " And thus *was* his behavior all the time he dwelt in the country of the Philistines. So Achish believed David, saying, "He has made his people Israel utterly abhor him; therefore he will be my servant forever."

a. **And David would say, "Against the southern area of Judah."** David didn't lie to Achish because he was ashamed of what he did. He lied to gain favor with Achish. He knew the Philistine leader would be pleased to hear that David raided his own people of Israel.

b. **David would save neither man nor woman alive, to bring news to Gath**: In his raids, David killed all the men and the women so his lie to Achish would not be exposed.

i. Much later in his life, David will have a far more notorious season of sin with Bathsheba, and end up killing her husband Uriah to cover his sin. Though that later event is far more famous, the root of sin that nourished it began way back in 1 Samuel 27. Here, many years before David killed Uriah to cover his sin, David killed these men and women in his raids to cover his sin. The roots of sin must be dealt with or they come back with greater strength.

c. **So Achish believed David, saying, "He has made his people Israel utterly abhor him; therefore he will be my servant forever."** Achish felt he was in a good place. David was trapped in a web and Achish was the spider. Achish believed that David burned all his bridges with the people of God. It all looks pretty dark; but David had not - and could not - burn his bridge with God.

4. (28:1-2) David takes sides with the Philistines against Israel.

Now it happened in those days that the Philistines gathered their armies together for war, to fight with Israel. And Achish said to David, "You assuredly know that you will go out with me to battle, you and your men." And David said to Achish, "Surely you know what your servant can do." And Achish said to David, "Therefore I will make you one of my chief guardians forever."

a. **Achish said to David, "You assuredly know that you will go out with me to battle, you and your men."** David had lied to Achish, telling him that he raided the people of Israel. Now David is forced to *live the lie* he gave to Achish.

b. **David said to Achish, "Surely you know what your servant can do."** Here, David seems *completely surrendered to the ungodly Achish.* He will fight for the Philistines, against Israel. We might wish that David was really operating as a "double agent" and he planned to turn on the Philistines in the midst of battle. But the text gives us *no reason* for such an optimistic perspective. David has come to a very low place.

i. To some degree, most every Christian has been where David is at in this back sliding state. We can *understand* what David is doing; but it is still wrong, and very dangerous.

ii. "But it pleased God to leave David to himself in this, as well as in other particulars, that those might be sensible demonstrations of the infirmities of the best men; and of the necessity of God's grace, and daily direction and assistance; and of the freeness and riches of God's mercy, in passing by such great offences." (Poole)

1 Samuel 28 - Saul and the Medium of Endor

The first two verses of 1 Samuel 28 connect with the previous chapter, so they are examined in the commentary on 1 Samuel 27.

A. Saul's distressing situation

1. (3-5) Saul's fear at the attack from the Philistines.

Now Samuel had died, and all Israel had lamented for him and buried him in Ramah, in his own city. And Saul had put the mediums and the spiritists out of the land. Then the Philistines gathered together, and came and encamped at Shunem. So Saul gathered all Israel together, and they encamped at Gilboa. When Saul saw the army of the Philistines, he was afraid, and his heart trembled greatly.

a. **Samuel had died**: Samuel's death was originally reported in 1 Samuel 25:1. Here, the fact is mentioned again to emphasize the spiritual vacuum left by Samuel's departure.

b. **Saul had put the mediums and the spiritists out of the land**: To his credit, Saul obeyed the commands in the Mosaic Law to cast out those who practiced occultic arts. God commanded that **mediums** and **spiritists** (those who either can or claim to contact the dead and spirit beings) should have no place among His people in passages such as Leviticus 19:31, 20:6, 27 and in Deuteronomy 18:9-14. Saul did this in his earlier days when he was still influenced by Samuel's leadership.

i. Things such as tarot cards, palm readers, horoscopes and Ouija Boards are modern attempts to practice forms of spiritism. They are dangerous links to the demonic, even if undertaken in a spirit of fun. Christians should have nothing to do with occultic arts or practices.

c. **Then the Philistines gathered together, and came and encamped at Shunem**: The geography of **Shunem** means that the Philistines made an aggressive attack against Saul and Israel.

i. "*Shunem*, in the Valley of Jezreel, was about twenty miles north of Aphek, the most northerly Philistine city. The fact that the Philistines had penetrated thus far gives an indication of their dominance over Saul's kingdom, and of their intention to press further east to the Jordan." (Baldwin)

d. **When Saul saw the army of the Philistines, he was afraid, and his heart trembled greatly**: Long before his downward spiral when Saul still walked in the Spirit, he was a man of great courage (as in 1 Samuel 11:6-11). Saul began to lose his courage when the Spirit withdrew from him (1 Samuel 16:14) and now after the death of Samuel his courage seems almost completely gone.

2. (6) God will not speak to Saul.

And when Saul inquired of the LORD, the LORD did not answer him, either by dreams or by Urim or by the prophets.

a. **When Saul inquired of the LORD, the LORD did not answer him**: Saul was in a terrible place. The Philistines threatened, Saul's courage failed, and now God was silent when Saul sought Him. Saul hoped God would speak to him through **dreams**, but God was silent. He hoped God would speak to him through the **Urim**, but God was silent. He wanted to hear from God through the **prophets**, but God would not talk to Saul.

b. **The LORD did not answer him**: This silence demonstrates that God will not always answer everyone who seeks Him; not when a man is in a place of judgment as Saul is. King Saul *has* rejected and *is currently rejecting* God's previously revealed will. Since Saul didn't care to obey God in what he already knew, God will not give him more to know.

i. At the very least, Saul knew that God did not want him hunting David, hoping to kill him. Saul said as much in passages such as 1 Samuel 24:16-20 and 26:21. Yet Saul disregarded what he knew to be God's will in this matter. If we want God to guide us, we must follow what guidance we *already* have from Him.

ii. When we reject the word of the LORD we can still be comforted by the fact that He speaks to us. As we continue to reject His word He may stop speaking to us - and we will lose even that comfort.

B. Saul consults a spirit medium.

1. (7-8) Saul seeks out a medium.

Then Saul said to his servants, "Find me a woman who is a medium, that I may go to her and inquire of her." And his servants said to him, "In fact, *there is* a woman who is a medium at En Dor." So Saul disguised himself and put on other clothes, and he went, and two men with him; and they came to the woman by

night. And he said, "Please conduct a seance for me, and bring up for me the one I shall name to you."

a. **Find me a woman who is a medium, that I may go to her and inquire of her**: It wasn't easy to find a **medium** in the land of Israel because Saul had previously put them out of the land. So Saul asked his staff to find him one and they suggested a woman in the city of **En Dor**.

i. Traditionally, this woman is known as *the Witch of Endor*. It may be appropriate to call her a witch but it is more accurate to call her a **medium** or a *necromancer* - one who makes contact with the dead. The Hebrew word for **medium** is *owb*, and it has the idea of "mumbling" or speaking with a strange, hollow sound - as if one were "channeling," with a dead person speaking through them. The Hebrew word has in mind the *sound* the channel makes as they speak. The English word **medium** has in mind the *concept* of a channel - they stand in-between the world of the living and the dead, and communicate between the two worlds.

ii. "*Endor* was only a short distance away, on the north of the Hill of Moreh, and accessible despite the Philistine forces close by." (Baldwin) Endor was "located four miles northeast of Shunem and thus dangerously close to where the Philistines were encamped." (Youngblood)

b. **Saul disguised himself . . . and he went**: As Saul sought the medium he brought upon himself a curse. God said in Leviticus 20:6: *And the person who turns after mediums and familiar spirits, to prostitute himself with them, I will set My face against that person and cut him off from his people.*

c. **Bring up the one I shall name for you**: Saul will ask the medium to channel the deceased prophet Samuel. He did this because he wanted to know what God might say to him. Saul is like a man going to a palm reader to hear the will of God.

i. This shows the depth of Saul's fall from God, and how it affected his mind. He obviously isn't thinking clearly here. Once Saul rejected the truth, he was likely to fall for even the most foolish deception.

2. (9-10) Saul answers the suspicions of the medium.

Then the woman said to him, "Look, you know what Saul has done, how he has cut off the mediums and the spiritists from the land. Why then do you lay a snare for my life, to cause me to die?" And Saul swore to her by the LORD, saying, "*As* the LORD lives, no punishment shall come upon you for this thing."

a. **Why then do you lay a snare for my life, to cause me to die?** The medium wondered if this was a government "sting" operation; but Saul assured her - swearing in the name of the LORD, no less - that she would not be punished.

b. **Saul swore to her by the LORD**: Saul's oath in the name of the LORD reminds us that spiritual jargon means nothing. As certainly **as the LORD lives** Saul was in complete disobedience and darkness. This is the last time Saul used the name of the LORD in the book of 1 Samuel and he used it to swear to a medium that she will not be punished.

3. (11-14) To the medium's surprise, Samuel appears.

Then the woman said, "Whom shall I bring up for you?" And he said, "Bring up Samuel for me." When the woman saw Samuel, she cried out with a loud voice. And the woman spoke to Saul, saying, "Why have you deceived me? For you *are* Saul!" And the king said to her, "Do not be afraid. What did you see?" And the woman said to Saul, "I saw a spirit ascending out of the earth." So he said to her, "What *is* his form?" And she said, "An old man is coming up, and he *is* covered with a mantle." And Saul perceived that it *was* Samuel, and he stooped with *his* face to the ground and bowed down.

a. **Bring up Samuel for me**: Why did Saul want to see Samuel? Considering the times Samuel strongly rebuked Saul (such as in 1 Samuel 15:22-29), we might think that Samuel was the last person Saul would want to see. Probably, Saul wanted to remember his "good old days" with Samuel, when the prophet was his guide and mentor (1 Samuel 9:25-26).

i. In the midst of his sin, depression and demonic influence, Saul forgot that Samuel was in fact his adversary when he slipped into sin (1 Samuel 13:13-14 and 15:22-29).

b. **When the woman saw Samuel, she cried out with a loud voice**: The medium was probably so shocked because she was a fraud, and most of her dealings with the spirit realm were mere tricks. Now Samuel *really* appeared from the world beyond and she was completely surprised to have a *real* encounter with the spirit realm.

i. In addition, we can say that this medium was familiar with the presence of demonic spirits but the presence of the Holy Spirit was probably unfamiliar to her. The holy presence of the Holy Spirit may have seemed terrifying to her. "The indications are that this was an extraordinary event for her, and a frightening one because she was not in control." (Baldwin)

c. **Why have you deceived me? For you are Saul!** The medium is also surprised because now she knew that she practiced her craft before the same king who drove out all the mediums and spiritists from Israel. She had reason to be afraid both of the real spiritual presence she saw and the king right beside her.

i. We are not told how the medium knew it was Samuel. It might have been something Samuel said when he first appeared. It might have been a word of supernatural knowledge, communicated to her either from God or from the world of the demonic.

d. **And the woman said to Saul, "I saw a spirit ascending out of the earth."** The Hebrew word translated by "**spirit**" in the New King James Version is actually the Hebrew word *elohim* - literally, "gods" but often applied to the One God in plural form. This indicates both the truth of the Trinity and God's greatness, which is indicated in Hebrew by the plural form. When the medium said she saw an *elohim,* she did not mean that she saw the One True God and she did not mean that Samuel was deified. Instead, speaking from her own pagan context, she called this appearing of Samuel an *elohim* because that was what it seemed to be in her pagan vocabulary. It was only *she* who called Samuel an *elohim.*

i. "She useth the plural number, *gods*, either after the manner of the Hebrew language, which commonly useth that word of one person; or after the language and custom of the heathens." (Poole)

e. **Saul perceived that it was Samuel**: However Samuel appeared, he was visible to both the medium *and* Saul. This wasn't a "crystal ball" appearance that only the medium could pretend to see. Nor was it a "voice in the dark" as in a séance. This was a real appearance of Samuel.

f. **It was Samuel**: This strange incident is controversial, and several different approaches have been used to understand this passage. Here are four of the most commonly suggested possibilities.

i. Some believe that *this was a hallucination of the medium.* But this doesn't make sense because it doesn't explain why the medium was so frightened. It doesn't explain why Saul also saw Samuel and why Samuel spoke to Saul, not to the medium.

ii. Some believe that *this was a deception by the medium.* But this also isn't an adequate explanation, for the same reasons given to the previous suggestion.

iii. Some believe that *this was a demonic impersonation of Samuel.* It is possible that the medium, with her occultic powers, summoned a demonic spirit that deceived both her and Saul. But this suggestion is also inadequate, because it does not speak to the issue of *motive.* After all, what advantage does Satan gain by "Samuel's" words to Saul?

iv. Some believe that *this was a genuine (but strange) appearance of Samuel.* This is the best explanation because it is supported by the reaction of the medium, who got more than she bargained for. It is also supported by the *truth* of what Samuel said (and the text says that *Samuel* said it). Some may say that it is impossible for Samuel to reappear in some way, coming from the world beyond back to this world. But

Moses and Elijah also came from the world beyond back to this world when they appeared with Jesus at the Transfiguration (Matthew 17:3).

v. Clarke makes an additional valuable point: "I believe that the woman of En-dor had no power over *Samuel*; and that *no incantation* can avail over any *departed saint of God*, nor indeed over any *human* disembodied spirit." Samuel really came, but not because the medium called for him. Samuel appeared because God had a special purpose for it.

g. **It was Samuel**: God allowed this strange appearance of Samuel because it accomplished two things. It re-confirmed the coming judgment upon King Saul in a dramatic way, and it taught the medium a powerful lesson about the danger of her occultic craft.

i. "I believe *Samuel did actually appear to Saul*; and that he was sent by the especial *mercy of God* to warn this infatuated king of his approaching death, that he might have an opportunity to make his peace with his Maker." (Clarke)

ii. When we close our ears to God He will find unusual - and perhaps uncomfortable - ways to speak to us. "That he did appear to Saul, there can be no question, but he did not come in response to her call. He was sent of God, for the express purpose of rebuking Saul for his unholy traffic with these evil things, and to pronounce his doom." (Morgan)

C. Samuel speaks to Saul.

1. (15-18) Samuel tells King Saul why the LORD will not speak to him.

Now Samuel said to Saul, "Why have you disturbed me by bringing me up?" And Saul answered, "I am deeply distressed; for the Philistines make war against me, and God has departed from me and does not answer me anymore, neither by prophets nor by dreams. Therefore I have called you, that you may reveal to me what I should do." Then Samuel said: "Why then do you ask me, seeing the LORD has departed from you and has become your enemy? And the LORD has done for Himself as He spoke by me. For the LORD has torn the kingdom out of your hand and given it to your neighbor, David. Because you did not obey the voice of the LORD nor execute His fierce wrath upon Amalek, therefore the LORD has done this thing to you this day.

a. **Why have you disturbed me?** Samuel's words would be in the mouth of anyone who left the place of comfort and blessing in the world beyond to come back to the earth. Samuel would rather be back where he was.

i. This is an indication to us of the *reality* of the world beyond. Though he passed from this world, Samuel was in a real place, living a real existence.

ii. Properly speaking, Samuel was not in *heaven*. Jesus explained in the story of the rich man and Lazarus (Luke 16:19-31) that before the finished work of Jesus on the cross, the believing dead went to a place of comfort and blessing known as *Abraham's bosom*. When Jesus finished his work on the cross, sin's penalty was paid for these believing dead and they were then ushered into heaven.

b. **I am deeply distressed**: Saul explained his problem to Samuel. First, **the Philistines make war against me**. But far worse than that is the fact that Saul knows that **God has departed from me and does not answer me any more**. Saul then revealed *why* he called for Samuel: **that you may reveal to me what I should do.**

i. **God has departed from me**: "God never departs from a man until the man has departed from Him. Then, in the interests of righteousness, God is against that man." (Morgan)

ii. **What I should do**: "Saul is asking for guidance when his course of action is obvious: he has to fight the Philistines. What he really wants is reassurance that all will be well and that he will win the battle." (Baldwin)

c. **Why do you ask me, seeing the LORD has departed from you and has become your enemy?** Samuel was on the LORD's side, so if the LORD wouldn't tell Saul what he wanted, he didn't have any reason to believe that Samuel would tell him. Perhaps Saul kept seeking, hoping that the news would get better, but it never did.

d. **As He spoke by me . . . the voice of the LORD**: Essentially, Samuel confirmed what God already said to Saul. The message of the LORD to Saul is disturbingly consistent, no matter which strange way God chooses to bring the message.

i. The test for any "spirit encounter" or "angelic revelation" is its faithfulness to the Biblical message. It doesn't matter what kind of impressive encounter one has with a spiritual being; even if *an angel from heaven* (or Samuel himself!) *preach any other gospel to you . . . let him be accursed* (Galatians 1:8).

e. **Because you did not . . . execute His fierce wrath upon Amalek, therefore the LORD has done this thing to you this day**: Samuel called Saul's mind back to what happened in 1 Samuel 15. In that chapter, Samuel told Saul "*The LORD has torn the kingdom of Israel from you today, and has given it to a neighbor of yours, who is better than you . . . For He is not a man, that He should relent*" (1 Samuel 15:28-29). Apparently, in the fifteen or so years since the events of 1 Samuel 15, Saul thought that perhaps the LORD would change His mind. Samuel told Saul that the LORD had not changed His mind at all.

i. Samuel makes this point exactly when he quotes from the 1 Samuel 15:28-29 passage with these words: **For the LORD has torn the kingdom out of your hand and given it to your neighbor, David**. God's word to Saul didn't change from the time He first said it until the time it would be fulfilled. Perhaps Saul thought that *time* would change God's mind; but *time* never changes God's mind. Our *repentance* and *genuine brokenness* may change God's mind, but never time.

ii. When the medium saw Samuel, she said he was *covered with a mantle*. The *mantle* was probably Samuel's robe, which would have identified him as both a prophet and a priest. In 1 Samuel 15:27, when Samuel announced that God would take the kingdom away from Saul, Saul grabbed Samuel's robe in desperation. The Hebrew word used for *robe* in 1 Samuel 15:27 (*meheel*) is the same word used for *mantle* in 1 Samuel 28:14. It is likely that when Samuel appeared before the medium and Saul, he wore this same torn robe to remind Saul that **the LORD has torn the kingdom out of your hand and given it to your neighbor, David**.

2. (19) Samuel tells Saul about his fate.

"Moreover the LORD will also deliver Israel with you into the hand of the Philistines. And tomorrow you and your sons *will be* with me. The LORD will also deliver the army of Israel into the hand of the Philistines."

a. **Tomorrow you and your sons will be with me**: Saul learned from Samuel that he would die the next day. In 1 Samuel 28:15, Saul asked to know *what I should do*. Samuel never told him what to do because it was too late to *do* anything. All Samuel told him was what would happen, and God's judgment was already in motion.

i. Before this time, Saul had plenty of time to repent but now time has run out. We can never assume that we will have as much time as we want to repent. The desire and opportunity to repent are gifts from God. If we have the desire and the opportunity today we must seize upon it, because they may not be there tomorrow.

ii. **You and your sons will be with me** does not mean that Saul was going to heaven and be with the believing dead. In the story Jesus told in Luke 16:19-31, the blessed dead and the cursed dead were both in the same general area. The believing dead were in the place of comfort knows as *Abraham's bosom* but the cursed were in a place of torment. Saul would be in the same *general* area as Samuel, but not the same *specific place*.

b. **The LORD will deliver Israel with you into the hand of the Philistines . . . you and your sons**: When judgment fell upon Saul it would also trouble the people around him. His sons and all Israel would also suffer.

i. "Can any person read this, properly considering the situation of this unfortunate monarch, the triumph of the enemies of God, and the speedy ruin in which the godlike Jonathan is about to be involved, without feeling the keenest anguish of heart?" (Clarke)

D. Saul's reaction and departure.

1. (20) Saul reacts with fear and a loss of all strength.

Then immediately Saul fell full length on the ground, and was dreadfully afraid because of the words of Samuel. And there was no strength in him, for he had eaten no food all day or all night.

a. **Because of the words of Samuel**: It wasn't just that Samuel told Saul that he would die or fall in battle before the Philistines. Far worse to Saul was the knowledge that the LORD was his adversary. Not only were the Philistines set against him, so was the LORD God. Knowing this was more than Saul could bear.

2. (21-25) The medium comforts Saul.

And the woman came to Saul and saw that he was severely troubled, and said to him, "Look, your maidservant has obeyed your voice, and I have put my life in my hands and heeded the words which you spoke to me. Now therefore, please, heed also the voice of your maidservant, and let me set a piece of bread before you; and eat, that you may have strength when you go on *your* way." But he refused and said, "I will not eat." So his servants, together with the woman, urged him; and he heeded their voice. Then he arose from the ground and sat on the bed. Now the woman had a fatted calf in the house, and she hastened to kill it. And she took flour and kneaded *it*, and baked unleavened bread from it. So she brought *it* before Saul and his servants, and they ate. Then they rose and went away that night.

a. **The woman came to Saul and saw that he was severely troubled**: It's a sad note when a practitioner of the occult comforts the King of Israel. But they were two of the same kind; each lived in rebellion to God, and each was under judgment from the LORD.

b. **And they ate**: The dinner Saul ate that night was like the last meal of a man on death row, waiting execution in the morning.

c. **Then he rose and went away that night**: Saul left this strange encounter resigned to his fate. "The additional information, that within twenty-four hours he and his sons would be dead, was no help at all to his morale. Indeed he would have been better without it. He did himself no good by doing what he had decreed to be unlawful. God's word stood and could not be altered. He should have believed it instead of thinking that by further consultation he could reverse its judgment. The Lord did not answer him, because there was no more to be said." (Baldwin)

1 Samuel 29 - The Philistines Reject David

A. The Philistine rulers object to David's presence among the Philistine army.

1. (1-3) Achish defends David before the Philistine leaders.

Then the Philistines gathered together all their armies at Aphek, and the Israelites encamped by a fountain which *is* in Jezreel. And the lords of the Philistines passed in review by hundreds and by thousands, but David and his men passed in review at the rear with Achish. Then the princes of the Philistines said, "What *are* these Hebrews *doing here*?" And Achish said to the princes of the Philistines, "*Is* this not David, the servant of Saul king of Israel, who has been with me these days, or these years? And to this day I have found no fault in him since he defected *to me*."

a. **Then the Philistines gathered together all their armies**: The battle lines were drawn in the previous chapter when the Philistines made a deep incursion into Israelite territory. The Philistines intented to deliver a death-blow to Israel and the two armies squared off in anticipation of battle.

b. **The lords of the Philistines passed in review . . . David and his men passed in review at the rear**: David is among the Philistines because when he was discouraged, he left the people of God and the land of Israel, and cast his lot with the Philistines instead (1 Samuel 27). David now finds himself in a place he thought he would never be: among the ungodly, ready to *fight against* God's people.

c. **What are these Hebrews doing here**: Leaders among the Philistines looked at David and his men and said, "They aren't one of us. They are Hebrews. They worship another God. We don't belong together!"

i. The Philistine leaders *could see what David was blind to.* David started to think and act like a Philistine, and was ready to fight with them against the people of God. But the Philistine leaders could see that this wasn't right, even when David couldn't.

ii. The Philistine leaders *knew who David really was* - that is, a Hebrew, part of God's people. David seems to have forgotten this but the Philistine leaders knew. David would have never slipped into this sinful place if he remembered who he really was and what his destiny was.

iii. F.B. Meyer made this observation based on the King James wording of these verses: "It is very terrible when the children of the world have a higher sense of Christian propriety and fitness than Christians themselves, and say to one another, 'What do these Hebrews here?' "

d. **Is this not David . . . who has been with me these days, or these years? And to this day I have found no fault in him since he defected to me**: It is a sad thing that a Philistine ruler defended David so confidently. David identified himself so much with the ungodly that Achish *knew* he had David in his pocket.

i. Hearing these words from Achish *should* have grieved David. To hear an ungodly ruler say, "David has been with me" and "I have found no fault in him" and "he defected to me" should have been a great wake-up call to David. It is as if an ungodly coworker insisted to others that you really weren't a Christian after all, because they saw how you lived.

ii. It is also important to see that Achish wasn't just making this up. David said as much in 1 Samuel 28:1-2 and Achish had reason to believe that David would fight with him.

2. (4-5) The Philistine leaders reject David.

But the princes of the Philistines were angry with him; so the princes of the Philistines said to him, "Make this fellow return, that he may go back to the place which you have appointed for him, and do not let him go down with us to battle, lest in the battle he become our adversary. For with what could he reconcile himself to his master, if not with the heads of these men? *Is* this not David, of whom they sang to one another in dances, saying: 'Saul has slain his thousands, And David his ten thousands'?"

a. **But the princes of the Philistines were angry with him**: The other Philistine leaders were not in agreement with Achish at all. They didn't trust David and they feared he would turn against the Philistines in battle, to bring himself back into Saul's favor.

b. **Is this not David, of whom they sang to one another in dances, saying**: The faith-filled victory over Goliath seemed like a distant memory for a backslidden David, but the Philistines remembered it well. The song of David's victory came back to haunt him again.

B. David heads back to Ziklag.

1. (6-7) Achish tells David to go home.

Then Achish called David and said to him, "Surely, *as* the LORD lives, you have been upright, and your going out and your coming in with me in the army *is* good in my sight. For to this day I have not found evil in you since the day of your coming to me. Nevertheless the lords do not favor you. Therefore return now, and go in peace, that you may not displease the lords of the Philistines."

a. **Surely, as the LORD lives**: "*As the Lord lives* is unexpected in a Philistine oath; can it be that Achish has committed himself to David's Lord, or is he being courteous to David in not swearing by Philistine gods? The latter is perhaps more likely." (Baldwin)

b. **Nevertheless, the lords do not favor you**: David thought he couldn't be happy or at peace in the land of Israel (1 Samuel 27:1). Now he finds that his "Philistine friends" won't accept him either. David has no home; he is trying to live in both worlds, so he has no home in either world.

i. No doubt, David didn't *like* being rejected by the Philistine rulers. Not many people like rejection. But God would *use* the rejection of ungodly people in David's life. Many people are hesitant to live out-and-out for Jesus Christ because they are afraid of the rejection of the ungodly. How much better it is to be all out for Jesus, and to trust that if the ungodly reject us, God will use it for good - for our good and for theirs.

ii. In many ways, David was in the worst place for any child of God. He had too much of the world in him to be at peace in the LORD, and he had too much of the LORD in him to be at peace in the world. God spoke to David through this, but David had to listen.

c. **That you may not displease the lords of the Philistines**: David used to **displease the lords of the Philistines** all the time. He used to be a mighty warrior for the cause of God, and he used to strike fear in the heart of every enemy of God. Now, David is concerned about displeasing **the lords of the Philistines**.

i. Is this the same David who fought Goliath? Could you imagine someone coming to David before that battle, and saying, "Excuse me David, I don't think you should do that. You might **displease the lords of the Philistines**." What do you think David's response would be? He might say, "Of *course* I will **displease the lords of the Philistines**. I *want to* **displease the lords of the Philistines**. I can't wait to **displease the lords of the Philistines**. Let me know if I ever stop displeasing **the lords of the Philistines**." But all that is a distant memory in this time of backsliding and compromise for David.

2. (8-10) David appeals to Achish.

So David said to Achish, "But what have I done? And to this day what have you found in your servant as long as I have been with you, that I may not go and fight against the enemies of my lord the king?" Then Achish answered and said to David, "I know that you *are* as good in my sight as an angel of God; nevertheless the princes of the Philistines have said, 'He shall not go up with us to the battle.' Now therefore, rise early in the morning with your master's servants who have come with you. And as soon as you are up early in the morning and have light, depart."

a. **But what have I done?** David seems genuinely disappointed that he will not be able to fight for the Philistines against Israel.

b. **He shall not go up with us to the battle . . . as soon as you are up early in the morning and have light, depart**: David wanted to fight with the Philistines against Israel but *God* wouldn't let him. David's heart is in a bad place, but God didn't abandon him. We should praise God for the times when He keeps us from sinning as bad as we want to.

3. (11) David returns to Ziklag and the Philistines army prepares to meet Saul.

So David and his men rose early to depart in the morning, to return to the land of the Philistines. And the Philistines went up to Jezreel.

a. **To return to the land of the Philistines**: The Holy Spirit made it clear to David. All these events were a wake-up call to David. He should have heard God speaking in many ways, but he didn't. Instead, he made his **return to the land of the Philistines**. It will take a dramatic crisis to bring David back to where he should be.

1 Samuel 30 - David in Victory Again

A. David's distress.

1. (1-2) Ziklag is plundered by the Amalekites.

Now it happened, when David and his men came to Ziklag, on the third day, that the Amalekites had invaded the South and Ziklag, attacked Ziklag and burned it with fire, and had taken captive the women and those who *were* there, from small to great; they did not kill anyone, but carried *them* away and went their way.

a. **Now it happened**: It certainly **happened**, but it didn't happen by accident. God had a purpose for all of this in David's life.

i. "*On the third day* indicates that David and his men covered about twenty-five miles a day on the march south from Aphek to Ziklag, where they would have arrived tired, hungry and expecting all the comforts for a welcome home." (Baldwin)

b. **The Amalekites had invaded the South and Ziklag, attacked Ziklag and burned it to the ground**: While David and his men were to the north trying to join the Philistine army, their own city of Ziklag was unguarded. The opportunistic Amalekites took advantage of the defenseless city, **attacked** it and **burned it to the ground**.

c. **Taken captive the women and those who were there, from small to great**: Not only was the city burned, but all their women and children were taken away. There is a touch of the LORD's poetic justice in all this. David brought this exact calamity on other cities. 1 Samuel 27:8-11 says during his time among the Philistines, David made his living as a bandit, robbing cities and *whenever David attacked the land, he left neither man nor woman alive*. The Amalekites were more merciful than David was.

i. God, who is great in mercy, does not discipline us as much as we deserve. Like a compassionate father He tempers the stroke of His hand with kindness and love.

2. (3-6) David and his men come upon the empty, burned city.

So David and his men came to the city, and there it was, burned with fire; and their wives, their sons, and their daughters had been taken captive. Then David and the people who *were* with him lifted up their voices and wept, until they had no more power to weep. And David's two wives, Ahinoam the Jezreelitess, and Abigail the widow of Nabal the Carmelite, had been taken captive. Now David was greatly distressed, for the people spoke of stoning him, because the soul of all the people was grieved, every man for his sons and his daughters. But David strengthened himself in the LORD his God.

a. **So David and his men came to the city**: As they came within a few miles of their city the hearts of David and his men must have brightened. As soldiers they were discouraged that they hadn't been allowed to fight with the Philistines. But they knew they were coming home, and home meant family and familiar surroundings. But that bright thought quickly turned black as night.

b. **And there it was, burned with fire**: Even off in the distance they saw something was wrong. Smoke rose from their city, but it wasn't the smoke of cooking fires. It was too much smoke for that, and the smoke was too black. They wondered why no one had come to greet them afar off - where were their wives and children? Weren't they glad to see them? But when they came to the city and saw it was a ghost town, a pile of burned rubble with no voice of the survivors, it seemed that everything was lost.

c. **Then David and the people who were with him lifted up their voices and wept, until they had no more power to weep**: All was lost. At this point, David had nothing more to support him. No one in Israel could help him. The Philistines didn't want him. His family was gone; all he owned was gone. Even his friends turned against him (**the people spoke of stoning him**). Every support was gone, except the LORD. That is a *good* place to be in, not a bad place.

i. David did not weep only because everything and everyone was lost. He also wept because he knew that he was responsible for it. No wonder **David was greatly distressed**. He is about as low in his backslidden state as a man can be; David is like the prodigal son who now sits in the pigpen.

d. **But David strengthened himself in the LORD his God**: It took a lot to bring David to this place, but now he is here - God is his only strength.

i. **David** strengthened himself in the LORD his God. This was backslidden and wayward David. Why would God strengthen him? Because God is rich in mercy and grace, and because David was now completely broken, ready to be filled. Sometimes we think we have to *achieve* God's blessing or strength, but David shows us another way.

ii. David **strengthened** himself in the LORD his God. He received the strength, and felt it flow through himself, and was bold enough to ask for it and receive it from God. Before this, he didn't see himself as weak but after coming home to a burned-out ghost town, David knew he was weak and needed God's strength.

iii. David strengthened **himself** in the LORD his God. He didn't wait for someone else to strengthen him. He didn't say, "Well LORD, if You want to strengthen me, that's fine. I'll just wait here until You do it." David knew that the LORD's strength was there for those who wait upon Him, so he strengthened **himself** in the LORD his God. God's strength was there for David all the time, but now he takes it for himself and will strengthen himself in the LORD his God.

iv. David strengthened himself **in the LORD his God**. This wasn't some kind of rah-rah cheerleader kind of positive thinking mumbo jumbo. This was the strength of the living God making itself real in the life and heart of a hurting man. This was strength for recognition, strength for brokenness, strength for repentance, strength for determination to win back what the enemy has stolen. This is the same strength that would raise Jesus from the dead!

e. **David strengthened himself in the LORD his God**: *How* did David strengthen himself in the LORD?

i. David could remember *God's love.* At this point of total loss, David now saw the love of the LORD in the rejection of the Philistine leaders. If God had not sent him back home through the rejection of the Philistines, it would have been months and months until he returned and the situation would have been far worse. That which stung him before became sweet to him now, and a most precious expression of the LORD's love.

ii. David could remember *God's promise and calling.* He could shake his head, clear the fog and say, "I am a man anointed by God, called by God, and promised by God to be the next king of Israel. I have a high calling and promise from God, and He hasn't taken it away. I need to start living according to that destiny."

iii. David could remember *God's past deliverances.* He could say, "This is a terrible spot, no doubt. But remember all the times when the LORD delivered me out of bad spots before? If He did it then, He will do it now. He didn't deliver me before to let me perish now."

iv. David took his only encouragement from the LORD. 1 Chronicles 12:19-20 gave David a reason for encouragement - men from the tribe of Manasseh came to him at this time, and stood with him when others turned on David. But that wasn't mentioned as encouragement to David at all. "God was beginning to cure his servant by a bitter dose of distress, and the evidence of the cure was that he did not encourage himself by his new friends, or by the hope of others coming; but he encouraged himself in the Lord his God." (Spurgeon)

v. What David *said in his heart* in 1 Samuel 27:1 got him into this whole mess; now, what he said to himself to strengthen himself in the LORD helped bring him out. "Some of the best talks in the world are those which a man has with himself. He who speaks to everybody except himself is a great fool." (Spurgeon)

B. David wins back what was lost - and more.

1. (7-8) David inquires of the LORD.

Then David said to Abiathar the priest, Ahimelech's son, "Please bring the ephod here to me." And Abiathar brought the ephod to David. So David inquired of the LORD, saying, "Shall I pursue this troop? Shall I overtake them?" And He answered him, "Pursue, for you shall surely overtake *them* and without fail recover *all*."

a. In 1 Samuel 30:6, *David strengthened himself in the LORD his God.* Now it was time to *do* something with that strength from the LORD. First, David uses that strength when he **inquired of the LORD**. Of all the time David spent among the Philistines, this is the first time we read of him seeking God in any way. During his time of compromise and backsliding, David simply didn't inquire of the LORD in this way.

b. **Please bring the ephod here**: David sought God with the help of the priest, almost certainly using the Urim and Thummim that were part of the priest's **ephod**. An **ephod** was a special apron that priests would wear, to cover over their clothing, so the sacrificial blood and gore would splash on the ephod, not so much on their clothing.

i. It is likely that this wasn't just any ephod; this was the ephod of the High Priest, which had the *breastplate of judgment* (Exodus 28:15) attached to it (Exodus 28:28). The breastplate had in it a pouch with two stones, known as *the Urim and Thummim* (Exodus 28:30). When David **inquired of the LORD**, he probably asked Abiathar to use the *Urim and Thummim.*

ii. If the Urim and Thummim were discovered today, God would no more bless their use today than He would bless a re-establishment of the Old Testament priesthood. The day for the Old Testament priesthood is past for us today, being perfectly fulfilled in Jesus Christ. But in David's day it was commanded of the LORD. The Urim and Thummim were effective because *God's Word* gave them. In seeking

God through the Urim and Thummim, David was really going back to God's Word for guidance, because it was the word of God that commanded their place and allowed their use. Today, if we have the same focus on God's Word, He will guide us also.

c. **Shall I pursue this troop? Shall I overtake them?** At one time David would not bother to even ask these questions. He would simply do it because when a soldier is attacked he attacks back. But in returning from his backsliding, David brings *everything* to the LORD. Nothing is done just because it was done before. He asks God about everything.

d. **Pursue, for you shall surely overtake them and without fail recover all**: God gave David something *to do* (**pursue**). Then, God gave David a *promise* in the doing (**you shall surely overtake them and without fail recover all**). When God gives us something to *do*, He also gives us a *promise* in the doing.

2. (9-10) David pursues the Amalekites who conquered Ziklag.

So David went, he and the six hundred men who *were* with him, and came to the Brook Besor, where those stayed who were left behind. But David pursued, he and four hundred men; for two hundred stayed *behind*, who were so weary that they could not cross the Brook Besor.

a. **So David went**: God told David to go and pursue them, and David did exactly that. Obedience to the LORD is often that simple.

b. **He and the six hundred men who were with him**: David's men were almost at a place of mutiny against him (*the people spoke of stoning him*, 1 Samuel 30:6). But now since he *strengthened himself in the LORD his God* (1 Samuel 30:6) and since he *inquired of the LORD* (1 Samuel 30:8) and since he did what God told him to do, his men are totally back on his side.

i. **David went, he and the six hundred men who were with him** implies that David said, "Men, I'm going. I have a promise from God for victory, and I'm going to believe it. It doesn't matter if you come with me or not, because God is on my side, and if I have to beat all the Amalekites all by myself, God's promise will not fail." Such faith stirred the hearts of the **six hundred men**, and they went with David.

ii. It was a magnificent sight - David and **the six hundred men** on the march again, this time not hoping to fight for the Philistines or for themselves, but off again on a mission from God. There wasn't an army on earth that could beat David and his **six hundred men** when they walked in God's will.

c. **For two hundred stayed behind, who were so weary that they could not cross the Brook Besor**: This might have discouraged David. As he pursued a significantly larger Amalekite army, he found that one-third of his men couldn't continue. But David didn't let this trial stop him. He set the one-third to work guarding the supplies, lightening the load of the 400 who continued and he set out again, full of faith.

i. "But mark this, he was not delivered without further trial . . . Many a leader would have given up the chase with one out of three of his troop in hospital, but David pursued with his reduced force. When God means to bless us, he often takes away a part of the little strength we thought we had. We did not think our strength equal to the task, and the Lord takes away a portion even of the little power we had. Our God does not fill till he has emptied. Two hundred men must be rent away from David's side before God could give him victory . . . Expect then, O troubled one, that you will be delivered, but know that your sorrow may yet deepen, that you may have all the greater joy by-and-by." (Spurgeon)

3. (11-15) David and his men befriend a helpless Egyptian.

Then they found an Egyptian in the field, and brought him to David; and they gave him bread and he ate, and they let him drink water. And they gave him a piece of a cake of figs and two clusters of raisins. So when he had eaten, his strength came back to him; for he had eaten no bread nor drunk water for three days and three nights. Then David said to him, "To whom do you *belong*, and where *are* you from?" And he said, "I *am* a young man from Egypt, servant of an Amalekite; and my master left me behind, because three days ago I fell sick. We made an invasion of the southern *area* of the Cherethites, in the *territory* which *belongs* to Judah, and of the southern *area* of Caleb; and we burned Ziklag with fire." And David said to him, "Can you take me down to this troop?" So he said, "Swear to me by God that you will neither kill me nor deliver me into the hands of my master, and I will take you down to this troop."

a. **Then they found an Egyptian in the field**: As David and the 600 men pursued the Amalekites, they came across a man collapsed in the wilderness. It would be easy and logical, to ignore this man because they had a "much greater" mission in pursing the Amalekites. But David and his men showed unexpected kindness and they **gave him bread and he ate, and they let him drink water**.

b. **Then David said to him, "To whom do you belong, and where are you from?"** David took a caring interest in this man. He showed simple care and kindness to a nobody. They didn't just give this Egyptian food and water; they gave him care and kindness.

c. **I am a young man from Egypt, servant of an Amalekite . . . we burned Ziklag with fire**: In showing unexpected kindness to this Egyptian, God showed David unexpected blessing. The Egyptian promised to guide David to the camp of the Amalekites.

i. "The emphatic 'we' at the beginning of v. 14 suggests that the slave participated personally in the Amalekites' raids." (Youngblood)

4. (16-20) David routs and spoils the Amalekites, winning back everything.

And when he had brought him down, there they were, spread out over all the land, eating and drinking and dancing, because of all the great spoil which they had taken from the land of the Philistines and from the land of Judah. Then David attacked them from twilight until the evening of the next day. Not a man of them escaped, except four hundred young men who rode on camels and fled. So David recovered all that the Amalekites had carried away, and David rescued his two wives. And nothing of theirs was lacking, either small or great, sons or daughters, spoil or anything which they had taken from them; David recovered all. Then David took all the flocks and herds they had driven before those *other* livestock, and said, "This *is* David's spoil."

a. **Attacked them from twilight until the evening of the next day**: As they caught the Amalekites in the midst of their victory celebration, David surprised the Amalekites. They figured that all the Philistine and Israelite armies were far to the north, preparing to fight each other.

i. **Twilight** is probably a bad translation here, and it should be *from dawn until evening of the next day*. "The Hebrew word *nesep*, translated 'dawn' in Job 7:4 and Psalm 119:147, has this sense here . . . Having noted the situation, David and his men took some rest and attacked at first light, when the Amalekites would be suffering from the soporific effects of the feast, and least able to defend themselves." (Baldwin)

ii. It was wise to attack the Amalekites when they were hung over from the party the night before. "Whom they found it no hard matter to stab with the sword, who were cup-shot before." (Trapp)

b. **David recovered all that the Amalekites had carried away**: Everything that the enemy took David took back. God gave him a complete victory, because David *strengthened himself in the* LORD *his God* (1 Samuel 30:6), David *inquired of the* LORD (1 Samuel 30:8), David did what God told him to do, and David showed unexpected care and kindness to others.

i. God's promise was proved true. When David inquired of the LORD, God promised *You shall surely overtake them and without fail recover all* (1 Samuel 30:8). The promise was fulfilled exactly, but it wasn't fulfilled as David sat back passively and said, "All right God, now You can do it." The LORD fulfilled His promise, but He used David's actions to fulfill the promise. God's promise didn't *exclude* David's cooperation, the promise *invited* his cooperation.

ii. "Brother, you will have to work and labor to extricate yourself from debt and difficulty, and so the Lord will hear your prayer. The rule is to trust in God to smite the Amalekites, and then to march after them, as if it all depended upon yourself." (Spurgeon)

c. **This is David's spoil**: God gave David *even more* than what He promised. He received **spoil** from the battle, beyond what was taken from Ziklag. This was blessing straight from the grace of God.

i. We should come to Jesus, and by our free will give Him everything we have, everything we are. We give our lives to Him and say, "This is Jesus' spoil." We give our gifts and abilities to Him and say, "This is Jesus' spoil." We give our possessions to Him and say, "This is Jesus' spoil." We give our praise to Him and say, "This is Jesus' spoil." We give our time to Him and say, "This is Jesus' spoil."

ii. Some wonder why David was allowed to keep the spoil of the Amalekites when Saul was expressly commanded to not keep any spoil from that nation (1 Samuel 15:1-3) and was judged by God for not obeying that command (1 Samuel 15:13-23). The answers are simple: First, David had no specific command from God to destroy all the spoil from the Amalekites, as Saul did. Second, David *recovered* what the Amalekites took from *others*, though he recovered far beyond what was taken from his city. Third, David was not acting as the king of Israel representing the LORD's nation, as Saul did. Simply put, in this case the rules were different for David.

C. The spoil from the battle is divided.

1. (21-25) The spoils are distributed equally among those who fought and those who supported.

Now David came to the two hundred men who had been so weary that they could not follow David, whom they also had made to stay at the Brook Besor. So they went out to meet David and to meet the people who *were* with him. And when David came near the people, he greeted them. Then all the wicked and worthless men of those who went with David answered and said, "Because they did not go with us, we will not give them *any* of the spoil that we have recovered, except for every man's wife and children, that they may lead *them* away and depart." But David said, "My brethren, you shall not do so with what the LORD has given us, who has preserved us and delivered into our hand the troop that came against us. For who will heed you in this matter? But as his part *is* who goes down to the battle, so *shall* his part *be* who stays by the supplies; they shall share alike." So it was, from that day forward; he made it a statute and an ordinance for Israel to this day.

a. **Now David came to the two hundred men who had been so weary they could not follow David**: When David was in swift pursuit of the Amalekites, 200 men among his company could not continue on. They made a camp where they were and lightened the supply load from the soldiers who continued. Now David returned to the **two hundred men** who stayed by the supply camp.

b. **Then all the wicked and worthless men of those who went with David answered and said**: When David returned, these men of the supply camp saw their own possessions among the spoils of battle and they wanted them back. The **wicked and worthless men** (apparently, there were some among David's men) protested, and said they could only have back **every man's wife and children**, but none of their possessions.

c. **My brethren, you shall not do so with what the Lord has given us . . . But as his part is who goes down to the battle, so shall his part be who stays by the supplies, they shall share alike**. David declared an important principle: the supply lines are just as vital as the soldiers and God will reward both "soldiers" and "supporters" properly.

i. Many people serve the Lord in invisible, behind-the scenes ways, often supporting a much more visible aspect of the Lord's work. God will support the hidden servant with the same reward as prominent servant.

ii. The **wicked and worthless men** looked at the spoil and said, "We fought for this spoil and it is ours." David looked at the spoil and said, "Look at **what the Lord has given us**." When you looked at it that way, how could you not share? When the Lord gave David a great victory he saw it as the Lord's victory more than his own.

d. **A statute and an ordinance for Israel to this day**: It became a standing principle in Israel. This principle should be declared and believed among God's people today.

i. There is encouragement for the **weary** here. "You Little-Faiths, you Despondencies, you Much-Afraids, you Feeble-Minds, you that sigh more than you sing, you that would but cannot, you that have a great heart for holiness, but feel beaten back in your struggles, the Lord shall give you his love, his grace, his favor, as surely as he gives it to those who can do great things in his name." (Spurgeon)

2. (26-31) David mends strained relationships.

Now when David came to Ziklag, he sent *some* of the spoil to the elders of Judah, to his friends, saying, "Here is a present for you from the spoil of the enemies of the Lord"; to *those* who *were* in Bethel, *those* who *were* in Ramoth of the South, *those* who *were* in Jattir, *those* who *were* in Aroer, *those* who *were* in Siphmoth, *those* who *were* in Eshtemoa, *those* who *were* in Rachal, *those* who *were* in the cities of the Jerahmeelites, *those* who *were* in the cities of the Kenites, *those* who *were* in Hormah, *those* who *were* in Chorashan, *those* who *were* in Athach, *those*

who *were* in Hebron, and to all the places where David himself and his men were accustomed to rove.

a. **When David came to Ziklag, he sent some of the spoil to the elders of Judah, to his friends**: David knew that his time among the Philistines strained his relationships with God's people. Now he knew he must do whatever he could to put things right again so **he sent some of the spoil to the elders of Judah**.

i. This is the final step in David's getting things right after his time of backsliding among the Philistines.

- David *strengthened himself in the* L*ORD* *his God*
- David *inquired of the* L*ORD*
- David believed God's promise
- David did what God told him to do
- David showed unexpected care and kindness to others
- David saw it as the LORD's victory
- David shared the reward with others
- David did what he could to mend relationships

b. **Here is a present for you from the spoil of the enemies of the LORD**: David sent spoil from the battle to more than 13 cities. Obviously, there was *spoil to spare* from the battle. In this David is a picture of his greater Son, Jesus Christ. When Jesus triumphed on the cross He won the greatest battle and He had "spoil to share." He shared the spoil with His people, as it says in Ephesians 4:7-8: *But to each one of us grace was given according to the measure of Christ's gift. Therefore He says: "When He ascended on high, He led captivity captive, and gave gifts to men."* Jesus has spoil from His victory to give you!

i. David is a remarkable picture of Jesus in this chapter. Note these five points of association:

- We are like David's men, David is like Jesus
- We are like the weary ones left behind, David is like Jesus
- We are like the Egyptian slave, David is like Jesus
- We are like the spoil David recovered, David is like Jesus
- We are like the elders of Judah, and David is like Jesus

1 Samuel 31 - The Death of Saul and His Sons

A. King Saul and his sons die in battle.

1. (1) The battle turns against Israel.

Now the Philistines fought against Israel; and the men of Israel fled from before the Philistines, and fell slain on Mount Gilboa.

a. **So the Philistines fought against Israel**: The Philistines attacked deep into Israeli territory (1 Samuel 28:4), and Saul's army assembled and prepared for battle at Mount Gilboa (1 Samuel 28:4). Because of his deep rebellion against the LORD, Saul was not ready for battle: *When Saul saw the army of the Philistines, he was afraid, and his heart trembled* (1 Samuel 28:5).

i. Instead of taking his fear to the LORD Saul made things worse by seeking God's voice through a spirit medium. Strangely, God did speak to Saul, but He spoke words of judgment through an unusual appearance of the prophet Samuel. Samuel told Saul that he and his sons would die the next day (1 Samuel 28:19). 1 Samuel 31:1 is the next day.

ii. The **Philistines fought against Israel**, and David wanted to be part of this group of Philistines (1 Samuel 29:2, 8). It was the LORD's mercy that did not allow David to join these enemies of the LORD.

b. **The men of Israel fled from before the Philistines, and fell slain on Mount Gilboa**: **Gilboa** was the location of the Israeli army camp (1 Samuel 28:4), meaning that the battle turned so badly for Israel that they were in full retreat back to their own camp.

2. (2) The death of Saul's sons.

Then the Philistines followed hard after Saul and his sons. And the Philistines killed Jonathan, Abinadab, and Malchishua, Saul's sons.

a. **And the Philistines killed Jonathan, Abinadab, and Malchishua, Saul's sons**: Tragically, Saul's sons were affected in the judgment of God against their father Saul. The brave and worthy Jonathan died as we might expect him to - loyally fighting for his God, his country, and his father the king unto the very end.

b. **Saul's sons**: Their death was tragic, yet important in God's plan. In taking the logical heirs to Saul's throne, God cleared the way for David to become the next king of Israel. We know that if Jonathan had survived he would have gladly yielded the throne to David (1 Samuel 18:1-4). But the same could not be said of Saul's other sons. God was also merciful to Jonathan, sparing him the ordeal of having to side with David against his own brothers.

i. "There was also a special providence of God in taking away Jonathan, (who of all Saul's sons seems to have been the fairest for the crown,) for the preventing divisions, which have happened amongst the people concerning the successor; David's way to the crown being by this means made the more clear." (Poole)

ii. As it was, David had to deal with Ishbosheth, the one surviving son of Saul before taking the undisputed throne of Israel (2 Samuel 2:8 through 4:12).

3. (3-6) The tragic end of King Saul.

The battle became fierce against Saul. The archers hit him, and he was severely wounded by the archers. Then Saul said to his armorbearer, "Draw your sword, and thrust me through with it, lest these uncircumcised men come and thrust me through and abuse me." But his armorbearer would not, for he was greatly afraid. Therefore Saul took a sword and fell on it. And when his armorbearer saw that Saul was dead, he also fell on his sword, and died with him. So Saul, his three sons, his armorbearer, and all his men died together that same day.

a. **The battle became intense against Saul**: Saul, struck by many arrows and **severely wounded**, knew the battle was completely lost. He pleaded with his armorbearer to kill him, and when he would not, Saul killed himself (**Saul took a sword and fell on it**).

i. In the way most people think of suicide, Saul's death was not suicide. Clarke explains well: "He was to all appearance mortally wounded, when he begged his armourbearer to extinguish the remaining spark of life . . . though this wound accelerated his death, yet it could not be properly the cause of it, as he was mortally wounded before, and did it on the conviction that he could not survive."

b. **All his men died together that same day**: As sad as anything was in this account, sad is the *absence* of any kind of sorrow or repentance or crying out to God at all on Saul's part. He was told the previous day that he would die (1 Samuel 28:19), yet he did not seem to prepare his soul to meet God in any way.

i. At the end of his life Saul became so hard in sin that he *did not want* to repent. Many people put off getting right with God until a later time, assuming they will still want to get right with God then. But that is a dangerous assumption because repentance is a gift from God and if it is here today it should be received today.

ii. "It is a very solemn thought! No career could begin with fairer, brighter prospects than Saul had, and none could close in more absolute midnight of despair; and yet such a fate may befall us, unless we watch, and pray, and walk humbly with our God." (Meyer)

c. **When his armorbearer saw that Saul was dead**: In 2 Samuel 1:4-10 an Amalekite came to David with the report that Saul had died in battle and that he actually delivered the death-blow to Saul. Does the Amalekite's statement contradict this passage, where it seems Saul killed himself? It may be that Saul fell on his sword, and life still lingered in him, so he asked this Amalekite to finish him off. Or it may be that the Amalekite simply lied and was the first one to come upon Saul's dead body, and that he told David that he killed him because he thought David would be pleased and he would be rewarded.

B. Aftermath of the Philistine's victorious battle.

1. (7) A significant defeat for Israel.

And when the men of Israel who *were* on the other side of the valley, and *those* who *were* on the other side of the Jordan, saw that the men of Israel had fled and that Saul and his sons were dead, they forsook the cities and fled; and the Philistines came and dwelt in them.

a. **They forsook the cities and fled; and the Philistines came and dwelt in them**: The victory of the Philistines was so complete that even those **on the other side of the Jordan** fled in terror before the Philistines. With the Philistine army occupying territory **on the other side of the Jordan**, they have cut Israel in half, drawing a line from west to east. The rest of the nation was ripe for total conquest by the Philistines.

b. **The men of Israel had fled and that Saul and his sons were dead**: This was a great defeat. When the leader (King Saul) was struck, it spread panic among God's people. Jesus knew this same principle would be used against His own disciples: *Then Jesus said to them, "All of you will be made to stumble because of Me this night, for it is written: 'I will strike the Shepherd, and the sheep will be scattered.'"* (Mark 14:27)

i. Saul's sin, hardened rebellion, and eventual ruin affected far more than himself and even his immediate family. It literally endangered the entire nation of Israel.

ii. This shows why leaders have a higher responsibility, because their fall can endanger many more people than the fall of someone who is not a leader. This is why the New Testament openly presents a higher standard for leaders, even saying they should be *blameless* for just cause before the world and God's people (1 Timothy 3:2, Titus 1:6).

2. (8-10) The Philistines disgrace the corpses of King Saul and his sons.

So it happened the next day, when the Philistines came to strip the slain, that they found Saul and his three sons fallen on Mount Gilboa. And they cut off his head and stripped off his armor, and sent *word* throughout the land of the Philistines, to proclaim *it in* the temple of their idols and among the people. Then they put his armor in the temple of the Ashtoreths, and they fastened his body to the wall of Beth Shan.

a. **To proclaim it in the temple of their idols and among the people**: Saul's tragic death gave opportunity for the enemies of the LORD to disgrace His name. Saul's death was used to glorify pagan gods and to mock the living God.

b. **They fastened his body to the wall of Beth Shan**: This was the ultimate insult against Saul. In that culture, to have your dead body treated this way was considered a fate worse than death itself.

i. You can go to the ruins of Beth Shan today, as the foundations to the city sit high on a hill overlooking the Roman ruins destroyed in an earthquake. It was high on that hill that the Philistines hung the decapitated corpse of King Saul in the ultimate humiliation.

3. (11-13) The men of Jabesh Gilead end the disgrace of Saul and his sons.

Now when the inhabitants of Jabesh Gilead heard what the Philistines had done to Saul, all the valiant men arose and traveled all night, and took the body of Saul and the bodies of his sons from the wall of Beth Shan; and they came to Jabesh and burned them there. Then they took their bones and buried *them* under the tamarisk tree at Jabesh, and fasted seven days.

a. **All the valiant men arose**: In a time of disgrace, loss, and tragedy like this, God still had **valiant men** to do His work. The men of Jabesh Gilead took down the bodies of Saul and his sons from their place of humiliation and gave them a proper burial.

i. Glory to God, He always has His **valiant men**! When one servant passes the scene, another arises to take his place. If Saul is gone, God raises up a David. If the army of Israel is utterly routed, God still has His **valiant men**. God's work is bigger than any man or any group of people.

b. **The inhabitants of Jabesh Gilead**: These valiant men are also recognized for their *gratitude*. Many years before Saul delivered their city from the Ammonites (1 Samuel 11:1-11), and they repaid the kindness God showed them from the hand of Saul. Upon taking the throne David rightly thanked these **valiant men** for their kindness to the memory of Saul, Jonathan and Saul's other sons (2 Samuel 2:4-7).

i. When David heard of Saul's death, he did not rejoice. In fact, he mourned and composed a song in honor of Saul and Jonathan (*The Song of the Bow*, 2 Samuel 1:11-27). In spite of all that Saul did against David, David spoke well of Saul after his death.

ii. Choosing this kind of heart showed David to be a true "Man after God's Own Heart." It showed that the years in the wilderness escaping Saul really were years when God trained him to be a king after God's own heart. Despite his sin, David never followed in the same tragic footsteps as King Saul.

The Book of 1 Samuel – Selected Bibliography

This is a bibliography of books cited in the commentary. Of course, there are many other worthy books on 1 Samuel, but these are listed for the benefit of readers who wish to check sources.

Baldwin, Joyce G. *1 and 2 Samuel, An Introduction and Commentary* (Leicester, England: Inter-Varsity Press, 1988)

Blaikie, W.G. *The First Book of Samuel* (New York: Hodder and Stoughton, ?)

Clarke, Adam *The Holy Bible, Containing the Old and New Testaments, with A Commentary and Critical Notes, Volume II – Joshua to Esther* (New York: Eaton and Mains, 1827?)

Cook, F.C. (Editor) *The Bible Commentary, 1 Samuel – Esther* (Grand Rapids, Michigan: Baker Book House, 1974)

Ellison, H.L. "Joshua - 2 Samuel" *Daily Bible Commentary, Volume 1: Genesis – Job* (London: Scripture Union, 1973)

Ginzberg, Louis *The Legends of the Jews, Volumes 1-7* (Philadelphia: The Jewish Publication Society of America, 1968)

Harris, R. Laid, Archer, Gleason L. Jr., and Waltke, Bruce K. *Theological Wordbook of the Old Testament* (Chicago: Moody Bible Institute, 1980)

Keil, C.F. and Delitszch, F. *Commentary on the Old Testament, Volume II – Joshua, Judges, Ruth, I & II Samuel* (Grand Rapids, Michigan: Eerdmans, 1984)

Maclaren, Alexander *Expostions of Holy Scripture, Volume 2* (Grand Rapids, Michigan: Baker Book House, 1984)

Meyer, F.B. *Our Daily Homily* (Westwood, New Jersey: Revell, 1966)

Meyer, F.B. *David: Shepherd, Psalmist, King* (Fort Washington, Pennsylvania: Christian Literature Crusade, 1977)

Meyer, F.B. *Samuel the Prophet* (Fort Washington, Pennsylvania: Christian Literature Crusade, 1985)

Morgan, G. Campbell *Searchlights from the Word* (New York: Revell, 1926)

Poole, Matthew *A Commentary on the Holy Bible, Volume 1* (London, Banner of Truth Trust, 1968)

Redpath, Alan *The Making of a Man of God – Studies in the Life of David* (Old Tappan, New Jersey: Revell, 1962)

Smith, R. Payne "1 Samuel" *The Pulpit Commentary, Volume 4 – Ruth, I & II Samuel* (McLean, Virginia: MacDonald Publishing, ?)

Spurgeon, Charles Haddon *The New Park Street Pulpit, Volumes 1-6* and *The Metropolitan Tabernacle Pulpit, Volumes 7-63* (Pasadena, Texas: Pilgrim Publications, 1990)

Trapp, John *A Commentary on the Old and New Testaments, Volume 1 – Genesis to Second Chronicles* (Eureka, California: Tanski Publications, 1997)

Youngblood, Ronald F. "1, 2 Samuel," *The Expositor's Bible Commentary, Volume 3* (Grand Rapids, Michigan: Zondervan, 1992)

Much thanks to the many who helped prepare this commentary. This last year has been a tremendous year of change for our whole family, and my gratitude goes out to my wife Inga-Lill and our children who give so much support in this and all the ministry. Jonathan - this one's for you! When I read about Jonathan in the Bible, it reminds me a lot of you - bold, trusting, and loving God. Thanks for being such a great Jonathan.

This book is the first time I received the capable proofreading help of Sue Long. Thank you Nick and Sue - you both are great blessings to Inga-Lill and I.

We use the same cover format and artwork for this commentary series, so continued thanks to Craig Brewer who created the cover and helped with the layout. Kara Valeri helped with graphic design. Gayle Erwin provided both inspiration and practical guidance. I am often amazed at the remarkable kindness of others, and thanks to all who give the gift of encouragement. With each year that passes, faithful friends and supporters become all the more precious. Through you all, God has been better to me than I have ever deserved.

After more than 20 years of pastoral ministry, David Guzik became the director of Calvary Chapel Bible College Germany in January of 2003. David and his wife Inga-Lill live near Siegen, Germany with their children Aan-Sofie, Nathan, and Jonathan. You can e-mail David at david@enduringword.com

For more resources by David Guzik, go to www.enduringword.com

More Commentary by David Guzik

In Print

Genesis (ISBN: 1-56599-049-8)
First Samuel (ISBN: 1-56599-040-4)
Second Samuel (ISBN: 1-56599-038-2)
Acts (ISBN: 1-56599-047-1)
Romans (ISBN: 1-56599-041-2)
First Corinthians (ISBN: 1-56599-045-5)
Second Corinthians (ISBN: 1-56599-042-0)
Hebrews (ISBN: 1-56599-037-4)
Revelation (ISBN: 1-56599-043-9)

Software

New Testament & More (ISBN: 1-56599-048-X)
This CD-ROM gives immediate access to thousands of pages of verse-by-verse Bible commentary through all of the New Testament and many Old Testament books. For ease of use, commentary is available in both Acrobat and HTML format. Also includes bonus audio resources - hours of David Guzik's teaching in mp3 format

www.enduringword.com

CPSIA information can be obtained
at www.ICGtesting.com
Printed in the USA
FSOW01n2147150218
44388FS